How the
Heather Looks

How the Heather Looks,

A JOYOUS JOURNEY TO THE BRITISH SOURCES OF CHILDREN'S BOOKS

JOAN BODGER

THE VIKING PRESS   NEW YORK

"William the Second" from *Kings and Queens* by Eleanor Farjeon, Copyright 1932 by Eleanor and Herbert Farjeon. Reprinted by permission of Harold Ober Associates Incorporated. Page 158.

"A Smuggler's Song" and "Puck's Song" from *Puck of Pook's Hill* by Rudyard Kipling. Reprinted by permission of Mrs. George Bambridge, The Macmillan Company of Canada Limited, Macmillan & Co. Ltd., London and Doubleday and Company, Inc. Page 172.

"I Never Saw a Moor" by Emily Dickinson from *The Complete Poems of Emily Dickinson*, edited by Martha Dickinson Bianchi and Alfred Leete Hampson. Reprinted by permission of Little, Brown and Company. Page 14.

To John and Ian, and to Lucy
who went back to find the door

Contents

How the
Heather Looks

Foreword

In 1958 our family came into a modest windfall—enough to put into effect a long-cherished dream of spending a summer holiday in England. My husband and I are each half English, we had each spent time in England as children, and each of us—by circumstance, education, and inclination—was steeped in English history and literature.

We cannot claim erudition for our children, but books, conversation, games, genes, and osmosis had made Anglophiles of them. Lucy, aged two and a half, knew her nursery rhymes, having learned them from Randolph Caldecott's *Picture Books* and L. Leslie Brooke's *Ring o' Roses*, both illustrated with scenes from English country life. She also knew Brooke's *Johnny Crow's Garden* and she had pored over the pictures in his *Golden Goose Book* and his illustrations in *A Roundabout Turn* by Robert H. Charles. When she was very young indeed she had been introduced to A. A. Milne's Pooh and Piglet and Christopher Robin, and she was quite well acquainted with the world of Beatrix Potter. It would be another twelve-month before she began to read, but could one truly say that she was illiterate?

Ian, almost nine, worried his teachers because he was a better listener than he was a reader, but he had managed to assimilate and accumulate an astonishing amount of lore. He was, in his way, as fond of history as his father, who holds a Ph.D. in the subject. He seemed unable to make anything of the mysteries of *Dick and Jane* (authors mercifully anonymous) but he liked to listen to *Beowulf* (also anonymous). His favorite indoor toys were wooden blocks, model soldiers, maps and dioramas. When outdoors, he and his friends engaged in elaborate war games which seemed to require that endless amounts of army surplus equipment be festooned from every knobby shoulder and hip bone. To the naked eye, these little wars may have seemed the ordinary contests between "good guys" and "bad," but it was Romans and Britons, Roundheads and Cavaliers, Napoleon and Wellington who waged their battles in our suburbia.

Ian also liked to draw. Sometimes he drew maps (of places both real and imaginary) but mostly he drew soldiers. In order to do a good job of it he pored over his own and his father's books. He especially liked Howard Pyle's illustrations of knights in armor. He also liked *Life's Picture History of Western Man*, the *Puffin Picture Book of Armor* by Patrick Nicolle, *Weapons, a Pictorial History* by Edwin Tunis, and Robert Lawson's illustrations for a children's version of *Pilgrim's Progress*. These were for looking, although he liked to hear the texts, too. For pure listening, Ian preferred Stevenson's *Treasure Island*, Grahame's *The Wind in the Willows*, T. H. White's *The Sword in the Stone* and Tolkien's *The Hobbit*. He also liked ballads and folklore, archaeology and history, and the verse and poetry of A. A. Milne, Robert Louis Stevenson, Alfred, Lord Tennyson, and Walter de la Mare.

Revealingly, his favorite poem was "The Land of Counterpane," by Robert Louis Stevenson.

Almost since he was born we had told Ian that he would be able to see "all that" when he went to England. Now, as Lucy was old enough to look and listen, we heard ourselves saying the same thing, with less conviction. Our children were so literal! They beseiged us with questions. Would we see where Rat and Mole had had their picnic? Could we climb to the Enchanted Place at the Top of the Forest? Would we go down to towered Camelot? Could we pay a call on Mrs. Tiggy-Winkle? Privately we adults told each other that of course such places did not exist in reality, but the children's faith was unfaltering—and unnerving. Perhaps, we said, a few of the places really did exist. Perhaps, we said cautiously, we could seek them out.

We began by writing letters to the British Travel Association and the British Information Services. Both agencies were exceedingly kind, but not very helpful. The information we needed was not in their files. Pig iron production—but not Piglet! It is true that there were all sorts of guides to "Shakespeare Country" and "Scott Country" and "Hardy Country," but these were not the landscapes sought by our children. We tried writing directly to authors. Some publishers would not forward letters, some authors would not answer, some authors were dead. We were undaunted. We did not want to be lion hunters. Places, not people, were what interested us. We would explore for ourselves.

I ransacked our old favorite books, going over the familiar ground like a detective in search of clues. The Arthur Ransome books, T. H. White's *Mistress Masham's Repose*, even the Pooh books, had maps in the end papers. Were they totally imaginary or could we orient them to an atlas? I searched out more information at the public library and found more books to bring home and read aloud to the children. My husband, who is a reference librarian, brought home biographies and autobiographies of children's authors for me to study. Perhaps something in a writer's life would give a concrete clue to the places described in his books. A kind friend presented me with a twenty-year back file of *Horn Book*, the magazine of books and reading for children. I combed these for details concerning the lives and works of authors and illustrators.

The more I read the more convinced I became that the children were right. Most places in children's literature are real. We could find them if we searched. All we needed was faith. I was reminded of a poem by Emily Dickinson.

> I never saw a moor,
> I never saw the sea;
> Yet know I how the heather looks,
> And what a wave must be.
>
> I never spoke with God,
> Nor visited in heaven;
> Yet certain am I of the spot
> As if the chart was given.

This book, then, is the story of how Ian and Lucy went to see for themselves "how heather looks." Ian and Lucy had the faith. It was left to their parents to arrange for passage and to invest in Bartholomew's *Road Atlas of Great Britain*.

1

Caldecott Country

We were bound for Whitchurch, just thirty miles down the road from Liverpool. A few hours before we had disembarked from a staid, broad-beamed Cunard liner which had taken more than a week to cross the Atlantic. While still on shipboard we had discovered a 1957 *Saturday Book* in the ship's library and had read a delightful article on Randolph Caldecott, the early illustrator of children's books. Whitchurch, we read, was the town in which Caldecott had lived as a very young man and scenes in the town and the countryside roundabout had been immortalized in his Picture Books.

In a last-minute decision we had set it as a cautious destination for our first day's journey. We were glad now that we had not been more ambitious. We had arranged months beforehand to rent a car at the docks, but when we were met by the car rental company's agent we discovered that by some mischance or inefficiency we could not be supplied with the kind of car we had requested. We knew, of course, that English cars are small, by American standards, but the car actually supplied must have been built for midgets. Somehow we managed to wedge ourselves and four suitcases into an impossible space and to set off undaunted. Well, almost undaunted. There was something peculiar about the gearshift which worked without benefit of clutch, but we told ourselves cheerfully that John would soon get the hang of it. He never did.

Now we were racing down the Great Chester Road, on the wrong side, it seemed to us, in a strange car which we barely knew how to rein in at the crossroads. We had hoped to see the famous arcades of Chester, but the road bypassed the town almost before we knew where we were, and town gave way to open countryside. Chester is where Randolph Caldecott was born and went to school. Thinking of him now as John tried to get the knack of shifting gears without a clutch, I was about to say that driving the new car put me in mind of the desperate John Gilpin on his runaway steed, perhaps Caldecott's most successful portraiture. Looking at the grim-set look in my husband's eye I decided to forego the literary allusion.

Instead, I turned my thoughts to Whitchurch. We planned to drive into town, consult the local librarian, take some Caldecott Picture Books out of the library or buy them in the local bookshop, and stroll about town identifying the house where he had lived, the familiar scenes he had sketched as background for the nursery rhymes. Ah, innocence! Suddenly, before we expected it, we saw a small brick building marked Whitchurch Council School standing by itself along the roadside. John stopped the car so Ian and I could go in and ask the teacher to direct us. I wondered what it would be like to talk to children who walked to school each morning over the very fields and country lanes made famous in the Caldecott illustrations. Did every household own a dog-eared copy or two, or did the teacher have the thrill and pleasure of introducing the books? If so, the experience must be akin to holding a child up to the mirror for the first time and letting him recognize what it is that the rest of the world holds dear.

It was a one-room branch schoolhouse that we had found. The children, sitting at double desks, stared at us, round-eyed. Ian hung back at the door, too shy to enter. Despite the calendar's claim to June, the air outside was chill and raw. Every door and window in the tiny schoolroom was open. The children sat with their feet on stone flags and I noticed that the walls were red brick, patchily covered with thin plaster. The thought flashed through my mind that even the children were burnished to the same hue as the bricks, as though they, too, had sprung from the clay. The boys sat with knobby red knees bare, gaping at Ian in his long flannel-lined blue jeans with turned-up cuffs. The young teacher had never heard of Randolph Caldecott. I explained as best I could, but she shook her head, not comprehending why Americans should come so far to look for a man who illustrated nursery rhymes. She obviously thought our quest frivolous and our interruption rude (which it may have been), but she suggested we continue into town and ask for more information at the Town Hall. Ian, who had blushed scarlet under the gaze of boys his own age, was glad to make his escape.

We came to the square-towered church at the top of the High Street and plunged down the hill into the town. The shops and inns were crowded, people spilling out of the buildings, over the narrow sidewalks, and into the streets. At last we saw a building marked Town Hall and John suggested that Lucy and I hop out while he and Ian found a place to park. I had to hold Lucy in my arms to breach the crowd near the doorway, but once inside we made our way easily to a dank little library on the ground floor. The girl at the desk said that the librarian was on holiday, and she wrinkled her brow in thought when I asked about Randolph Caldecott. She had seen a book about him somewhere in the library, but it was not in the children's section. She went to look in the shelves and came back with Henry Blackburn's *Randolph Caldecott: A Personal Memoir* written in 1886, the year Caldecott died. I settled gratefully to taking notes, resigning myself to the stark fact that none of Caldecott's own books was to be had.

Randolph Caldecott was a bright, handsome, pleasant boy when he came to Whitchurch in 1861. Not much is known of his early childhood except that it was a happy one and that he was head boy at the Henry VIII grammar school in Chester. There he is remembered as having spent hours drawing, modeling from clay, and carving from wood. He, like us, must have come down from Chester on the Great Road on the day he first came to Whitchurch. Perhaps an apprentice job in a bank does not seem to us ideal for a fifteen-year-old boy who loved beauty and the out-of-doors, but young Caldecott fell in love with Whitchurch from the very first. As careful and thorough with a column of figures as he was with his own drawings, he does not seem to have been in a state of rebellion against his apprenticeship. His zestfulness soon endeared him to his fellow workers and townspeople alike, for he made friends easily and joined in the life of town and countryside. His biographer and close friend, Henry Blackburn, reports that he took lodgings "in an old farmhouse about two miles from town where he used to go fishing and shooting, to the meets of hounds, to markets and cattle fairs."

At this point in my reading Lucy became restless. I took the book back to the desk and went out with her into the cobbled courtyard in the rear of the building. Travel with a two-year-old can be complicated, but it has its compensations. Because of Lucy I had left the musty library and we now found ourselves in the middle of a market fair, watching and listening in fascination as the hawkers cried their wares—cheap crockery, sharp knives, plastic shopping baskets. Before our very eyes we saw the end of an era as many a farmer's wife rushed to buy the new garish pink or blue synthetic carryall in preference to her old hand-caned basket. My only comfort was uncharitable. The plastic handles looked as though they would break easily and in that case they could not be mended.

Caldecott must have loved Whitchurch especially on days such as this, when the inns were filled to overflowing, when red-faced farmers argued the price of a bull on every street corner, when the farmers' wives came to gossip and haggle at the stalls in the market place or the little shops that line the High Street. I have never seen so many beautiful babies. Beside them Lucy, usually considered rosy, looked a trifle pale and unhealthy. I found that Lucy, in her fleece-lined pale pink snow suit, and I, in my Joseph's colors raincoat, were being stared at and studied, even as I was studying the local inhabitants. (This was the sort of scene that Caldecott would have loved to dash off for the pages of the *Graphic*!) The women, on that rainy day, bore little resemblance to the "lasses" in the Picture Books. They wore navy blue mackintoshes or brown or black wool coats, and they covered their heads with plastic hoods. The bare-kneed children wore high black boots and navy blue mackintoshes belted with a wide buckle at the waist. Only the men, and especially the old ones, seemed unchanged by time. True, the fabrics they wore were transformed by a century's progress, but their silhouettes were the same as that of the old gaffers in *Daddy Darwin's Dovecote.* The stained and colorless mackintoshes reached only to the knee, for all the world cut on the same lines as the peasant smocks worn a century ago. Boots had replaced gaiters, but the hats (whatever their shape on the day of purchase) were as round and limp as the one worn by the farmer who sows his corn in *The House that Jack Built.* And everywhere was the same broad, beefy countenance, also made familiar by that same farmer.

John and Ian came shouldering their way through the crowd and we held a family council. The car had been parked in the inn yard at the Swan but there were no rooms for hire. We had arrived in Whitchurch on the day of semiannual cattle market. Farmers had flocked there from all over Shropshire and beyond. It was already afternoon. We should decide about a night's lodging, but we were too tired and hungry to make decisions. We bought tomatoes from one stall, cheese from another, and made our way back to the car to drive out into the country.

Down a narrow lane we found a wide (though muddy) spot to park near a gate, and pulled over for a picnic. Never had food tasted so good! After nine days of elaborate menus aboard ship we reveled in this simple fare and the freedom to eat it when and where we chose. The children sat astride the gate and gazed across the misty fields to wide horizons and rolling hills beyond. A blackbird sang out, the notes hanging like dewdrops in the still air. Suddenly, we heard a "whuffle" and the sound of heavy hoofs coming toward us down the road. A huge horse, similar to the one in *A Farmer Went Riding,* came into sight over the hedges. Two ruddy-faced boys

sat upon his broad back, not astride but with one pair of feet
dangling "port," the other, "starboard." Like the country
people whom we had seen in the market place, they wore
boots to their knees. Their bony young wrists and hamlike
hands shot out from rough tweed sleeves bespangled with
drops of mist. They seemed all of a piece with their heavy fet-
locked steed, but one of the boys slid from the Percheron's
back and unfastened the gate. No word was spoken. The children scrambled down quickly and we all watched in silence as
the giant horse was led around our little car. I do not think
any of us would have been greatly surprised to see the Ford
Anglia crushed like an egg shell beneath one of the hoofs. In a
moment boys and steed were lost to sight along the hedge,
but we stood staring, as though we had seen a vision. This was
pure Caldecott!

We drove back into Whitchurch and counted ourselves
lucky to find a hotel room for ourselves and Lucy at the
Old Vic, and a tiny, chintz-hung room for Ian in a respectable pub a few doors up the street. The motherly middle-aged
barmaid said she would see that he was tucked in properly at
night and that she would bring him his breakfast in the morning. We then set out to explore the town and to find if anyone
could give us a clue to where Randolph Caldecott had lived.
The town museum was like a family attic, filled with stuffed
ducks, an embroidered waistcoat, a magnificent Ark with Mr.
and Mrs. Noah and one hundred animals hand carved from
wood. A few faded brown ink sketches by Caldecott hung on
the wall. The old woman who acted as char and custodian
knew only that he had been a famous man, but where or why
she was not sure. John was almost sure he had seen similar
sketches in the hallway at The Swan, so we walked down

the hill to Watergate Street. There could be no doubt. The Swan was the original of The Angel, the inn to which the *Three Jovial Huntsmen* had repaired after the chase, but the proprietor's wife knew little beyond that. She suggested the newspaper office. The editor remembered that Caldecott had died "in Florida—you know, one of those South Seas places," because he had read it in an old book by Blackburn that had been kicking around the office until he presented it to the library. We seemed to have gone full circle.

Back in our room at the Old Vic, I stood at the window and looked down at the street. An estate agent's office was almost directly across from us and it occurred to me that this was a place that might have in its files the facts of who lived where, when. John was still game, so out we went again. Two extremely young men (not much older than a certain bank apprentice must have been) came to the counter to wait on us. Glancing about, I seemed to recognize the establishment of Mrs. Mary Blaize, the lady pawnbroker satirically described in Oliver Goldsmith's rhymes and further brought to life by Caldecott's illustrations in *The Great Panjandrum Picture Book.* It seemed not unlikely that she would have dabbled in real estate on the side, her sense of business being unerring. The two young men explained that their employer was away "on assessments," but they would do their best for us. Yes, they had heard of Caldecott, but surely we were not interested in so minor and uninteresting a person? Everyone else who came to town inquired about Edward German, the composer, a truly famous person who had owned a very grand house, besides.

The two young men could hardly hide their disdain at my ignorance, but wishing to be polite they turned the conversation to sports. Once again they had me at a disadvantage, and once again my husband stepped in to rescue the tattered remnants of American reputation. The talk switched back and forth from Newport to Henley, from Wimbledon to the World Series. It occurred to me that Whitchurch clerks have changed very little from Caldecott's day. Evidently the young men of the town have always lived and breathed the air of the sporting world, although I was willing to wager that neither of these two gentlemen had ever ridden forth to hounds on a lumbering farm horse, or tramped miles over the snowy fields to hunt rabbits. They looked as though they gleaned their knowledge from the "telly."

Finally we were able to extricate from them (after some checking in the files) that Caldecott had lived at Wirswell: "Under the railroad bridge, sharp to the left, up the bank." We would have to inquire among the houses when we got there. But were we absolutely sure that we did not want to take a run out to see Edward German's place? When they auctioned off Mr. German's estate ("the most splendid auction ever held in these parts, sir!") there had been a cardboard box full of sketches by Caldecott. ("Just scraps of paper, you know.") No one had wanted them particularly, and the young men remembered that the estate agent had been quite annoyed because he had hoped for some bidding. Finally the whole box was sold off to someone who rather fancied the hunting scenes.

"Pity you weren't there," said the young man pleasantly, "I think he paid only a couple of guineas for the lot!" John claims he had to support me, pale and tottering, from the office.

Getting to sleep that night was difficult. The crowds continued to mill about directly below our windows, and although it seemed at least two hundred years since we had left our ship that morning, our beds seemed to pitch and toss as though we were still on the Atlantic.

The next morning we woke to the sound of a pony clopping by. Lucy nearly fell out of the window in her excitement. The little cart below us, bright and shiny in the morning sun, was filled with bottles of fresh milk. How different the High Street looked! The town was absolutely deserted. We learned that during the night all the cattle had been driven out of town and, after the pubs closed, the crowds had left too. There was a rap at our door, and Ian came bouncing in. Why weren't we up? He had already had his breakfast, but he would have a second one with us. He evidently felt that he had really seen Life. The noise at the bar had kept him awake until after ten o'clock, but as soon as closing time was called the motherly proprietress had gone up to tuck him in.

I left the family at the breakfast table and sallied forth to do a little shopping. Coming out of the hotel, I looked up the street toward the square-towered church at the top. Now that the narrow sidewalks were no longer so thronged that one had to fight for foothold, I could appreciate that we had walked into *The Great Panjandrum Picture Book* the day before, and had not been able to realize it. Whitchurch had scarcely changed since the Great She Bear had come walking down the High Street. The church was the same, and surely the little shops were equally untouched by time.

This was the morning that I was to be initiated into the mysteries of British shopping. The little basket over the She Bear's arm, I was soon to find, was almost a necessity. Nothing comes ready wrapped in English villages, and it cost three pence for a flimsy paper bag to carry one's purchases in. I went in and out of the little shops, learning as I went. Fruit is bought at the florist's. (Of course! He owns a greenhouse.) Canned and frozen food one buys at Woolworth's. I had to go back up the hill to the butcher in order to buy butter. Outside and in, the butcher shop was decorated with blue and white tiled pictures of sheep and cattle. The meat was set out on great slabs of marble without benefit of refrigeration. Although everything was scrupulously clean, I seemed to be much more aware that life's blood must be spilled, oozed, and dripped about unless we all turn vegetarian. The butter was set out in great tubs. Which did I want? New Zealand . . . Guernsey . . . Shropshire? I chose the local product and watched while the butcher weighed out a quarter of a pound, then asked him where I could buy bread. That all depended, he said. Did I just want bread, or did I want Hovis? The shop down the street was licensed to sell Hovis and (glancing at the clock) it should be just coming out of the oven now.

Down the street I went again and into a dusky little shop marked by a green and gold "Hovis" sign. I knew at once where I was. Bunches of millet hung from the ceiling and the walls behind the counter were lined with small drawers. With difficulty I restrained myself from shouting out "What! No Soap!" and glancing over my shoulder to see if the Great She Bear would "pop her head into the shop." Nothing so exciting happened—yet. The rosy-faced girl behind the counter explained that the bread was not out of the oven, but if I would care to wait. . . . She swept an indignant tortoise-shell cat off the chair and I sat down, wondering idly if this cat was a descendant of the one "who killed the rat who ate the malt that lay in the house that Jack built." Almost at the same instant the door opened, a woman came into the shop with a dog on a short thick chain, and the cat sprang up to the counter arching its back. No wonder! For here was the very dog who had worried the cat (and who was later "tossed by the cow with a crumpled horn"). All my life I had believed that the excruciatingly ugly brindle bulldog in the Caldecott illustrations was a product of the artist's imagination or, at best, a unique specimen of dogdom. Before the day was out I was to see two or three more of the same breed and to learn that this is the famous Whitchurch brindle, born and bred to a life of herding cattle and noted, despite the unfortunate mishap depicted in *The House that Jack Built*, as being an excellent work dog.

I had hardly recovered from the start of recognition before the dog was dragged back out of the shop by its owner. The cat, its back still arched, took several minutes before it would risk climbing down from its perch. The little shopgirl excused herself to run back behind the shop to look at the ovens. A moment later she was back again, skipping into the shop, tossing and juggling a loaf of bread before her. Her sleeves were rolled above the elbow; the revelation of round, firm arms making her more than ever "pure Caldecott."

"That be jolly hot, that!" she said, and wrapped the loaf in a piece of newspaper for me to carry. Oh, how good it smelled! And it was better than a fur tippet to carry against the chill. I bought a wedge of cheese (cut carefully with a string that dangled from the ceiling) and some hundreds-and-thousands out of a big glass jar with a beautifully japanned lid. It was not so much that I thought the children would enjoy the candy that prompted me to do so, but the fun of seeing the delightfully unself-conscious way the girl moved about among ancient shop fixtures and modern advertisements. Some of the containers had probably been on the counter when Randolph Caldecott came to town.

John and the children were waiting impatiently by the time I got back to the inn. What on earth had kept me? The car was all packed and we wedged ourselves in among the suitcases and started out for Wirswell. Too small to be a village, it was not even marked on our map. There could not have been more than half a dozen houses in the district. But where to begin? There was a large Tudor manor house with "Tarrick Hall" marked over the mailbox. It might have belonged to the Master of the Farmer's Boy. It seemed the most likely repository of local lore. I walked to the house and rang the bell. A little parlormaid answered, complete in uniform and ribbons, and said she would consult "the master." An imposing gentleman came to the door and informed me that no Mr. Caldecott lived in the house. I tried to explain that Mr. Caldecott had been dead these many years, that he had been a famous illustrator, but that when he was a young bank clerk in Whitchurch he had boarded with farmers in Wirswell. "I knocked at the door merely to inquire. . . ." I thought the gentleman was about to have apoplexy.

"Madam," he said, "we do not take boarders. You have been misinformed. This has always been a very *important* house. The present Earl of Harlech was born here. I was assured of that when I bought the place. But we do not show the room to visitors. . . ." I beat a hasty retreat down the drive to where John and the children were waiting in the car.

This left only three or four other houses to be accounted for in Wirswell. They all seemed vaguely familiar and the largest (now an old people's home) seemed to us very like the one from which the "maiden all forlorn" issued forth to do her milking. Later inquiry brought us a letter from the Clerk of Whitchurch Urban District Council in which he informed us that Caldecott had lived "at Hinton Old Hall which is on the outskirts of the town and quite close to Wirswell. . . ." No doubt we saw it even if we could not immediately identify it. If only we could have had a complete set of the Picture Books in hand!

We were not the only ones who have set out to explore Caldecott country. In his biographical memoir Henry Blackburn quotes a letter from an unnamed pilgrim who preceded us:

> During occasional rambles in this and the neighboring country of Chester, more especially in the neighborhood of Whitchurch, I have been interested in the identification of some of the original scenes pictured by Mr. Caldecott in his several published drawings. Thus:—
>
> Malpas Church, which occupies the summit of a gentle hill some six miles from Whitchurch, occurs frequently—as in a full page drawing in the *Graphic* newspaper for Christmas, 1883; in *Babes in the Wood*, p. 19; in *Baby Bunting*, p. 20; and in *The Fox Jumps Over the Parson's Gate*, p. 5.
>
> The main street of Whitchurch is fairly pictured in *The Great Panjandrum*, p. 6, whilst the old porch of the Blue Bell portrayed on p. 28 of *Old Christmas* is identical with that of the Bell Inn at Lushingham, situated some two miles from Whitchurch on the way to Malpas. . . .

It seems strange that Caldecott did not consider himself a good landscape artist and refused several commissions to do such work. During his trips to the continent it was the people who captured his fancy and set his pencil going; châteaux and cathedrals he left to others. Occasionally, as in the sketches of Parliamentary scenes for *Pictorial*, he would have another artist "fill in" the architecture. I cannot think why. The world he created in his children's books certainly does not lack veracity. Although he was gifted, ambitious, and experimental, he seems to have set certain limits for himself. His Breton folk bear little resemblance to the tortured peasants of van Gogh and Gauguin; his eye for the foibles of high society is as keen as Lautrec's, but he lacks the savagery. One would wonder if he had ever heard of the Impressionists, yet when he died Vincent van Gogh was among those who paid him tribute in a letter of condolence written to his widow.

Caldecott left Whitchurch in 1867, when he was twenty years old, to go to Manchester where he clerked in a bank, joined an artists' club. From Manchester he went on to success in London and made several continental sketching tours with his friend Blackburn. In 1886 he and his wife sailed for the United States, hoping that the Florida climate would alleviate his tubercular condition. He continued to send off cheerful notes and sketches to the *Graphic*. The people he saw during a stopover in Washington fascinated him, especially American Negroes and the pioneer types he saw in the rotunda of the Capitol. He even managed to take part in a fox hunt in Maryland, his caustic pencil recording a countryside already beset with outdoor advertising. A few weeks later he died in Florida. He was barely forty.

If ever a man truly loved a place, that man was Caldecott and that place was Whitchurch. One might almost say he was in love with it and that his Picture Books represent some of the most delightful love letters in the world. The green triangle made by Whitchurch, Malpas, and Wirswell is almost unbearably dear and familiar to anyone who knows his Caldecott. The fields and lanes gave us the feeling of homecoming that John and I were to discuss many times. Each of us had one English-born parent, and we were brought up on more or less the same books. Now we found ourselves in a countryside we had shared unknowingly. Those enormous pigs! Those fawn-colored cows! The broad-faced farmer striding across his fields! We knew them all. The feeling went beyond our childhoods into the ghostly past.

Now, as John drove our car through the very countryside made known to us along with our nursery rhymes, I glanced at the children, covertly watching their reactions. Ian, even as John and I, seemed to be struggling with a half-remembered dream, but to Lucy the line between shadow and substance offered no problems. Although she had been born only thirty months before, she had spent a great deal of that time in Caldecott country. How many times she had sat on my knee (as she was doing now) so that we could open wide the book and let her enter in. So many people had argued against our taking her on this trip to England, that we had become dubious ourselves. Lucy's whole life, ran the argument, was taken up with eating and sleeping and diapers. She would not care where she was, nor would she remember where she had been. Now, studying her bright little face, I was made humble. Lucy could accept absolutely that she had entered a world where she was already at home. She was the only one among us who did not need a guidebook.

2
The Open Road

From Whitchurch we drove south. We hoped to reach Chepstow by nightfall so were determined not to stop more often than we could possibly help. We ate our lunch of bread and cheese in the car but by afternoon everyone was hungry again so we stopped at a "tea chalet." For the first time I began to realize the difficulties of traveling with American children in England. Ian and Lucy seemed to grow before my very eyes. They were noisy, brash, ill mannered, strangely dressed, and enormous! There were other children present, but one would scarcely know it. They ate their bread and cake and drank their tea—silently. Their round blue eyes gazed at us in astonishment, but no one pointed or asked questions. They spoke when they were spoken to. Heavens! Our children talked all the time! But far worse than the collective gaze of the children was the attitude of their parents. The noisier and messier my children were, the more determined they were not to notice us. Before the trip was done I was to develop a much tougher skin, but now I could hardly wait until John had paid the bill and we could beat a retreat.

The stop for food had done us good, but the children were
still cramped and crowded in the back seat. We decided that
we would have to jettison cargo somewhere or we would never
make it to Cornwall. We drove through lovely vales and came
to Shrewsbury, thronged with Saturday shoppers. We drove
on, up into the hills that led to the Welsh Marches, then
down again into Ludlow Town. We threaded our way through
streets so narrow that shoppers had to crowd into doorways to
let our tiny car go by. The road makes a sharp Z in the middle
of the town and Ian, glancing back, caught a glimpse of his
first real castle. I wish we had been able to stop, but a policeman waved us on, and in another moment or two we had shot
out of the bottleneck into open country again.

It was late afternoon when we drove into Monmouth. Lucy
and I headed for a sign marked Public Convenience, but John
and Ian strolled over to look at the statue of Sir Harry Royce
who stood with airplane in hand. Suddenly, above them, in
the portico of the town hall, they spied another Harry—Harry
of Monmouth. The king's nose was chipped, his garments
were worn, and the pigeons had given him a collar of dirty
ermine. But he was not entirely forgotten. Ladders and
scaffolding stood about, and it was evident that not only was
he destined for a good cleaning, but someone had been regild-
ing his crown. By the time Lucy and I returned from our excursion, Ian was gazing up at him as at an old friend.

Just a few months before our trip we had taken him to see
Sir Laurence Olivier's magnificent and classic film, *Henry V.*
How he had loved it! But of course this was not his first intro-
duction to that particular king for we owned a copy of Marcia
Brown's *Dick Whittington and His Cat.* On our return from
the theater Ian had rushed upstairs to find the book and

brought it down in triumph. There, on the last page, was Richard Whittington, "thrice Lord Mayor of London," and, to do him honor, his most distinguished visitors, Henry V and his little French queen. Studying the spare black and mustard block prints that make the illustrations, Ian noticed and pointed out to us something that had hitherto escaped us. In some of the pictures we could see what was going on inside the houses at the same time we saw what was happening in the street. It was as though the wall had been sheared away. Of course Ian, like most children, had drawn that way for years, but recently he had become much more conventional. And like most recent converts, he tended to be critical. I tried to show Ian that this X-ray technique of Marcia Brown's was not lack or oversight, but an attempt to get the "feel" of the fifteenth century by using the techniques of contemporary illustrators. Hastily rummaging through our shelves, I was able to find *Life's Picture History of Western Man,* containing a reproduction of the Duc de Berry's *Book of Hours.* Studying those jewel-like pages, we suddenly realized that whoever designed the unforgettable sets for the motion picture had turned to this same source. Why, here in "February," was where the Welsh captain had argued with his allies. . . .

We had known that we were a trifle mad to take Lucy on a literary tour of England, but some people had even argued against our taking Ian. Why not wait until he was older? Until he had read more? Until he had developed a sense of historical perspective? Now we were vindicated. Ian stood in that ancient empty square and gazed upward, his face a study in delight. Above him stood the king—proud, imperious, though a little battered. Perhaps his fossil heart was momentarily quickened by the homage paid by a small American boy in the square below. An old magic was at work. Given the chance, Ian would have laid heart and sword at Henry's feet, willing to follow him anywhere.

We drove across the bridge that leads out of the town, and now the road led between high, wooded hills and around ox-bow bends. We seemed to be the only car on the road, and in the late afternoon shadows it was easy to imagine ambushes and raiding parties, the glint of steel and clash of armor. We came to a tiny deserted village of stone cottages, the roofs caved in and covered with vines. An old man with a staff in his hand and a dog at his heels stood by the side of the road and watched our car go by. He looked like a figure out of Wordsworth. In a little while the valley widened, we passed green fields and comfortable farmhouses, then suddenly our hearts leaped. Ahead of us the fretted ruins of Tintern Abbey seemed to float toward us in the translucent air.

I felt then that I had come home. My grandfather's house was but five miles from Tintern. My mother had filled my childhood with tales of all the country around and I, in turn, had passed them on to Ian. Alas! We had come too late. It was just six o'clock and a man was clanging the gate shut and turning a key in the black iron lock when we turned into the parking lot.

We decided to drive on to Chepstow and spend the night there in an old inn where my family had spent a week when I was a little girl. I painted a glowing picture of it to John and Ian. There was a high-walled garden where my sisters and I had played shuttlecock; there were blue and white tiles surrounding a window or fireplace (I could not remember which), and I could still remember an upstairs drawing room with a glass-fronted bookcase which contained the best ghost story I had ever encountered. But when we came to it I would not have recognized the old inn except for a sign above the door. Where were the old stone stairs that had gone up one side of it? A huge, red brick cinema had been built so close that there was not room for the outside stair now, hardly room to slip a knife blade between the buildings. Where was the quaint walled garden? Gone, gone under blacktop. Reluctantly we went inside. Lucy, tired of being cramped in the car all day, broke loose from my grasp and ran down the corridor. I managed to waylay her on the first landing of the staircase. As I turned to come down again I found myself gazing straight into a blue and white tiled alcove. Lucy was as enchanted as I. Here were Mr. and Mrs. Noah; here were Adam and Eve. The tiles were extremely old—seventeenth century, perhaps—but their colors, their freshness, their naïveté seemed like the morning of the world. No wonder I had remembered them, however vaguely, over all the years. This was the place! We signed the register.

That night, after I had tucked Lucy in bed, I tried to find the drawing room and the book containing the ghost story so that I could read it to Ian. But the old drawing-room fireplace had been replaced by a sterile "electric fire," and there was not a book to be seen. The room was empty, most of the guests evidently preferring the bar downstairs or the television in the lounge. The marvelous ghost story (which I had never finished) was lost forever. I returned to our rooms on the fourth floor. The Saturday night cinema, just the other side of the wall, was in full blast. There was no use trying to sleep. John and I spent the time until midnight packing and repacking our belongings, trying to pick out what we would need for

our camping trip in Cornwall, relegating the remainder to two
suitcases we planned to leave in Chepstow. Sometime after
midnight we crept into bed and fell into troubled sleep.

Next morning our car crept down the steep, cobbled streets,
then across the quiet river. Looking back, we saw the walls and
turrets of Chepstow Castle reflected in the Wye. To Ian, the
sight was almost unbearably frustrating. Here was another
castle he was not allowed to visit. What was the good of coming to England at all, he asked dramatically, if we were going
to drive by every interesting thing we saw? In vain we pointed
out to him that we had promised to reach St. Agnes, Cornwall,
by Monday, in order to claim our reservation, and this was
Sunday. We had made far too many stops, and now we were
behind schedule. In the resulting argument I somehow failed
to keep my eye on our trusty Bartholomew's *Road Atlas of
Great Britain*, and we missed the turn to the ferry that was to
give us a shortcut across the Severn.

"We can turn around at the first wide place on the road," I
said reassuringly, but miles went by with no wide place appear-
ing. "Oh, well!" said John at last, "We might as well drive on
to Gloucester and double back from there." Lucy sat up suddenly and took her thumb out of her mouth. "Am I sick?" she
asked. Hastily I felt her forehead. "No," I said, "you aren't
sick." I knew enough to be firm. But Lucy was not to be put
off. "I don't *want* to go to the doctor." I tried to soothe her.
"We aren't going to the doctor. For Heaven's sake! Whatever
gave you *that* idea?" Lucy stopped in mid-howl. "Doctor
Foster," she said. "Daddy said 'Doctor Foster,'" For a moment we were all puzzled, then we began to laugh. It had
taken Lucy to remind us that Gloucester was not just a dot on
the map, but a place fabled in song and story:

Doctor Foster went to Gloucester
In a shower of rain.
He stepped in a puddle right up to his middle
And never went there again.

Then, of course, Ian remembered Beatrix Potter's *The Tailor of Gloucester*. Craftily he pointed out that since we had not stopped at the castle we *must* find the place where the Tailor had lived. John hesitated. "We'll see when we get there," he said, but when we crossed the bridge and came to the big intersection he did not take the road to Bristol. Instead, he drove straight into the heart of the old city. Off to our left we could see the lovely tower of the cathedral. The tailor had lived near the cathedral, we remembered, but although we tried several narrow Sabbath-emptied streets, our little car seemed to go in circles, never quite finding a way to penetrate the maze. Then we saw a sign marked Westgate Street, a name familiar from the book. We turned down the narrow way where the old houses seemed to lean over and touch foreheads above us. The street ended in a tiny square or court surrounding an ancient cross. A stone-arched gateway yawned across the way and through it we could glimpse grass and flowers. Miss Potter tells us that although the Tailor's shop was in Westgate, ". . . he lived quite nearby in College Court, next the doorway to College Green. And although it was not a big house, the tailor was so poor he only rented the kitchen. . . . He lived alone with his cat; it was called Simpkin."

Would John let us stop and explore? I would not blame him if he decided not to. It seemed too much to ask, especially after my failure to watch the map. We crept around the square in our tiny car to a halt in front of the old archway.

"Look! There's Simpkin!" he shouted, his voice full of sudden wonder and delight. He was as surprised as we at his own enthusiasm. And sure enough, there in the arch was a haughty tortoise-shell cat shaking rain water from his paws in such a disgusted and Simpkin-like manner that there could be no doubt.

John parked the car and opened the doors so we could stumble out and stretch our legs. Rain had been falling, but now it had stopped and watery sunlight began to shine through. Before our delighted eyes we saw the College Green and the old cathedral made bright in blinding sunshine. The children ran ahead of us and out of the archway, eager to revel in sun and grass and flowers. John and I strolled in their wake, marveling at houses already old "in the time of swords and periwigs. . . ." The houses were very old, but each one was tended with loving care. Every garden was mowed and clipped and crowded with flowers, every diamond pane sparkled in the sunlight. Morning service was being conducted in the cathedral. We could hear the voices of the choir and, peeking through the great doors, we had an impression of vast depths, flickering candles, and shards of sunlight filtered through stained glass.

We started back toward the gate and noticed Simpkin stretched full length upon a wall, soaking up warmth and sunlight. He lay with one eye closed, the other a mere green slit, but we were well aware that he was watching us. The children came running back along the paths and we seized the opportunity to herd them through the archway and into the car again. Simpkin, pretending haughty disdain, had leaped down from his wall and followed us out to the car. Ian leaned out to wave him an especially fond farewell.

It was in 1902, soon after the publication of *Peter Rabbit*, that Beatrix Potter visited Gloucester and heard the story of an old tailor who had left a coat unfinished, and the next day discovered it completed except for one buttonhole. Whoever (or whatever) had done the work, had pinned a note: "No more twist." There was something in this little mystery that intrigued Miss Potter. She sketched the house in College Court where the old tailor was said to have lived, and the old buildings in Westgate Street where he had had his shop. Her passion for old furniture and architectural detail set her to working on drawings of the interiors of the old cottages too. She wrote down the story in an ordinary copy book and sent it off to her former governess's little girl, Freda Moore, sister to the little boy for whom she had written *Peter Rabbit*. The letter that went with it appears as the dedication in the book:

My Dear Freda:
  Because you are fond of fairytales, and been ill, I have made you a story all for yourself—a new one that nobody has read before.
  And the queerest thing about it is—that I heard it in Gloucestershire, and that it is true—at least about the tailor, the waistcoat and the
    "No more twist."

Miss Potter was too shy (and too proud) to badger her publishers with another book so soon after the publication of *Peter Rabbit*. She herself paid for a private edition and eventually a copy made its way into the hands of Norman Warne. He liked the book but was hesitant to print it without abridgment. Miss Potter set about to write and rewrite, to polish her prose and to place each word and phrase in proper and precise relationship. Then she was ready to set the jewels. The scenes of Gloucester she had done the year before, but to make the exquisite studies of eighteenth-century clothes and embroidery she went to South Kensington Museum where she must have spent hours transposing the richness and texture of the needleman's art to paint and paper. The resultant illustrations have almost the effect of *trompe-l'oeil*. I have seen a small child reach out and wonderingly touch his finger to the page.

> The stitches of those buttonholes were so neat—*so* neat—I wonder how they could be stitched by an old man in spectacles, with crooked old fingers and a tailor's thimble.
>
> The stitches of those buttonholes were so small—*so* small— they looked as if they had been made by little mice!

We drove back to the main intersection in Gloucester and took the road to Bristol. It was late afternoon when we threaded our way through Bristol's unmarked streets. We were thankful to be tackling it on a quiet Sunday. On the map the city looks too far inland to be much of a port, but its sheltered access to the sea makes it a major one. We crossed the Avon where ocean-going vessels rode the tide, and remembered that it was from here that the *Hispaniola* sailed, and where Jim Hawkins first met Long John Silver. We looked in vain for Master Silver's "Spy-glass," a little tavern with a large brass telescope for a sign. We all agreed that it sounded an ideal place to stop for a meal: cheerful and clean, with new red curtains at the windows and a freshly swept floor. John said he would be perfectly willing to share a table with Black Dog and have a one-legged pirate do the cooking for him. In fact, he was so hungry he would be amenable to anyone's doing the cooking!

John peered hopefully into each window as we passed, but every wayside tea place seemed to be closed. Just before coming to Bridgewater we began to see those strange and (to us) un-British notices: No Gypsies and Gypsies Not Served Here. We had seen signs like these before, of course, directed against another and larger minority in the United States. Our liberal reflexes were in perfect working order; we felt our hackles rising, even as at home. But it was disconcerting, now that we were faced with it, how little we knew about gypsies or "the gypsy problem." It was not until we had returned to the United States and I had spent some hours poking about in the files of the British Information Services in Rockefeller Center, that we were able to fill out our scanty store of knowledge.

We found out later that there are approximately a hundred thousand "travelers" who roam the English roads and countryside, although only one third of them are true Romany. There is probably not an English gypsy today who can speak the pure language that is said to have come from India centuries ago, but the Anglo-Romany language is still unique in itself. With few exceptions, it would seem foolish to claim respectability—by ordinary Anglo-Saxon middle-class standards —for the average gypsy. Although he lives by a strict social code of his own, he does not necessarily apply this code to the "gorgio." It is perfectly permissible, for instance, to lie, cheat, beg, steal, trespass, and poach as long as the victim is nongypsy. Gypsies must pose a ticklish problem for local authorities, especially since many of them steadfastly refuse to send their children to school for fear of separating them from their Romany heritage. In recent years, the encroachments of suburbia and the building of council houses on once-free common lands has steadily cut into their camping sites and forced the issue of tolerance on the local level. Despite the efforts of the government, when gypsy children *do* go to school, they are more often than not put into segregated classrooms.

But driving along the Bridgewater Road that Sunday afternoon, we could only rely on our memories to supply us with gypsy lore. John remembered stray bits from George Borrow's *Romany Rye* and *The Little Minister* and Ian asked us not to forget the gypsy whose shoe figured so prominently in the *The Borrowers Afield*. And then there was the *Impractical Chimney Sweep*: he was only half-gypsy, but in the end he married a gypsy girl. But what Ian remembered best of all was the picture in Arthur Rackham's *Book of English Ballads*. The next moment we were all trying to sing as much as we could remember of "The Gypsy Laddy":

> Last night you slept on a goose-feather bed
>   With the sheet turned down so bravely, O.
> Tonight you will sleep in the cold, open field
>   Along with the Raggle, Taggle Gypsies, O.

We felt the song especially apropos since we ourselves were bound for Cornwall to camp out on the moors. We had arranged to rent a caravan and rather fancied ourselves as wayfarers, albeit somewhat in the amateurish way of Mr. Toad in *The Wind in the Willows*. John warned us, however, that it would not be tonight that we would be sleeping in the "cold, open field." We were far behind schedule and would have to stop soon to search for more civilized lodgings. John and I both were busily peering for Bed and Breakfast signs when Ian suddenly called out, "Hey, look! Gypsies!" We looked to where he was pointing and, sure enough, saw a whole encampment on the other side of the road.

John stopped the car, evidently resigned to missing deadlines, and we made our way across the road to peer through a wire fence. Some of the "caravans" were what we would call modern trailers, but down at the brook, in one corner of the field, were several suitably romantic types, their shafts resting on the grass, smoke curling from their chimneys.

Nowadays, having done a little reading and research, our family rather prides itself as expert on the subject and we would like to think that we can just cast a glance over a gypsy wagon and be able to tell you immediately where it came from, its relative cost, and who built it—rather like old sailors being able to tell a ship's identity by the cut of her jib. But at the time when all this book-learning would have served and we could have put it to the test, we did not know the difference between a Reading wagon (the largest) and a Fen (the smallest, and now virtually extinct). Indeed, we were so ignorant that we did not know that the term "caravan" is never used by a true gypsy. He calls his house-on-wheels a "living wagon." The misnomer seems to have been first applied by Dickens when describing Mrs. Jellicoe's van in *The Old Curiosity Shop*.

The wagon that now caught our eye was painted green and yellow, its barrel-shaped body flaring out to about six and a half feet at its widest point. It was rather small, so perhaps it was a Leeds wagon, built by Bill Wright & Sons, although I seem to remember that the high painted wheels were outside the body. An old woman, wrinkled and nut brown, sat on the steps at the opening and stared at us. A collection of children pressed close to her, peering out at us with bright, dark eyes through tangled hair. (Brian Vesey-Fitzgerald, in his book *British Gypsies,* writes that Romany children are the happiest and most spoiled in the world.) The children tumbled and struggled like so many puppies, striving for a seat closer to the grandmother or the better to see the gorgios, but the old woman sat unmoving and stared straight at—or through—us with eyes as bright as any of the children's. An old black dog leaped down from the interior and came running toward the fence, sniffed once or twice at us, and returned to the children. He did not bark, but neither did he wag his tail.

In the end it was we who were discomfited. We could not simply stand there and stare as though we were watching animals in the zoo, although the old grandam seemed to find us infinitely amusing. We were told later that we should have offered money and perhaps she would have let us take a picture, but this seemed a poor way to begin a friendship.

I am certain that if the fence had not intervened Ian and Lucy would have tried their best to make friends, but I also have an idea that the old grandmother might have hustled her own brood into the wagon. It struck me that she had a decidedly low opinion of us gorgios.

During World War II the British government exhibited great imagination in putting everyone to work, and even the gypsies' peculiar skills and arts were woven into the scheme of things. A man who can walk up on a rabbit, seize it and wring its neck, then make a quick getaway is admirably suited for detonation work, where nerve and deftness count. Former tinkers were set to making small airplane parts and their wives and daughters went to work in factories where they were re-

nowned for their dexterity. The New Forest gypsies set up
their own factory under the dappled shade of the King's Oaks
and subcontracted to make small parts for munitions and air-
planes. Even Petulengro, king of the British Romany tribes,
offered his royal services. He possessed extraordinary knowledge of every flower and herb in England and he gave a series
of talks over the BBC on the uses of herbs and foods from the
wayside.

When one considers that in totalitarian countries the
"gypsy problem" has been solved by simple extermination, it
is heartwarming to know that the Briton's exasperation is
rarely more than just that. There is something in the Englishman's heart that quickens to true eccentricity, and if the
gypsy's right to be himself is threatened, then every Englishman hears the tolling of the bell. Someone, somewhere is
bound to Ask Questions.

Months later, when we were home in the United States,
John ran across such a someone in Hansard's *Parliamentary
Debates* while perusing some research of his own. Knowing
that I would be interested, he jotted down a few notes to
bring home to me. It would seem that on June 20, 1956, a
certain Mr. Dodd (Erith and Crayford, Lab.) informed the
Minister of Housing and Local Government that a serious position had arisen because of the enforcement of laws which
made no allowance for the protection of traditional gypsy
sites. The problem could not be adequately dealt with by
local authorities, but only by the government. . . .

Mr. Godfrey Nicholson (Farnham, C.) argued that it
would be a great tragedy if "this historic and picturesque
community were squeezed out by the growing pressure of in-
dustrialization and the bureaucratic system. . . ."

Mr. Powell (H. and L. G.): "I am too great an admirer of George Borrow not to agree with that." (Cheers.)

But Mr. Dodd was not to be put off so easily: "In view of the unsatisfactory nature of the Answer I beg to give notice that I shall raise the matter . . . after I have raised the matter of white bread." And sure enough, a few days later Mr. Dodd is at it again: "Is the Minister of Education aware that gypsy children are not being taught to read and write? . . . that they are being placed in separate class rooms?"

To this Sir D. Eccles seems only able to respond: "As long as gypsies are gypsies their children's education will be a problem."

But do not think for one moment that Parliament had heard the last of this. The gypsy is not without allies, for according to Hansard's the hearing would be resumed when new evidence would be introduced on behalf of the Commons, Open Spaces and Footpaths Preservation Society. Surely the gypsy has nothing to fear as long as the C.O.S. & F.P. Society (or its equivalent) exists in Britain!

We stopped that night at a farmhouse just outside Taunton. It had been a busy day, the car was misbehaving, and John was tired. We had had enough of hotels, so the Bed and Breakfast sign in the window of a clean and comfortable old house was more than we could resist. Our instinct proved right, for we were shown to a pleasant room with a double bed for ourselves and two smaller beds tucked back under the eaves for the children. The bathroom was down the hall and the maid would bring hot water for shaving in the morning. It was very like the tourist homes one used to stay in before the advent of the motel, the only difference being that the owners included a hearty breakfast in the price for a room. We could have supper, too, but it would be a few shillings extra.

The next morning, after a wonderful country breakfast, John took the car into Taunton for repairs, and the children and I explored through a gate in the wall of the garden. We found ourselves on the towpath for the old Taunton-Bridgewater Canal. Bridges arched at regular intervals, geese and ducks paddled in the osiers, cows stood knee-deep in dew-wet grass. Ian gathered stones and skipped them over the surface of the canal, while Lucy and I wandered along behind, stopping to talk to a cow, a tethered goat, and a family of young pigs. It was the first time that our suburban-reared Lucy had ever been so close to real live farm animals, and to her it was a most important event. I was a little ashamed of myself for having neglected her education. The morning was so sparkling that we walked a good mile or so without even realizing it— and then it began to rain. The heavens simply opened, and we were drenched through in a minute. I called to the children to creep in under one of the arched bridges and while I took a firm grip on Lucy we huddled together and listened to the rain drumming above us and saw the canal rise perceptibly higher at our feet. We finally decided that we must return to the farmhouse. Of course, no sooner did we get back to our room than the sun shone out more gloriously than ever. John had been caught in the rain, too, so we had to take time for hot baths and a change of clothes all around. We had learned another lesson: when in England, never venture anywhere without rain gear.

We were late getting started again and although the car had spent the morning in a garage its temper did not seem one whit improved. We still had almost one hundred miles to

go, and although in America such a run would mean only two
or three hours, in England it seemed to take forever. Before
leaving home in the United States we had been pleased to
realize how short the distances must be from one landmark to
another in England, but now that we were actually scuttling
along the narrow roads in our tiny car it seemed as though we
ourselves had been reduced to scale. It must have been a state
of mind, but we felt as though we were making a transcon-
tinental journey or that we had wandered out of Bartholowmew's England into Tolkien's *Hobbit* country.

Hour after hour we drove through mist or rain under lower-
ing skies. The children were too tired even for crankiness. I
remember the green hills giving way to great brown sweeps of
moor and long stretches of roadside, where we saw almost no
evidence of human habitation and only a few sheep, as wild as
mountain goats. Once in a while, when the rain lifted, I
would see a high crag or tor in the distance, and sometimes, in
the hollows, the gray glint of a tarn. We were pleased to discover how easily a lifetime of reading enables one to fit the
right words to the landscape. We had climbed to what must
have been almost the highest point on the road when I saw an
inn, a large, low, rambling building with beetling roof and a
board that creaked in the wind. Glancing back, my heart
missed a beat when I read the sign: Jamaica Inn. The day before we might have stopped, but now we flew past as though a
pack of smugglers were at our heels. At least, I thought, we
could not be too far from the sea.

Tired, cold, hungry, we crept into St. Agnes in the late
afternoon. The address we had been given was Beacon Cottage which, I had assumed, indicated a lighthouse nearby. We
stopped in the village to inquire the whereabouts of such a

landmark, only to learn that the entire hill, on whose inland flank the village was perched, was known as The Beacon.

We started out again, skirting the hill and following the line of the coast. We stopped at a lonely farmhouse where a weather-beaten sign advertised cream and I made my way to the door, quite a distance from the road. A tall woman with crinkly red hair and a long narrow face answered to my knock. She looked like pictures of the first Queen Elizabeth. She recognized the name of our landlady and directed us farther down the road to "the next house."

"The lane's to the left. You can't miss it," she said, but we passed it several times before we realized we must open a farm gate first. The way led through a tunnel of wind-flattened pines, then we were in a circular drive, a gaggle of protesting geese running ahead of our car, and a huge, chained watchdog setting up a raucous bark. For a long moment we sat in the car, too numb with cold and fatigue to make a move. Then the door of the house opened and a bar of yellow light fell across the stone doorstep. A cheerful voice called out, "Why, it must be the Bodgers!" And then, "Come along inside, gypsies. We've been waiting for you."

3

A Peak in Narnia

It was dark under the trees in the farmyard and the light from the door had temporarily blinded us so that we could not quite make out who had called out. Now a woman moved toward us, dressed in old trousers, a velvet jacket, heavy brogues. For all this, our landlady was incontrovertibly feminine, her hair wrapped in shining silver coils around her head, her complexion soft and rosy as a young girl's. How heartwarming to be greeted at the end of a long journey! Although we had been in England for several days, I don't think we had spiritually arrived until we heard that cheery welcome and saw the accompanying smile.

Mrs. S. led us through the dairy-kitchen and into a parlor. After days of ocean-liner and hotel life, nothing could have been more homelike. We sat around the heavy round table and relaxed in the luxury of not having to watch the children's manners while we talked to our hostess. We were fascinated by her vast accumulation of West-Country lore. She seemed interested that we had stopped down the road to ask directions and was glad that I had had a chance to see "a true Cornish woman." The crinkly red hair, white skin, and long head were truly characteristic. Alas, her own family was not Cornish, although most of her ancestors *were* Celtic. This last was absolutely prerequisite to understanding Cornwall and the Cornish. She patted Lucy's red hair approvingly and inquired gravely into our own ancestry. She was relieved to find we both had Welsh blood in us. From our mothers? That was even better. The Welsh were an interesting people, too, and, of course, the Highlanders. All of them, like the Cornish, had been pushed back into the mountains and the deepest pockets of the island. Her own family, she said, had come originally from England. It was as though she spoke of another country, and I gathered that although her family had been on the farm for several generations she and the neighbors regarded her family as newcomers. She would show me the house later, she said. Part of it had been built in the 1100s . . . she would show me the beams . . . but of course it had been added to . . . modernized. We were in the new part now. Looking about me I surmised that the modernization had taken place in the eighteenth century.

We went out again, into the dooryard. The dog strained at his chain and barked at us. Mrs. S. apologized for having such a brute, but both the local police and her husband had strongly advised it. Cornwall was the last refuge of kings and scoundrels, and a large camp of "incorrigibles" had been established just a mile or so away—"people who never adjusted after the war, you know." As for the kings and nobility, they had run away to Cornwall all through history—and long before.

We went through a door in a wall and came out into a large meadow. Set in a ring about the grassy center was a score or so

of prosaic metal "trailers." Our hearts sank. Was one of these
to be our gypsy caravan? Ian looked as though he were about
to cry, and I gave him a warning glance, although I felt much
the same way myself.

I have wanted to live in a caravan ever since I was ten years
old and read a book called *The Slow Coach*, by E. V. Lucas.
It is about a family of English children who receive a caravan
delivered to their door by mistake, and who set out along the
dusty roads on a series of delightfully pastoral adventures.
The book has that same Robinson Crusoe quality that the
Arthur Ransome books have, although it was written a generation earlier and is long out of print. I had not been able to
find a copy to read to Ian, but I think I managed to communi-
cate some of its charm by telling him about it and by finding
substitutes. We read *Doctor Dolittle's Caravan* by Hugh Lofting and *The Fairy Caravan* by Beatrix Potter. We almost
knew *The Wind in the Willows* by heart.

It was with some trepidation that we followed Mrs. S. as
she escorted us past the campsite. Then she started up a path
that led out of the meadow and up toward the hill (or
Beacon) that reared up behind the farm. "Come along, gypsies. It's time to see your caravan." Hope sprang up again in
our breasts and we hastened to keep up with her. Above the
furze bushes we could see the top of what surely must be our
new living quarters. We pushed on and came into a wedge-
shaped clearing hedged all about with tough, twisted gorse
and furze. A heavy, straight-sided wagon stood there, the
wooden body painted green and perched high on silver-
aluminum wheels. There was a flight of wooden steps leading
up to the door in its side.

It was obvious that much thought had been given to the interior of the wagon. The sleeping quarters were divided from the "drawing room" by a partition which would be of great help in allowing people to have naps. There were three windows: one in the rear between the two tiers of bunks, and one on each side giving us lovely views of moor and sea. Inland we looked out upon our little clearing and then straight upward toward the Beacon which seemed to spring up as suddenly as Childe Rowland's Dark Tower. Seaward we had a breathtaking view of the gray Atlantic and we could see the winking lights of St. Ives curving to the southwest.

There was a writing table under the west window and a kerosene lamp with glass chimney. The front (or north) end of the wagon was fitted out with cupboards and a dresserful of colorful pottery dishes which our hostess gravely informed us were "for aesthetic purposes only" and not to be used in any circumstances. As a concession to the fact that we were American she had placed a small kerosene stove to the right of the door, although it was not part of the usual furnishings.

The principal difference between ours and a true gypsy wagon, of course, was that we had no cooking facilities within the wagon. Mrs. S. led us down the steps and across a small clearing recently hacked from the gorse and heather (we could see the twisted white roots, still raw) to what she called the "Bend or Bump." We all—except Ian and Lucy—bowed our heads and walked into an abandoned chicken coop. It had been hauled up on the hillside, scrubbed clean, whitewashed inside, and converted into a kitchen. The former roost served as a backbreakingly low and narrow counter all along one side, and the dishes and utensils were stacked neatly in the former nesting boxes. A large oilcloth-covered table was shoved under the eaves, surrounded by old omnibus seats. Jars and buckets of clean water had been brought up from the tap in the meadow, and there was—wonder of wonders—a gas stove, served by a large tank outside.

We were enchanted. This was what we had dreamed of. To think that even for a moment we had had any fears of not being "primitive" enough! The light from the row of windows above the roosts was beginning to fade, so we moved outdoors and over to the caravan again.

Mrs. S. had supplied us with blankets and sheets, and we made our beds and started to unload the car. We could not bring the car all the way up to the clearing, so it meant a long haul, but since we were to stay in the caravan for two weeks we felt it wise to empty the car completely. Our great concern was our laundry, which had grown to alarming proportions.

Lucy ran about at our heels, sniffing ecstatically at all the wonderful moor smells. She had taken off her shoes and I decided it was not worth it, in the wet grass, to struggle to put them on again. Ian had run off to explore. No sooner had he disappeared from sight than Mrs. S. arrived with more blankets, a copy of Robert Hunt's *Popular Romances of the West of England*, and warnings against letting the children wander down to the cliffs (they were apt to crumble), over to the chimneys (they were part of an old mine—very dangerous), or up on the hill (more mines and a neurotic horse). She was genuinely surprised that we had not known about the Beacon. She opened the old green and gilt cover of the book she had brought us and showed us the frontispiece by Cruikshank: "The Giant Bolster striding from the Beacon to Carn Brea—a distance of six miles." The hill above us was the second highest pinnacle in all low-lying Cornwall and had been used as a place for signal fires or celebrations since time began. The

Phoenicians were guided by lights on the Beacon when they came in search of tin, the Romans built a sentry post there, and pyres had been made ready to signal the coming of the Armada and an invasion from "Old Boney."

We looked up at the peak above us with awe and respect. Our caravan, in its lonely place on the moor, was closer to the top than any other dwelling. All about us the earth was pockmarked and scarred with mines and old ruins, although our untrained eyes saw only gorse and grassy hillside. Perhaps there were other things our eyes could not see—the ghost of a young Roman sentry, for instance, lost on the edge of the world somewhere between midnight and morning. . . .

I made supper of bread and butter, milk, and scrambled eggs. Ian reappeared in the nick of time to claim his share. His face was glowing, and I could see that the temptation for him to wander and explore was balanced only by *my* temptation to forbid him to go anywhere by himself. We explained to him the dangers of being caught in the steepsided coves at high tide, and he himself seemed quite sensible about the perils of mines and tunnels.

In the days to come my resolve sometimes failed me when I thought of the rain-drenched crumbling earth on the edge of a cliff or old shaft, but we let Ian wander over the moors to his heart's content, up to the Beacon and down to the sea. Who could forbid a child the right to Earth and Sky and Water? I remembered how the young mother in E. Nesbit's *The Railway Children* had given in in similar circumstances and let the children walk the rails, although it was against her better judgment. Because she was an "honest and honourable Mother" she had to admit that she, too, had done dangerous things when she was growing up. After she had finally given the permission to wander, the author, in one of her characteristic asides, confides:

> . . . and I daresay you think that she ought not to have said it. But she remembered about when she was a little girl herself, and she did say it—and neither her own children nor you nor any other children in the world could ever understand what it cost her to do it.

That night we slept in our narrow shelflike bunks with five blankets apiece over us—and never have I been so cold. Dawn finally came, and with it bright sunlight streaming through the skylight above us. We dressed as quickly as possible and crept out the door. The air outside was warmer than the air within. In a few minutes I had a kettle on to boil and we made breakfast. Supplies were so low that it was obvious that we must do some shopping in the village.

It was not only food that we needed. We realized that the children's shoes would be in a constant state of wetness as long as we lived on the moors, and it would be sensible to buy extra pairs of that cheap and sturdy variety of sandals sold all over England. I could remember them from my own childhood hanging in strings—like onions—outside the doorways of seaside shops. St. Agnes did not disappoint us—we found them at the local shoe store. At the draper's we bought a warm nightgown for Lucy, a schoolboy cap and a blue jersey for Ian.

On our way back to the car we noticed that a lorry parked next to the butcher's was being decorated with flowers. Obviously great doings were afoot, and when we stopped to read a placard in front of the Methodist Chapel we learned that the

annual St. Agnes Floral Fete would be held that very evening.
A queen would be selected from candidates between the ages
of ten and twelve years, all entrants being "members of this
parish." Teas, minerals, and Cornish pasties would be on sale.
"Minerals" we interpreted as meaning soda pop, but it was
the promise of Cornish pasties that won us over. We already
knew about those envelopes of pastry filled with a mixture of
meat, potatoes, carrots, and turnips. We had read about them
in Dorothy Spicer's *From an English Oven,* a book of folklore
and cookery, and had tried the recipe for ourselves. Upon rereading George MacDonald's *The Princess and the Goblins*
soon afterward we decided that Cornish pasties were probably
the mainstay of the hot lunch which Curdie's mother packed
for him to take into the mines.

We drove back to our caravan and I spent the afternoon
washing clothes in a bucket, hanging them to dry on the
spiny gorse bushes that ringed our campsite. Lucy and John
went to sleep in their bunks, Ian went exploring, and I spread
a blanket out on the grass, meaning to read and to write letters. The earth smelled of ferns and sweet grasses intermingled with tiny, almost microscopic, pink flowers. Sleepy in the
hot sun, I recalled that the date must be very near Midsummer's Eve and I wondered if the Fete had always been held so
close to the solstice.

In the early evening we bundled into the car and drove off
toward the village. Parking the car on the outskirts, we
glimpsed the procession coming down the High Street. First
came the constable, tall in uniform and helmet, his truncheon
held out in front of him like a scepter. He walked in solemn
cadence to the music, a few paces ahead of the village band.
Next a sad little last year's queen was borne along on the

butcher's lorry. All the little boys in the village seemed to be hanging to the tail gate and Ian promptly ran off to join them. Lucy, with a two-year-old's love of music, danced along with the little girls at the end of the procession, but as she grew tired her father picked her up and carried her. The village was more than a mile behind us when we came to the gates of an old country house. Tents were pitched on the lawn inside. We paid our sixpences at the gate (we discovered later that Ian had simply surged in on a wave of little boys), and found ourselves on the grounds of the Cornish Home for Unwed Mothers. We were mildly surprised, but remembering Mrs. S.'s description of Cornwall as a final refuge of fugitives and banished kings we bowed and smiled at the smock-clad young ladies who had crowded to the low-set French windows opening onto the lawn.

We mingled with the villagers, ate cold pasties, drank warm Coca-Cola, and voted for the queen. We had almost decided that this was no more than the usual dull church outing when, suddenly, three young men in tight, tight blue jeans leaped upon a platform. One of them held an enormous guitar and before John and I could quite grasp the situation, the trio launched into "The Jail House Rock," à la Elvis Presley. The new queen tapped her foot, the displaced queen smiled for the first time, the little princesses swayed back and forth on the platform. The villagers on the lawn broke into wild gyrations, the unwed mothers clapped their hands and cheered. A few elders looked on sourly, but most seemed to be enjoying the spectacle even if they did not participate. There followed "The Purple People Eater" and "You Ain't Nothin' But a Houn' Dog." The crowd went wild. John and I hardly dared look at each other when the Methodist minister, his face beaming and benign, called out to his flock: "I see we're all real gone tonight!"

We awoke the next morning to the sound of a gale and the patter of rain on the skylight. The storm lasted two days, then took another day to blow itself out. It was peaceful in the caravan. We slept for hours, especially John, who was still worn out by the rush of correcting exams before we left home. Somehow the ocean liner, with its constantly hovering stewards, had not been half so soothing as this solitude on the moors. I found a stack of old Penguin books in one of the lockers and began to gnaw a bookworm's trail through them. John and Ian continued to peruse the green and gilt copy of Robert Hunt's *Popular Romances of the West of England: the Drolls, Traditions and Superstitions of Old Cornwall*. I do not know whether it was the effect of those old tales, our isolated life, or our rich Celtic blood, but we became true believers.

We read how the Giant Bolster, having fallen in love with St. Agnes, was outwitted by her when he promised to fill a hole over Chapelporth way with his life's blood. He didn't know it was bottomless. Chapelporth was just around the curve of the next bay, and we promised ourselves that we would one day go see the hole which is still there in proof of the tale. We read about Dorcas, the poor woman who flung herself into a mine near St. Agnes and whose ghost haunts the village and nearby moors. Later, Mrs. S. was briskly positive in confirming the ghost's existence. Dorcas is often seen, and she rather makes a nuisance of herself down at the Railway Inn by turning certain pictures to the wall. We soon learned to differentiate between the varieties of Small People: Spriggans and Piskies, Knockers and Browneys (*sic*). It seemed quite natural to believe that we were especially vulnerable to their pranks and visitations, living as we did so far up the flanks of the most storied hill in Cornwall. It was comforting to know that we could protect ourselves by "turning the cloak," and none of us ventured out after dark without carefully turning jacket or sweater inside out.

The Knockers, who live in the mines, were especially interesting to us since they were so obviously related to the goblins who haunt George MacDonald's books. Although we knew that MacDonald had lived in the north of Scotland, we were convinced of Cornwall's being spiritually, if not geographically, a part of that strange, dim landscape that forms a background to his works. C. S. Lewis, in a preface to a collection of excerpts from MacDonald's letters and sermons, freely admits that it was the writings of the Scottish mystic that stirred his interest in Christianity, and acknowledges his debt to him. This being the case, we could not help feeling that Narnia was not too far off.

I shall always be grateful to the storm in Cornwall that drove us inward on ourselves. The quality of light being almost the same at ten in the morning as it was at ten at night, we lost all count of time. The soporific swaying of the wagon, the utter stillness of the moor broken intermittently by sounds of wind and rain, the glimpses of a shifting, shadowed landscape gave us the feeling of having embarked upon a long voyage.

English children's literature is filled with tales of children who fly back and forth in space and time. We had read the E. Nesbit books, and Mary Norton's *Magic Bedknob*, but we were not to discover Hilda Lewis's *The Ship that Flew* until we were home again. But best of all, our family agrees, are the *Narnia* books by C. S. Lewis. These are filled with symbol and inner meaning on one level, but stand as rousing good adventure stories on quite another. However, it is doubtful that any child who reads them would not recognize the root-stirring undercurrent of mysticism even though he could not put a name to it.

Joanna Field, in her self-analytic *A Life of One's Own*, writes how one day she thought it would be amusing to draw a map of her life, to show in pictures what she felt had been the most important things in it. To her amazement she discovered herself drawing a scene from childhood—a river, a ruined chapel, a little spring. But even more amazing, she found that part of her mind assigned to these familiar landmarks a new significance. Although she would have sworn that she, an intensely practical and scientific person, could remember nothing of folklore or mythology, the chapel had become the Chapel Perilous from *Morte d'Arthur* "although I could not remember a single fact about the chapel. . . ." The little river was the Styx, a dot (or safety pin?) on the floor of the spring was Odin's eye. What struck her particularly was the way in which her thoughts took material from anywhere and everywhere in order to find a form in which to become "clothed and visible." She then went on to remember arguments she had heard against reading fairy tales to children. Weren't they a waste of time? Children have enough work cut out for them just to discover what are the facts of the world, without having the issue confused with fantasy. After the experiment, Miss Field was suddenly convinced that it is not only the facts about the world that children need to know, but facts about themselves, and it is only through imaginative symbols of fantasy that they can at first find and then express their knowledge of themselves.

As for *our*selves, peering out of our caravan for a glimpse of the mist-shrouded Beacon, every gorse-clothed indentation, every rocky outcropping was a reminder of the pagan and Christian past and had a dimension in time as well as space. We had come upon the landscape of our dreams. We slept and ate and read, washed socks, and slept again—and awake or dreaming we would never be quite the same.

The weather cleared, but not for long. "Absolutely shocking," said everyone in the village. They shook their heads and complained that England was not what it used to be. The fruiterer explained that "things as would be right for harvest are not yet in the ground," and Mrs. S. and her sister were anxious about the first haying. The hired mowers and their itinerant helpers would arrive on an appointed day and it would be a matter of luck whether or not the weather was right.

One day, when Ian and I had scrambled up to the Beacon, we decided to take a less steep path back to the caravan and started off along a rarely trodden track that led through the fields. After a few feet we found the way strewn with some curiously woven grasses that looked somewhat like the cross one is given to take home on Palm Sunday. Later we learned that we had found a trail of gypsy *patens*, a sort of secret sign language blazing the way to a good campsite or, more likely in this case, a chance for employment in the hayfields. Here was still another use for the Beacon. I wondered how many centuries the gypsies had used this hilltop as a rendezvous and message center.

Although it was too early for school to be out officially, Ian had found two boys who were staying in one of the metal caravans in the meadow. Their mother was a laundress (like Mrs. Ruggles in *The Family from One End Street*) and their names really were Roland and Nigel—the very ones that Mr. Ruggles decided *not* to inflict on the twins. The family owned a motorcycle with a sidecar and were off on excursions most of the day, the older boy (who had a broken arm) sitting behind his father on the pillion; the mother, younger boy, and dog encased under a transparent dome in the sidecar. They had ridden all the way from Bristol this way, Mrs. Ruggles explained, although she *had* been rather worried about Nigel's safety, handicapped as he was with a cast!

In the evenings the boys and Ian played cricket in the meadow or sat and read Nigel's comic books. Or Ian and Roland, who were of the same age, ran about the moor playing cowboys and Indians together. Mrs. Ruggles (whose real name I cannot remember) and I had many heart-to-heart talks down near the water tap and once she came up to our caravan for a cup of tea. She was worried about Roland because he had a terrible stutter. Everyone, including his own brother, made fun of him, she said, and that was one of the reasons they had taken their holiday early this year, to give him a rest from school. I thought it interesting that the school therapist had recommended it. The curious thing was that although Roland continued to stutter as badly as ever when speaking to the rest of us, his speech was almost entirely free when he played with Ian. Mrs. S., who had once been the educational director of Cornwall, was the first to notice it.

"I do love Americans," she said. "Especially the children. They are so polite." Polite! I was dumfounded. I thought of those public meals with my ravenous and uncoordinated children, their habit of talking anytime and anywhere, the commotion we seemed to cause just walking down a village street.

"Polite?"

"Why yes," said Mrs. S. "They are what I call *truly* courteous. So outgoing, you know. I wish our English children could be like that. American manners seem to come straight from the heart." I was to hang onto her words like a talisman for many a day to come.

Mrs. S. was most interested in our "literary tour" and assured John that if we wanted to see the river bank of *The Wind in the Willows* we must by all means go to Fowey and row up the river there. Mrs. S. had been a friend of "Q" (Sir Arthur Quiller-Couch), who in turn had been close friend to Kenneth Grahame. She said that once "Q" had taken her and James out in a rowboat and pointed out some of the literary landmarks for their especial benefit. When John brought this back to me, I am afraid I rather discounted it. Why, Kenneth Grahame had spent almost all his life along the Thames! Would that I had heeded, . . . but at the time I thought that either Mrs. S. or John must be mistaken, or that this was a further example of Cornish chauvinism.

Mrs. S. had also much to say about Lyonesse, the lost land that is said to lie off Cornwall. She told fascinating tales of fishermen who look down through the waters and see the roofs of ancient houses and the spires of churches. We could witness for ourselves the uneven struggle between land and sea. As we walked along the cliff edge we could see where rocks had dropped down into the steep coves below, or where the sea had carved caves and gullies into the cliffs, and we could hear the sounds of earth and rocks rattling down through the darkness to splash in the sea when we leaned over the shafts of old mines along the cliff tops. Several times we took the children for picnics along the cliffs. There we would seek shelter from the cold wind and sit and munch hard-boiled eggs and look out to sea and talk. Sitting with our backs to the rock, Ian and I would discuss what Mrs. S. had had to say about Lyonesse or the tales we had read in Hunt's *Popular Tales* and wonder if it was true that fishermen had heard church bells tolling beneath the waves or, looking down on a summer's day, had seen mermaids swim through coral-encrusted windows. Ian was far less credulous than I. Lucy, playing with pebbles or bits of wood nearby, seemed neither to listen nor take part, but months later when we read *Father Bear Comes Home* she was more than usually attentive.

"I saw a mermaid," she said quite firmly. Challenge only made her adamant. "I did too," she said. "We sat on a rock and ate egg shells, and I saw a mermaid with green hair!"

"Well," said Ian, "if she was going to see one, that was the place."

Among all the fact and folklore in Hunt's *Popular Tales*, we read about a "lost chapel" over Perranporth way. According to Hunt, the great sand dunes near Perranporth had shifted so that "toward the end of the last century" a "reputable person" had reported seeing the walls of the original oratory established by St. Parin in about 490 A.D. But Hunt wrote his book in 1865, and we were doubtful that it would be worth while to go in search of walls that might by now be buried under sand again. Mrs. S. assured us, however, that the chapel had been unearthed several times since, and that it was now freed of the surrounding sands and protected from them by a concrete shell. All we had to do, she said, was to find the little lane branching off the main road along the coast. "Just follow the line of rocks marked with white paint."

But of course it wasn't as easy as all that. Every once in a while, when we reached a marker, we would stop to rest and argue which way the white blaze meant us to go. It was rather like a treasure hunt. Ian and Lucy would run ahead, circling and sniffing like puppies, then Ian would run back to report if he had found another marker. We had almost given up finding the chapel, when there was a shout from Ian. Running to catch up with him, we came over the shoulder of a dune and looked down into a little hollow onto a low, crude building of cinder blocks. We stumbled down the slope and stepped aside just in time to let a middle-aged man and his wife come out of the only opening. The woman seemed a trifle dazed, perhaps from the sunlight. "It makes you feel fair queer," she said. They had been searching for the chapel for several days, walking all the way from Perranporth across the sands. We stood watching as they trudged off and disappeared over the dunes behind the church, toward the sea.

I had never heard of St. Parin before coming to Cornwall. In fact, I had never heard of most of the Cornish saints. St. Petrock, St. Crantock, St. Kea—who are they? They are not Roman Catholic, nor even Anglican. John pointed out that when St. Augustine arrived in Kent, there were already Christian communities in Wales and Cornwall. The Celtic saints were not men canonized by Rome, but hermits or anchorites come as missionaries from Ireland. What we were seeking was something that Puck, in *Puck of Pook's Hill*, would call "older than England," for it was purely Celtic-British, not Anglo-Saxon.

According to a guidebook we bought in Perranporth, St.
Parin probably came from Ireland in the fifth or sixth century.
Legend says he floated in on a millstone, but it is more likely
that he arrived in an Irish coracle (a round boat made of
stretched skins), and he may have brought his altar stone
with him. Celtic altar slabs were often round, whereas those
in Anglo-Saxon churches are rectangular. Parin was evidently
a hard-working saint. Not only did he cope with wolves and
pagans, but with all the powerful demonology of Cornwall.
The guidebook credits the good and practical anchorite with
instructing his followers in the art of smelting tin, although
history indicates that tin-smelting has been going on in Cornwall since the Roman occupation. Nevertheless, local legend
has it that St. Parin discovered the art by accident when his
hearth "black as coals" was heated more than usual one night
and suddenly set forth a stream of white metal. After his death,
Parin's saintly relics became an object of veneration not only
for Christians from all over Cornwall, but for pilgrims from
Ireland and Brittany, too. During the Middle Ages the relics
were carried in an annual parish procession and the church
records show that in 1433 money was set aside to repair and
reset the jewels in the box containing Parin's head. No one
seems to know what ultimately happened to the box—or the
head—but when the little chapel was rediscovered in the nineteenth century a headless skeleton was found buried under
the altar.

We ducked our heads and went into the chapel and waited
for our eyes to grow accustomed to the gloom. There was not
much to see, really. The cinder-block building was small, but
there was another structure within it. Thick walls of small
stones haphazardly placed rose to about waist height, tracing

the outlines of a building that could not have been much larger than a medium-sized living room. A low stone bench ran around the wall, and there was an altar at one end where someone, surprisingly, had placed a bouquet of wild flowers. We looked down at our feet. We were standing on slate above the sandy floor, and a spring bubbled up through the sands. Barefooted Lucy had already discovered it and was happily wiggling her toes in the water. It was dark and cool and dim and quiet, except for the children. We shooed them out into the sunshine again. Far away we could catch the sound of the sea and, perhaps, the scream of a gull. Then silence again. We waited, as though expecting something. I thought of Aslam and the trumpets of Narnia. I tried to remember what it was that C. S. Lewis had written in *The Last Battle*:

> "I thought the house had been destroyed," said Edmund.
> "So it was," said the Faun. "But you are now looking at the England within England, the real England just as this is the real Narnia. And in that inner England no good thing is destroyed."

We began to feel the awesomeness of what we had found. These were the original four walls left standing from that dim, distant time of early Christianity in Britain. The oratory was so small, so remote, one wondered how its teachings could have existed, much less survived.

Outside, the children ran wild in the winey air and sunshine where bees bumbled among scant blossoms of gorse and vetch. Suddenly, we heard shouts from Ian and at the same moment Lucy started to scream. We stumbled out into

the harsh brightness of sand and sun. Lucy, running around
the church, had cut her foot on a rock half-buried in the sand
and it had begun to bleed. Ian, going white and red by turns,
tried to explain. "Lucy was going around the church widdershins and I tried to stop her and she thought I was chasing
her just to be mean. . . ."

I knew what he was trying to tell me and why he was so
upset. Just the day before I had been telling him and the Rug-
gleses the story of "Childe Rowland," perhaps the oldest tale
in Joseph Jacobs' *English Fairy Tales*. Ian must have heard it
a hundred times, because it is my favorite tale for telling. The
story is so old that it is in the form of cantefable, part rhyme,
part prose:

> Childe Rowland and his brothers twain
>   Were playing at the ball,
> And there was there sister Burd Ellen
>   In the midst among them all.
>
> Childe Rowland kicked it with his foot
>   And caught it with his knee;
> At last as he plunted among them all
>   O'er the church he made it flee.
>
> Burd Ellen round about the aisle
>   To seek the ball is gone,
> But long they waited, and longer still,
>   And she came not back again.
>
> They sought her east, they sought her west,
>   They sought her up and down,
> And woe were the hearts of those brethren,
>   For she was not to be found.

Of course what had happened was that Burd Ellen had run around the church "widdershins"—the opposite way to the sun—and had been carried off by the King of Elfland. One by one the brothers went in search of her, but it was only Rowland, the youngest-best, who was able to rescue her. In *King Lear*, Mad Edgar says, "Childe Rowland to the Dark Tower came." The "Dark Tower" was "a green hill all ringed about by terraces." The story was already old enough by Shakespeare's day for him to take for granted that his audience would recognize a reference to it.

In the scholarly "Notes and References" which Jacobs includes at the end of his collection, he suggests that pixies, piskies, and pechs (the last is the word for "fairy" in Scotland) may well have been Picts who were driven into hiding and who became mound dwellers.

> If, as archaeologists tell us, there was once a race of men in Northern Europe, very short and hairy, that dwelt in underground chambers artificially concealed by green hillocks, it does not seem unlikely that odd survivors of the race should have lived on after they had been conquered and nearly exterminated by Aryan invaders and should occasionally have performed something like the pranks told of fairies and trolls. . . .

> Altogether it seems not improbable that in such a tale as Childe Rowland we have an idealised picture of a marriage by capture of one of the diminutive non-Aryan dwellers of the green hills with an Aryan maiden, and her recapture by her brothers. It is otherwise difficult to account for such a circumstantial description of the interior of these mounds, and especially of such a detail as the terrace cultivation of them. . . ."

Although I do not think that modern archaeologists agree wholeheartedly with this theory, there is still scientific credence given to much of it. I could not blame Ian for being so apprehensive when he saw Lucy running widdershins about that ancient chapel. Anything could happen among those sand dunes and, as if to prove it, now Lucy was suffering the consequences with cut and bleeding foot. We all went back into the chapel and Lucy dipped her foot into the water bubbling up through the sandy floor. John bound it up with a clean handkerchief while Lucy's screams subsided to sobs and her sobs to sleepy silence. In a few minutes she was asleep in her father's arms. The water must have great curative powers for, although she bore the scar for weeks, the cut never became infected and gave no further trouble. The strangest part of the episode is the effect it had on Lucy. She often speaks of it, asking, "Do you remember? Do you remember the time we went into a church and it had a brook right in the floor and I went wading . . . ?" It is as though she were struggling to recall a dream.

But at the time she hardly stirred as we set out to retrace our steps to the car. A few yards away we turned to look back at the chapel. It had disappeared again, behind the dunes. Like others before us, we had thought it a myth, but we know now that it is there—that we did not imagine it. It may be lost again for centuries, only to reappear as a fragment left over from the childhood of Faith. Perhaps it will always be there in Lucy's consciousness, half-buried, but imperishable as rock beneath the sands. After all, it is not every child who stumbles on the upthrust peaks of Narnia.

4

In Quest of Arthur

We had been living for two weeks on the moors, purifying ourselves in the wilderness. Now we were ready to set out on a quest. We were seeking King Arthur. There are so many Arthurs, and he is claimed by so many places all over Britain that it is difficult to know where to search. There is Arthur's Chair and Arthur's Cup, Arthur's Quoit and Arthur's Stone; the places where he and his knights are said to lie buried or sleeping range all the way from Scotland to the Scilly Isles.

Ian was the most excited. He had suffered an attack of medievalism at an early age and had not yet recovered. Now, as we drove north along the coast of Cornwall, he suddenly came out with "Boy! I can hardly wait until we get to Camelot!"

Camelot? John explained to him that we were bound for Tintagel, the place where Arthur was born and which he left when still in swaddling clothes. Then we were going on to Glastonbury, the Isle of Avalon, where Arthur went to die. He didn't know about Camelot. . . .

Well, how about that place in *The Sword in the Stone*? The castle where Arthur had lived when he was a little boy and people called him Wart, and Kay had been his foster brother and Merlyn was their tutor and they had had all those wonderful adventures? Guiltily we had to admit that we did not know where that place was either. (Since then I have decided it must have been Castle Ludlow in the Welsh Marches, the very one we had hurried by on our way down to Cornwall.)

Waves of gloom emanated from the back seat. I tried to explain to Ian that although King Arthur was depicted in medieval costume the real or historical Arthur had actually been a Roman-British chieftan who lived in the sixth century and who had never heard of a knight for the simple reason that knights had not been invented by then. If he had had some sort of headquarters it was certainly not an elaborate castle or even as big a place as a Roman fortification, but something much more primitive that would be almost impossible to rediscover. It was a bitter pill for Ian to swallow, although John tried to be comforting by pointing out that the man who rallied the last of Roman Britain to fight off the Danes and Saxons must have been unique to have had so many stories attached to him. Ian was interested in spite of himself, but it was a complex notion and his enthusiasm died down entirely when he found that there was nothing real to which he could attach Arthur's ghost. The final blow came when he asked about the Isle of Avalon and we had to tell him it is no longer an island. Why, he wanted to know, had we bothered to come to England?

We drove into Tintagel and paused where the incoming roadway makes a sort of T with the main street. Straight ahead of us was a building with a large sign announcing itself as "King Arthur's Hall." John's and my heart sank. The building was uninspired pseudo-Gothic, obviously Victorian. We dared not point this out to Ian but slunk past it in search of a restaurant that would serve us a really civilized meal, our first in two weeks.

Refreshed and replenished, we went in search of lodgings. The enormous hotel at the cliff's edge so repelled us that we turned inland and went back along the main street to the far end of the village. There we found a small, neat house with bright yellow gate, cockleshell path, and a Bed and Breakfast sign. We were admitted by a pleasant young farm wife who said she had two bedrooms vacant, plenty of hot water, and a drying cupboard. This last proved to be a cupboard in the bathroom, next to the hot-water pipes. That evening we reveled in hot baths. Next morning I washed clothes while John and Ian went to do a little shopping and exploring. I soon exhausted the possibilities of the drying cupboard and asked leave to hang the rest of the clothes outside on the lines I had spied in the farmyard. I thought wistfully of my washing machine and dryer at home—especially when I looked up at the sky—but there were compensations: Lucy was exchanted by the ducks and geese, turkeys and hens, pigs and tethered goat, all of which she could watch in the meadow just beyond the low stone wall that bordered the neat little yard.

I was just pinning the last sock to the line when John and Ian returned from the village where they had bought a few toothbrushy sort of things in the shops, and a garish picture of King Arthur's last battle with his wicked son, Mordred. They had purchased it at King Arthur's Hall. Ian had enjoyed himself, but John, born and raised in Hollywood, murmured an aside to me, "Phony as Forest Lawn!"

Looking at the sky, we decided to start off immediately in

search of Tintagel's famous castle, and not wait for lunch. We
were learning! We hurried down the street toward the cliff
tops again and found a steep path marked by a faded Youth
Hostel sign. The path led down into what, in California, we
would have called a canyon. Dusty rock walls trapped the
noon heat all around us, but in a few moments the path
began to follow the bed of a lusty little stream and the hillside was covered with green. Lucy sat down in the path and
pulled off her sandals. We came to a slab of slate flung across
the stream as a bridge. Lucy sat down again to dabble her toes
while Ian amused himself by playing "Pooh-sticks"—throwing
tiny twigs into the water on one side of the bridge and watching to see which came out first on the other. The children
were loath to leave, but we crossed the brook and took the
path that led up onto the flank of the opposite hillside. We
turned a corner and felt the cool sea breeze on our faces. The
path was hardly more than a sheeptrack although here and
there we were helped by a man-made step. Up and up we
went, walking in single file, the children ahead of us. We began to see outcroppings of ruins, hoary with moss and lichen,
then the path would curve again and we would wonder if we
had mistaken natural rock for man-made wall.

Suddenly we came out on a wide plateau, the blue-green
grass beneath our feet smooth as a richly textured rug. Lucy, in
her bare feet, ran straight ahead to where an ancient wall
marked the limit of the lawn. We followed hastily and peered
over the parapet. It seemed to have grown of itself out of the
cliff, stone on stone. A sheer precipice dropped fearsomely to
the rocks below where green waters swirled. Sea gulls hung
screaming as though suspended by a thread, their orange bills
scarlet-tipped. Strong gray wings held them motionless just

beyond our reach in the updraft of air at the cliff edge. In-
stinctively I reached out to grasp Lucy's coat while John,
almost at the same moment, noticed that Ian had started up a
flight of steps leading to nowhere but eternity. He called to
him, but Ian did not heed. John ran to the steps, grabbed him
by the scruff of the neck and we retreated to the entrance to
the sward. It was then we noticed the sign posted there by the
Ministry of Works: "Parents are requested to discipline their
children." How very un-American!

John had a little talk with Ian. The Ministry of Works, he
said, had made this place neat and accessible, repaired the
outer walls, built paths, maintained steps, engaged in archaeological research, but had not made it child-proof. This was not
Disney Land, but the real, real thing. If Ian wanted to see
more of it (or anything else interesting in England, for that
matter) he would have to learn to obey instantly and to use
his common sense.

Our little party returned cautiously to the ramparts to look
abroad. We were on a headland jutting out to sea. Far to the
south we could see St. Agnes Beacon, the hill on which our
caravan had been "anchored," thrusting its dome skyward.
Except for that one hill we could see how definitely the
southern part of Cornwall sloped off to the lost lands of
Lyonesse. Ian was tugging at our coats, begging us to walk
over to the other side to see the view he had glimpsed from
his steps. Looking straight down we could see a tiny cove with
great caves yawning on either side of it. The brook we had followed made a final leap down to the sands in the form of a
waterfall, and ran among scattered rocks to the sea. All this
was wild and romantic enough, but now we realized that we
were seeing only part of the castle. The headland had been

cut through by the sea and a steep wooden staircase led down from our plateau to the bottom of a deep V, then another staircase led up the other side of the V to the other half of the castle. That was the Inner Ward; we were standing on the Lower Ward. We learned later that in the thirteenth century a bridge was built between the two parts of the castle. Before that the narrow, natural causeway could be held by three men. As we watched, the clouds that had sagged over the horizon all morning moved inland and everything was soaked with a sea mist. I thought with a pang of my clothes on the line; we were all hungry, and Lucy was ready for a nap. We decided to explore the Inner Ward another day, preferably without Lucy.

Next day dawned clear and we started out again, but in opposite directions. John and Lucy were bound for Trebarwith Sands to take advantage of the sunshine and natural bathing pool, Ian and I to explore the Inner Ward and the cove beneath the castle. Ian was so anxious to be off that I let him go ahead of me. He promised faithfully that he would wait for me on the sands of the cove and that on no condition would he start up the spider-web stairs or do anything else foolhardy.

The path was steep and I was hot and breathless now that the sun shone again. I slowed down and decided to read the guidebook as I went along and I began to relax. But halfway down the trail and halfway through the guidebook I began to feel a trifle nervous. What was all this about dangerous tides, dark caverns, treacherous hidden pools? When I arrived at the spot where the brook began its tremendous leap to the sands below, I stood anxiously scanning the sands and rocks for the sight of a small boy in blue jeans, pale blue jersey, and English schoolboy cap. Ah, there he was! I shouted, but what with the sound of the waves and the waterfall he could not possibly hear me. Seen from this lower level, the beach was much larger than I had thought. There were several people hunting shells and pebbles or strolling on the shingle. The tide was coming in, but so far there did not seem to be much danger. Then I saw Ian doing just what I feared the most. He walked over to the mouth of a large cavern and peered inside. I saw him hesitate and look about him, then disappear. What was it the guidebook had said? "It is not always wise to attempt to explore this cave without a torch as occasionally there are deep pools not easily seen in the dim light of the cave. . . ." And somewhere else, on another page, something about "Safety first: Bathe from the centre of beaches . . . observe care at all times. At all beaches the tide reaches the cliff at high water."

I waited a few minutes to see if Ian would emerge, then decided that I must start down at once and look for him. The path wound around between rocks, and I could not keep either the cave or the beach in sight at all times. I finally reached the coarse sands, cursing the heavy camera that hung like a millstone around my neck. I hurried over to the cave mouth and peered inside. It was immense. This was Merlyn's cave tunneling all the way under the Inner Ward. I stepped inside and called Ian's name. There was no answer, only the sound of great seas booming hollowly afar off, then the sound of water gurgling from the pebbles. I moved ahead cautiously through the gloom. The sand turned to pebbles and round, flat pieces of slate, and when I came to a chain of half-submerged boulders lying along the cave floor, I climbed up

on them, my feet splashing in little pools. It was like walking
along the backbone of a sleeping dragon. The way grew
darker, then I turned a corner and saw light ahead and a patch
of sky. There was still a length to go, but having come this far
I was determined to make it to the end of the tunnel and, if
need be, rescue Ian from the incoming tide in the next cove.
If only I knew whether he were ahead of me! I splashed and
climbed and slithered onward. Wet and tired and cross I
came out of the cave's mouth and found my way barred by
giant boulders. I climbed to the top of one and looked up at
the cliff. There were the white-breasted gulls of yesterday
hanging motionless far above me. I could just make out the
heads of some sightseers looking over the castle wall. I wondered if they could see me, or if I looked like part of the rocks
below. I tried to judge the tide. The cove was already lost to
the waves, except for a thin crescent of pebbles along the
cliffs. Even if Ian did go into the cove he could not have made
it around the next headland. The tide was coming in too fast
for that. I sat on the rock to rest and to try to think. I had
seen Ian go into the cave, of that I was sure, but had he come
out again while I was scrambling down to the beach? It was
just barely possible. A huge wave, green and foam-flecked,
came hurtling in on the tide and in a moment I was drenched.
I scrambled down from my high perch and started back to the
cave. The tide had crept higher even while I sat on the rocks
outside, and now I did not even try to keep myself dry. I
reached the dragon's back and in the half darkness it seemed
to me that it rose and fell with the shadows on the wall, and
the heaving of the waters was caught in scales and ripples on
its flanks. I fairly ran out of the cave mouth and onto the

gritty sands. There was Ian, sitting and talking to a young couple with a little girl of about Lucy's age. They gazed at me in wonderment.

"Mommy, where have *you* been?" asked Ian. "I waited and waited and you didn't come."

"And where have *you* been?" I asked, not to be outdone. "Didn't you go into the cave? I distinctly saw you go into that cave and I expected to meet you there."

Ian shook his head in bewilderment. "Was I supposed to meet you in *there*? It's kind of spooky!"

I sat down on the sand. My knees felt weak. The young couple explained that Ian had been playing by himself and had seemed a little lost, so they had invited him to join them. He had asked them and several other people if they had seen me, but of course no one had. I told them of my experiences in the cave and we all had a good laugh. If mine was a little hollow I hoped they could forgive me. We sat and talked for a few minutes while I tried to wring out my bedraggled skirt, then Ian and I said good-by and set out at last to climb the steep zig-zag that led from the beach to the Inner Ward, to see if we could find, at last, a clue to the real Arthur.

Geoffrey of Monmouth, writing a good seven hundred years after the historical event is supposed to have occurred, is the first to mention Tintagel in connection with Arthur and as his birthplace. In his day a Norman castle was built on the headland. Under it workmen found the remains of a Celtic monastery or collection of hermitages such as the early Welsh and Irish saints inhabited. The promontory would have made a natural fortress, especially as there are several wells on the island. It seemed a perfect place for the Duke of Cornwall to have put his wife for safekeeping from the lustful Uther Pendragon, and if there were already a company of hermits there, so much the better. It is Malory, writing in the fifteenth century, who tells us:

> When the duke had this warning, anon he went and furnished and garnished two strong castles of his, of the which the one hight Tintagil, and the other castle hight Terrabil. So his wife Dame Igraine he put in the castle of Tintagil, and himself he put in the castle of Terrabil, the which has many issues and posterns out.

The Inner Ward of Tintagel has only one "issue and postern." Ian and I climbed the steep and winding path, holding tightly to the handrail in some places and picking our way carefully where steps had been cut into the living rock. An amazing number of others were making the pilgrimage, most of them British, but a few foreigners, too. The path had been constructed in 1852 when the poems of Tennyson and nineteenth-century romanticism rekindled an interest in anything to do with Arthur, and now it is under the care of the Crown. We came at last to the gate, paid our shillings to the uniformed guard, and stepped onto the green and rolling carpet of the Inner Ward. Ahead of us was a Norman arch, broken walls and merlons, and unfinished steps leading into thin air. The whole place brought to mind those steel engravings by Maclise in old editions of the *Idylls of the King* and the lines from "Enid":

> He looked and saw that all was ruinous.
> Here stood a shattered archway plumed with fern;
> and here had fallen a great part of a tower,
> Whole, like a crag that tumbles from the cliff,

and like a crag was gay with wilding flowers:
And high above a piece of turret stair
Worn by the feet that now were silent, wound
Bare to the sun. . . .

Ian and I set out to explore the ruins. The island was larger
than we had thought. There were several walls, and it was
treacherously pitted with ankle-wrenching rabbit warrens.
The rabbits, the guidebook said, had been imported and bred
as a part of the food supply for the medieval monks. Despite
the map at the entrance and the careful explanations in the
guidebook, we found it difficult to keep the overlapping buildings and reconstructions straight in our minds. There were the
Celtic hermitages, the medieval halls, the Norman chapel, the
fourteenth-century prison, the fifteenth-century fortifications,
the nineteenth-century reconstructions. But what matter?
Here was physical proof of how Celtic legend could be incorporated in Geoffrey of Monmouth's *Historia*, how Malory
could provide a foundation for Tennyson, T. H. White, and a
host of others.

On our last evening in Tintagel we took the walk to St.
Nectan's Glen. It reminded me of some lines from Coleridge:

But oh! that deep romantic chasm which slanted
Down the green hill athwart a cedarn cover!
A savage place! as holy and enchanted
As e'er beneath a waning moon was haunted
By woman wailing for her demon-lover!

I was struck afresh by the way in which the landscape
seemed to fit the topography of my dreams. We came at last
to a waterfall. The stream, making a tremendous leap from

the height, had hollowed out a little basin halfway down
where it swirled and foamed for a moment, then leaped forward again through a perfectly formed circle cut through a
curtain of rock. It was the sort of place where one could expect to find a hermit's cell or, running a wild boar to its lair,
come upon the Green Knight.

The next morning we set out on Quest again, bound for
Glastonbury. We stopped in Camelford, not because we
wanted to but because traffic was tied in a knot by a herd of
cows gone astray in the middle of town. We were so bemused
that we forgot to watch for Slaughter Bridge, the place where
Arthur is said to have received his mortal wound from Mordred. Ian almost screwed his head from his neck trying to get
a better look out of the rear window. I think he was hoping
for blood stains, but the bridge that now spans the Camel is
of modern brick. Dozmary Pool, where Sir Bediver flung Arthur's sword, Excalibur, is on Bodmin Moor, near Camelford.

Glastonbury is just a few hours from Tintagel, but it took
us three days to get there. We drove north, cutting inland,
until we reached the coast again at Bideford Bay. We stopped
at Clovelly—everyone stops at Clovelly. It was terribly
quaint, but self-consciously so. There were crowds of people
dutifully climbing up and down the steep stairstep streets,
peering in shop windows and eating ice-cream "cornets." Except for the donkeys, the place reminded us of Carmel, California. The donkeys are used to carry loads up from the quay,
and for sixpence one can buy a ride for a child. We thought it
a charming idea, but Lucy, usually unafraid of animals,
howled during her entire sixpence 'orth. She was sleepy, and
after the ride when we were halfway back to the car she found

one of the few level spots in Clovelly—a wide, sunny doorstone—and she lay down and promptly went to sleep. John carried her the rest of the way up the hill.

Back in the car, we looked at our map which showed us that we were near the town of Westward Ho. Of course! This was the very countryside from whence Sir Amyas Leigh and his brave men of Devon had embarked on their voyages. Ian was too young to appreciate Charles Kingsley's *Westward Ho!* but John remembered it fondly and was anxious to turn off the main road to see if there were a house or a Kingsley museum we might have missed. The town proved rather disappointing, but thumbing through the Guide to the National Trust I came across reference to yet another old favorite, Rudyard Kipling's *Stalky & Co.* Kipling went to school here, but his happiest hours were spent in a gorsey hideaway along the cliff edge to which he and a company of friends would repair to read and talk and smoke forbidden cigarettes and stare out to sea. Now that I knew how close his school was to Tintagel I could better appreciate the intensity of Kipling's lines from *Puck of Pook's Hill:*

> I've seen [says Puck] Sir Huon and a troop of his people setting off from Tintagel Castle for Hy-Brasil in the teeth of a sou'westerly gale, with the spray flying all over the Castle, and the Horses of the Hills wild with fright. Out they'd go in a lull, screaming like gulls, and back they'd be driven five good miles inland before they could come head to wind again. . . It was Magic-Magic as black as Merlin could make it and the whole sea was green fire and white foam with singing mermaids in it. And the Horses of the Hills picked their way from one wave to another by the lightning flashes! *That* was how it was in the old days!

The strip of land along the cliff edge, where Stalky & Co. once skulked, has been presented to the National Trust as a memorial to Kipling. How Stalky would have enjoyed the irony—that the myopic Beetle should be the one so memorialized! We would have liked to stop and explore but we still thought we were in a hurry.

We crossed the River Taw and stopped for petrol in Barnstaple. Lucy and I crossed the road to look at a bookshop and the shopkeeper, recognizing that we were Americans, showed us some guides to Exmoor and seemed to take it for granted that we would spend several days exploring it. It seemed rude to explain to him that we intended merely to skirt it as quickly as possible in order to drive on to Glastonbury. Just as John and Ian entered the shop he reached into a case and brought out a copy of *Lorna Doone*. The book was illustrated with photographs of places mentioned or described in the novel, and I could see John weaken before my eyes. "Might take a look at just a few of the places," he said, and when the man went on to talk of wild ponies and sheep-dog trials and badgers and red deer and otters; Ian was completely captivated. We did not know it then, but the bookseller had not only sold a book, he had talked us into two whole days in Exmoor.

I am glad he did. I cannot give a clear account of our wanderings there because we seemed to spend most of our time being lost, but no matter, since the countryside was wild and beautiful. We never did find the wild ponies or see a red deer, but once we came upon a little stone bridge near an old mill and the children put on their bathing suits and went swimming in the river. Later, from maps and pictures and careful reading and rereading of the book, we found that they had been paddling within a few yards of where *Tarka the Otter,* of Henry Williamson's beautiful story, was born.

To us, the most amazing thing about this West Country was first its wildness and variety. There are bleak moors, hidden valleys, thick forests, deep swift rivers, beautiful little villages, and trim little seacoast resorts. It is a whole world in itself and I suppose that is why writers have been attracted to it. We did not find the waterfall up which John Ridd climbed when he first met Lorna Doone, but we did find Doone Valley, where the outlaws had lived. It is so narrow that whenever two cars meet, one of them has to back up. The next day we found the farmhouse which is supposed to be the one where John Ridd lived, and we stopped at Oare church nearby. Lucy was sleeping in my lap, but Ian and John went inside to see the interior and the window through which Carver Doone was supposed to have shot Lorna as she stood before the altar in her bridal clothes. John had read bits of the book aloud the night before, but did not realize how literally Ian had taken it until he begged to be allowed to look for bullet holes.

Surely among the most unusual books about Exmoor—"by children, about children, and for children"—are the *Oxus* books written by Katherine Hull and Pamela Whitlock when they were fourteen years old. Using Arthur Ransome's books about the Lake Country as a springboard (rather than a model), the two girls while at boarding school planned and executed a complete manuscript about a group of children riding and camping on Exmoor. They sent their unwieldy efforts to Mr. Ransome, asking his advice about presenting it to a publisher. At first suspicious that he was the victim of a hoax and that the book was really the product of an adult imagination, Mr. Ransome proceeded with caution. To his amazement he discovered that the two girls had written the entire book in secret, using the backs of old exercise books so as not to arouse suspicion by the purchase of large supplies of paper.

Cautioning the young authors to secrecy, Mr. Ransome took the manuscript to his own publisher and then entered into further correspondence with them about the practical aspects of editing, cutting, and having the manuscript typed. He himself wrote the introduction, setting forth the history and evolution of the book and including some of the correspondence. One paragraph, which he quotes in full, should be learned by heart by all would-be writers:

> You may think there is an excessive amount of red ink splashed over the typewriting, but we tried to cross out four main things. Firstly, any parts which were misleading or didn't fit into the story. Secondly, any unnecessary and drivelling descriptions. It's funny how when writing you feel you have to make points clear and then, on reading it over, you find it is all repetition. Thirdly, we got rid of all useless words like rather, quite, very definitely, etc.; and any words which we disliked, such as children, graceful, poised, etc. Lastly we knocked out all the passages we loathed but which somehow managed to squirm their way in.

I wonder what an imaginative English teacher could do by supplementing the indestructible *Lorna Doone* with readings from *Tarka the Otter* (such beautiful, taut prose) and the youthfully zestful *Oxus* books? The last are out of print, but those who knew them when young are tenaciously loyal to their memory. Girls, especially, respond to these stories. I once read that Mrs. John F. Kennedy, when asked about her favorite books as a child, answered that she had liked most

some books about camping and riding on Exmoor. There were
no titles given, but in answer to my written inquiry, her secretary wrote that Mrs. Kennedy wished to inform me that the
Oxus books were indeed her favorites as a child, and that they
had been given to her by her grandmother.

5

Down to Camelot

We had been lost in the Forest Sauvage and had wandered about like King Pellinore, but we had not forgotten our Quest for Arthur. Perhaps we had been dazed or mazed or bewitched because we hardly knew what to expect at Glastonbury and it was only afterward that we discovered how much we had missed. I will not go so far as to say that everything went wrong, but nothing seemed to go right either.

As we drove toward the town we saw a great hill, the ancient tor, that stuck up from the surrounding landscape and seemed to dominate all the country around with its tower atop, but when we actually drove into the narrow streets that strange green hill seemed to have disappeared. We parked the car and walked into the Abbey grounds, only to be taken aback by the number of souvenir shops and books stalls just inside. The Abbey is under neither the Crown nor the National Trust and there seemed to be no authorized guidebook. Not that there wasn't all sorts of "literature" for sale, most of it making the most extravagant claims! We finally chose a comparatively innocuous little pamphlet and hoped for the best. King Arthur seemed farther away than ever.

I know now what was wrong. We were approaching Glastonbury from the wrong point in time, the wrong point of view. We were too sophisticated, we thought we knew more than we really did. It was all very well to tell Ian that of course there would be no island, that the marshes had been drained centuries ago; to intimate that it was childish to think of Avalon in such literal terms. Why an island? What difference did it make? But an island is distinctive, individual. An island is magic. And, of course, we should have known to tell Ian that it was not so very long ago that the marshes were drained away, that a fairly large lake, five miles in circumference, was still on the maps as Meare Pool in the seventeenth century, and that even in the nineteenth century an intricate system of ditches and drains was needed to keep the land from being lost again.

In 1892 an antiquarian became curious about some mounds in the area, discovered that workmen had unearthed bones and artifacts while tending the dikes, and subsequently directed the excavation of two amazing "lake villages" of the same type that had been already discovered in Switzerland. Large piles had been driven into the peat to support a man-made island of immense logs held together by a cement of clay. The village which had once existed at Godney was about three acres in size and connected to the mainland by a draw-bridge and causeway.

The people who lived there flourished about 300 B.C. Jacquetta Hawkes, in a beautiful little book called *Early Britain*, paints an idyllic sketch of what life must have been like in the lake villages. They were Bronze Age people, similar to those described by Rosemary Sutcliff in *Warrior Scarlet*, although Miss Sutcliff's red-haired, freckle-faced hero lived high on the Sussex downs several hundred years before the lake village was built. But Drem and his people were of the same La Tène culture, and it is with a pang that I realize we could have visited the Glastonbury Museum and seen examples of the marvelously wrought collars and bracelets and delicate fibulae with which the Celts adorned themselves.

The nearest dry land to the lake villages was the site of the present town of Glastonbury. It was here that the drawbridge and causeway gave access, where the lake dwellers kept their flocks and tended their small plots. It was also, probably, where they buried their dead. According to Geoffrey Ashe (in *King Arthur's Avalon*), although the Celts did not have a unified religion they did have two beliefs concerning the afterworld. Either the soul passed into a sort of fairyland by way of a hill, or it migrated to a Celtic version of the Greek Fortunate Isles, presided over by Avallach, Lord of the Dead. This second concept was the more popular because of the belief that spirits cannot cross water.

So now we have it: a unique community protected by a glassy lake, an island surmounted by a curious green hill. I have one more idea to add, not entirely my own, since T. H. White gave a clue to it in his book, *The Godstone and the Blackamore*. Could it not be, he asks, that the islands to the west of Ireland are those to which Oisin was transported? And could not the one where he found eternal youth be the one where the tannic peat bogs are known to have preserved the bodies of whoever fell or was buried in them? Jacquetta Hawkes writes that although we shall probably never know the full extent of the beauties of Celtic weaving and leatherwork, the bogs of Glastonbury have yielded up a treasure in bone and wooden artifacts that was preserved by the peat. Would not this peculiarity add to the concept of a place where a warrior king, such as Arthur, could retire with his wounds and wait through the centuries until he should be called again?

But we were not even dimly aware of all this as we wandered about and tried to orient ourselves. The Abbey, dismantled when Henry VIII broke with Rome, has suffered centuries of vandalism and is almost a total ruin. We entered the Lady Chapel and stood uncertainly, trying to get the feel of the place. The ruins of this chapel stand over the spot where once stood another chapel made of wood and covered with lead. This, in turn, was built to protect a tiny oratory made of wattle and daub, incredibly old, incredibly holy. It is believed to have been St. Joseph's chapel, built by Joseph of Arimathea, contemporary of Christ. Legend has it that after the Crucifixion he and a band of followers fled to Britain, that he built a chapel at Glastonbury, and that he preached the gospel there.

Caroline Dale Snedeker's *The White Isle*, which is still popular, communicates something of the history and mysticism of Glastonbury along with believable characters and a good plot. *The White Isle* is the story of a family of patrician Romans who were exiled to Britain. Lavinia, the heroine, is kidnaped by bandits, then rescued by a band of early Christians who take her to Glastonbury where she learns something of their religion. The description of a first-century Holy Communion service as a simple communal meal is especially interesting.

There is, of course, that other legend about Joseph of

Arimathea: that when he fled to Britain he brought with him
the cup used at the last supper and later used to catch the
blood of Christ. This is the Holy Grail about which clusters
so much legend, mysticism, speculation, and heresy. The
knights of Arthur's Round Table vowed to seek for it, but
only Galahad was pure enough to see it in a vision. The Blood
Spring on Chalice Hill is supposed to flow from it, but archaeologists claim that the well casing is older than Christianity
and that it might even be Egyptian. It seems always to have
been regarded as either magic or holy and there is some supposition that the Druids used it in their rites. There is so
much to explain—and so much unexplainable—at Glastonbury that figurative as well as literal quagmires abound. It is
probably best to accept that Glastonbury is a sort of geographical point of intersection for Druidical magic, Eastern
mysticism, and Early Christianity, and to let it go at that.

Moving about among the green lawns and golden stones we
could understand why Eleanore Jewett had chosen Henry II's
time as the period for *The Hidden Treasure of Glaston*. Most
of the ruins date from Henry II's time because it was in that
reign that a great fire destroyed the earlier buildings. The tiny
wattle chapel was the most appalling loss of the fire. Although
Henry II bent every effort to restore the Abbey to greater
magnificence, he could do no more than commemorate the
place where St. Joseph's original chapel had stood. The king,
perhaps more than any of his subjects, realized it as a *national*
loss.

Even in 1154, when Henry Plantagenet became king, the
Welsh were still uneasy under Anglo-Norman rule, still muttering of the time when Arthur should return from Avalon
and lead them to victory against the English. Henry II real-

ized that what his empire lacked was a national mythos, and he was not unwilling to turn the Arthurian legend to his own advantage. As Geoffrey Ashe says, the problem was "to preserve the hero but lay the ghost." Henry learned from a Welsh bard that not only was Arthur definitely buried at Glastonbury (and that Glastonbury, therefore, was the true Avalon), but that the grave could be found between two small pyramids on the Abbey grounds. Henry seems to have let this idea lie fallow for a year or two, but in 1184, when the great fire burned most of the Abbey to the ground, it seemed a logical time to do a little digging.

Twelfth-century archaeology was a haphazard affair. It was not until 1190 or 1191 that the monks got around to investigating the designated spot. King Henry was so interested that he sent his own steward to supervise. It may have been the steward's idea that the area be roped off and curtained. The work proceeded at the leisurely pace typical of the time. Weeks went by before a workman's pickax struck a stone slab seven feet down. On the other side of the slab a leaden cross was set loosely into the stone, a cross on which was written: HIC JACET SEPULTU INCLYTUS REX ARTURUS IN INSULA AVAL-LONIA. "Here lies buried the renowned King Arthur in the Isle of Avalon." As Geoffrey Ashe points out in his book, a grave usually has the name of the person buried and perhaps the date, but why the *place?* It seems terribly convenient for Henry!

But the monks kept on digging. Sixteen feet below ground level their spades and picks struck something large and wooden. Now, this is the odd part: if, as Geoffrey Ashe points out, they had found nothing but wished to pretend they had found something, they would have invented an elaborate

stone coffin suitable to Arturus Rex. From their point of view
a wooden coffin must have been disappointing. They probably
did not know that the Celts sometimes buried their dead in
hollow oak trunks. From our point of view, it at least proves
that Glastonbury was used as a Celtic burying ground, but to
the monks the find must have been a surprise—even if the
leaden cross was not. Carefully the monks cleared away the
earth, and just as carefully pried open the coffin. They peered
in and saw a jumbled skeleton. One of them picked up a shin
bone and measured it against the knee of the tallest monk
present. It measured a good three inches longer. A giant must
have been buried there! At his feet were other bones—
smaller, feminine. Local legend tells that a shaft of light fell
on the skull and something shone in the sunlight. A monk
reached out to touch the golden hair of Guinevere just as it
fell away into dust.

There is another tradition, equally strong, that the Queen
founded Amesbury Abbey as her retreat and was buried there.
But that is the way with Arthurian legends—as soon as you
think you have caught one and can nail it down, it slips away
or conflicts with something else.

Hot and tired and confused our family stood on the green
grass by a heap of tumbled stones and tried to imagine that
here had once been the high altar. We had come, we had
seen, we had wanted to believe. We longed for epiphany. Ian
tried not to fidget as John read from a metal plaque:

"Site of King Arthur's tomb; in the year 1191 the bodies of
King Arthur and his Queen were said to have been found on the
south side of the Lady Chapel. On 19 April, 1278, the remains

were removed in the presence of King Edward and his Queen to a black marble tomb on this site. This tomb survived until the dissolution of the Abbey in 1539."

We had come to Glastonbury on Quest, not hoping for the Grail but, much more humbly, Arthur. So far we had not found him.

We moved back toward the gate and, because our family is incapable of passing even a shelf of books without pausing to take a look, we stopped to browse for a minute among the stalls and fell into conversation with one of the booksellers. Tentatively I asked her a few questions. If this was Avalon, where was Camelot? She answered that some people thought that it might be Winchester, the ancient capital where kings were crowned before the building of an Abbey at Westminster. She seemed to hesitate, as though trying to make a decision. "There *is* a place, but it's hard to find. It's not a real castle, you know, just a sort of hill fort—with terraces." She paused, almost as though she regretted having said anything at all.

Ian, who had been looking at post cards, now turned his full and glowing attention upon us. A hill with terraces? Like the one in *Childe Rowland?* The woman smiled. "If you really want to see it I'll tell you directions. I always hesitate because people are often disappointed. It's a long way to go and they expect so much more when they get there."

Ian was wild to set out at once, but thanks to the warning of a long drive we stopped in Glastonbury for high tea. We also decided to search early for a Bed and Breakfast place to spend the night. The afternoon shadows were long as we drove through the flat countryside, a strange green and golden light suffusing all the landscape. It occurred to us that the road was really a long causeway over reclaimed land. After a while the road cut through an air base which stretched for miles on both sides of the road. Since this was all Crown land there were no farmhouses or inns. We came at last to six Nissen huts, the same shape as our Quonsets, that were set in a row not far from the main gates of the air base. One of them had a Bed and Breakfast sign in the window. We passed it, thought better of it, and turned back. Perhaps it was not romantic or quaint or charming, but it was a place to lay our heads.

Our landlady proved to be a widow whose soldier son was stationed in Cyprus and who lived alone. The place was clean and neat, had a "telly" in the parlor, and modern plumbing off the back hall. She was amazed to learn that we planned to go out again, even more so when she found out where we were going. "That's no proper castle," she said. "There's a nicer one along the other road," and she insisted on giving us the directions to a Norman keep. She had never been to Queen Camel herself, although she had lived in the Nissen hut for twenty-five years. Her son had bicycled over with his friends one day. "He was a great one for learning things from books," she said.

Ian had fallen heir to the son's room for the night. There was a shelf of books under the bowed roof: a children's encyclopedia, much worn; Quennells' illustrated histories; some school stories; some old Henty's, and A Boy's Malory. He had been on Quest, too.

We drove out into the long twilight. It was almost nine o'clock, but in that latitude we still had an hour or so until total darkness. Lucy was sleepy but we wrapped her in a blanket and took her along. We lost ourselves several times, threading through narrow country lanes and even going around in a circle once. The closer we got the less use we found the directions given to us in Glastonbury. The little village which we sought seemed so far off the beaten track that it might have fallen off the edge of the world. For once our Bartholomew's *Road Atlas* failed us, but this was only because the print had become almost microscopic. Cadbury Castle actually has an official existence.

And then we saw it! On our left a great dark hill thrust its way up into the sky. It was tiered like a wedding cake with cows grazing on the receding "layers." A thick wood surmounted the hill and great trees thrust themselves out to break the symmetry of the lower flanks. We half circled the hill and came into a village of apricot-colored plaster and well-kept thatch. The entire population seemed to be in the local pub, hoisting its well-earned evening pint. A boy came out of the pub door and climbed on a motorcycle. We asked where there was a path up to Cadbury Castle. He stepped on the accelerator and the motor gave a deafening roar. He was anxious to get away. "You've already passed it," he said, "but there's nothing there. Naught but mud and nettles. And it's not a proper castle." Then with a final roar he drove off.

We found the path ourselves and parked the car as close as possible to its base. John persuaded me to leave Lucy to sleep on the back seat. She seemed deep in slumber and I told myself that if she called I would hear her on the quiet air. We scrambled up the hill and came to a gate. Ian was there before us, sounding out the letters painted faintly across it. "Beware of the . . ." The rest was obliterated. What were we to beware of? Dogs . . . bulls . . . dragons? A stile had been placed beside the gate, so we concluded that other human feet had trod before us. Not only human feet. Our way had been churned to mud by generations of cattle.

We soon found ourselves caught in a groove. I suppose that each "layer" had been hollowed out to shoulder height so that a warrior could run safely around the entire hill, able to throw flaming arrows or deadly slingstones at the enemy below. In order to climb higher we would have to cut toward the center, just as a knife cuts through a cake. Alas! It was not easy. There seemed no direct path to the summit. We labored up over the edge of each tier, down into a trough, then up to the edge of the next. Once John and I stopped to measure the circumference of an immense old ash pushing out from the hillside. Our finger tips barely met. The shadows under the great trees were almost black and we gave up trying to avoid the nettles. As Shakespeare knew, the barbs do not sting if one has the courage to grasp the leaf quickly and tightly, but we had to brush by and could only squeak and groan in undignified anguish.

Then we came to the top of the hill, a great hollow filled with waist-high golden grass. The air was hot and humid. Ian stripped off his plaid shirt, knotting it over his shoulder and under one arm. He had become a desperate Briton. He found a long stick to use as a spear and ran about, as small boys will, completely caught up in the game. John and I looked out over the flat countryside, peering through the strange greenish twilight. Far away on the horizon we thought we could see Glastonbury. If Cadbury had really been the Celtic chieftain's fort, then it would make sense to bury him at Avalon. We began to believe again.

Christina Hole, in her book *English Folk Heroes*, has some interesting things to say about Cadbury. The top of the hill is known as King Arthur's Palace and a track leading from the hill to Glastonbury is known as King Arthur's Causeway. The fort must have been of strategic importance during Roman-British times. When a party of archaeologists made ready to investigate the mound in 1890, they found the local legends still vigorous. In the little villages that skirt the hill there was no doubt that this was Camelot. One old man was quite in earnest when he told them that the King was sitting inside the hill with all his knights, playing at chess, and if you climb the hill on St. John's Eve you can peep through golden gates and see him there. Others said that on winter nights a troop of horsemen ride 'round and 'round the hill, then gallop off toward Glastonbury. They claimed that silver horseshoes had been found as evidence. The archaeologists found no horseshoes, although they did find Roman coins. They also found the gates, just where the old man had pointed. By a curious freak of folk memory, the whereabouts had been preserved although the road leading to it had been obliterated by ploughing and a planting of ash trees three hundred years before.

The historical Arthur must have lived about the time that the edges of the Roman Empire were crumbling and the legions ordered home. The Romans had been in Britain more than four hundred years. One can make a parallel with English or Anglo-Indian families brought up in the Far East who spoke and wrote in English, whose manners and dress were English, who thought of themselves as English—yet who had never been to England. And so it was with the Roman-British who were suddenly faced with orders to return to Rome or, even more difficult, to defend some other part of the Empire. Many of them had lived for generations on farms and in villas in the English countryside. There were commercial ties not easily snapped. Even more compelling, there were wives and children who would be left to the mistreatment of Saxon barbarians.

Rosemary Sutcliff has caught this feeling of decay and indecision in her young people's novel *The Lantern Bearers*. Her hero, Aquila, is a Roman officer who discovers, at the last moment, that he is more British than Roman and decides to stay and keep alive the remnants of civilization in Britain. This is only the beginning of the story, for almost as soon as he returns home to the family villa the Saxons arrive to burn and pillage; his father is killed and his sister abducted. He himself is carried off to thralldom by the "wolves of the sea" and years pass before he is able to return to Britain. Eventually he makes his way into the mountain fortress of Wales where the last remnants of culture still exist alongside the Celtic culture previously sent into exile, before the coming of the Romans. Perhaps it was men like Aquila, embittered patricians, who disciplined the wild Celtic forces and attempted to forge them into a fighting unit. In Miss Sutcliff's story their leader was Ambrosius (a historical figure), the last official representative of Roman authority, and young Artoris (Arthur) was his nephew. Aquila has to conquer his own bitterness in order to realize that something more than force and vengeance is needed if there is going to be any hope in the Dark Ages ahead, and in this he influences the young Artoris.

Historians now generally agree that if Arthur existed he was not a king at all, but a mercenary commissioned by the several British princes who remained to hold back the Saxons. Under the Romans there had been an office and title of *Comes Britanniarum*. The holder of it commanded six mounted mobile regiments whose range covered all of Roman Britain. Arthur may have held this office under the new weak and divided authority. The seafaring Saxons knew nothing of cavalry or the discipline that goes with it. It has been surmised that somehow Arthur scraped together the last remnants of Roman military skill, that under his tutelage and inspiration smiths were made cunning again, and that with a picked force of armored men on horseback he was able to maneuver his mobile troops quickly from one part of Britain to another and to keep back the darkness for at least another half century.

We stood on the ramparts of Cadbury Castle, the crumbling tower that had once been Camelot, and watched Ian joust with shades as well as shadows. Generations of small boys have responded to Arthur's magic. Surely he must have been real, and surely he must have been more than a brilliant general to have inspired Malory's splendid medieval word tapestry, *Le Morte d'Arthur*. There must have been some especial strength in that homespun backing to support the rich embroidery, else the whole pattern would have long since unraveled.

Toward the end of *The Lantern Bearers*, one of the characters says:

I sometimes think that we stand at sunset. . . . We are the Lantern Bearers, my friend; for us to keep something burning, to carry what light we can into the darkness.

And then we read, Aquila said "an odd thing":

I wonder if they will remember us at all, those people on the other side of the darkness.

As we drove toward our lodgings I glanced at Ian. His face was aglow and he was chattering away to his father. Somehow he had been able to reconcile his old concept of Arthur with something vital found at Cadbury. I thought of T. H. White's contention that the Matter of Britain must be looked at through the innocent eyes of the young, the "pure eyes of absolute truth." In the last scene in *The Once and Future King*, Arthur—waiting through the night before his last battle—talks with his little page:

> Thomas, my idea of those knights was a sort of candle, like these ones here. I have carried it for many years with a hand to shield it from the wind. It has flickered often. I am giving you the candle now—you won't let it out?

And then, "The little boy kneeled down to kiss his master's hand—his surcoat, with the Malory bearings, looking absurdly new . . ."
"My lord of England," he said.

Somewhere above, in the darkness, I could hear a plane going overhead; only then did I remember the surrounding aerodrome. What must it have been like here during the war, when all of England was blacked out and great battles were being fought in the skies above? I shivered and drew Lucy's blanket tighter. What would it be like in the wars to come? But Ian was still chattering happily. He had been down to towered Camelot! After the last battle is fought, the last knight dead—oh, surely there will always be one small page left to tell the tale, to keep the candle burning in the wind!

6

The River Bank

We drove north again, taking several days to reach the banks
of the River Thames. I remembered a book my Uncle Roger
had read to me when I was a little girl. It was called *Three
Men in a Boat* and chronicled the adventures of three Victorian bachelors afloat on the Thames in something called a
"camping punt." I described the craft to John as a sort of
large rowboat with a tentlike contraption that could be pulled
over it at night or in the rain. I remembered my Uncle Roger
telling me that he had once hired a camping punt, but I
had no idea whether such a curious hybrid still existed, much
less where we could find one. Then, just before we left for England, I came upon a 1954 *Saturday Book* in which Edward
Ardizzone had recorded—in characteristic sketches and callig-
raphy—the experiences of his wife, small son, and himself on
a five-day trip on the Thames. The punt was exactly like the
one I remembered from *Three Men in a Boat* and Mr. Ardizzone mentioned explicitly that the trip started from Salter's
Boat Yard, Folly Bridge, Oxford. I began to make plans forthwith.

I did not know that John, in his quiet way, had decided that he had had enough of camping. In complete innocence I put my best dresses in the suitcase to be sent ahead by rail to Tunbridge Wells, and reserved space in the other suitcases for our oldest and warmest clothes. John insisted on packing for himself. It seemed to take forever. When he put something in, I took it out; when I took something out, he put it in. We behaved, in short, rather like George, Harris, and J. of *Three Men in a Boat* when they packed for their camping trip. Although no one put butter in the teapot, Ian weighted the suitcases with a ballast of stones he had picked up in Merlin's Cave at Tintagel, and Lucy packed the remains of a marmalade sandwich.

We came upon the Thames at Maidenhead and gazed about the red brick suburb in curiosity. Hugh Lofting, author of the *Doctor Dolittle* books, was born in Maidenhead and lived there until he was sent off to school at the age of eight. Like the hero of his many books he kept a collection of pets in the house and garden, and even (as his exasperated mother was to discover) in the linen cupboard. Perhaps Maidenhead is the model for Puddleby-on-the-Marsh, home of the great John Dolittle.

Three miles away (and a generation earlier) Kenneth Grahame had lived at Cookham Dene. On the surface there seems to be not much in common between Lofting's books and Kenneth Grahame's, yet the same river flowed through both their childhoods. Both men preferred animals to people, both never recovered from a mistrust of "grownups" ("Olympians," Grahame called them). Both men hated the commercial-industrial age, yet Grahame became Secretary of the

Bank of England and Lofting was an engineer, graduate of Massachusetts Institute of Technology.

We drove on to Marlow and stopped to look at The Compleat Angler, a justly famous inn with a view of the weir. We guessed that it was far too expensive and we drove on again. I was hoping for a farmhouse, but we were in a far more sophisticated part of England than hitherto. The likelihood of finding a Bed and Breakfast sign in a window was about on par with expecting one in Scarsdale, New York or Evanston, Illinois or Beverly Hills, California. We stopped at several inns but each time I turned them down because they were too expensive, or the manager did not seem to like children, or the location was too far from the river. I found myself regaling Ian with the adventures of the *Three Men in a Boat* and how they had found themselves in a similar plight. They had passed by one place because it did not have honeysuckle growing over it, and another because Harris did not like the looks of a man's boots and his red hair. Finally, when they realized they would have no place to lay their heads, they had rushed back to the first inn only to find that there was not even room on the billiard table.

The story seemed to impress John. "I'll go into the next place," he said, in a voice that brooked no argument, "and I'll make the decision."

We were rolling over the bridge at Henley as he spoke. At the far end, on the right, was a large inn or hotel with a red lion rampant above the door. John parked the car and disappeared inside. The children and I sat and waited. Lucy was soggy from sleep and I was soggy from Lucy. It seemed a long time before John came back. He appeared with a porter who politely opened the car door for me. Suitcases, books, maps, toys, jackets, sweaters, chocolate wrappers, raincoats, umbrellas immediately fell onto the cobbles of the innyard. The porter showed admirable composure. Fastidiously he plucked two suitcases from the mess and started toward the door while I tried to organize the rest of the clutter into manageable bundles. John took the sleeping Lucy and one of the zipper bags, Ian took his sketchbook and soldiers, and I staggered along under coats, jackets, and assorted stuffed toys.

We had arrived at tea time. The patrons of the Red Lion paused with cups half raised and sugar tongs in mid-air to watch our progress across the lobby. The ladies, I noticed, were in afternoon frocks; the gentlemen wore white flannels and blue blazers combined in a sort of yachting costume. I was acutely aware that my skirt was too long, my sweater baggy, my sockless feet in a pair of old loafers.

Grimly I followed John up three flights of stairs. Anyway, I told myself, we could steal off early in the morning, rent our boat, and be gone before any of these people ever saw me again. We had reached the third-floor landing and went down a long hall. At the end of it John flung open a door and ushered us into a large bedroom which, I saw by crossing to a window, was directly over the front corner of the hotel where five lanes of traffic came together. Proudly John showed me another bedroom, for the children, and an almost-private bathroom.

"How do you like it?" asked John. I started to reply, but I had to wait while a motorcycle turned the corner at our hotel. The sound of its motor seemed to be redoubled by some accoustical phenomenon that had to do with the river and the height of the opposite bank. At length I was able to say that I liked the rooms (except for the noise) and that I wished that I could wash a few clothes in the bathroom. I doubted if the clothes would dry overnight.

"What do you mean?" asked John. "I've paid for the rooms and four meals a day. For a week. In advance."

I was either struck speechless or the noise of another motorcycle drowned out my reply. Just as well. It was Ian who saved the day. He had come into our bedroom and was leaning out, trying to touch the heraldic red beast that reared itself above the main entrance to the hotel, just below our window.

"Poop, poop! Poop, poop, yourself!" he said to two small automobiles snarling at each other across the intersection. "Hey!" he said, turning to us, "Wasn't it at the Red Lion where Toad had his lunch and stole the motorcar?"

Although I hated to admit it, civilization has its compensations. In Henley I was able to window-shop for clothes and antiques, to have my hair cut, to browse through bookstores. Although our rooms were noisy, they had a pleasant view of the bridge and river and we could watch the swans glide by, and the motor launches, and the sculls. In addition, we were not far from London.

As the days wore on I tried to tell myself that the Red Lion was not really so bad. We were just across the street from the river and could easily hire a trim little boat, complete with scrolled arm rests and cushions, to scull about in, for all the world like Rat and Mole in *The Wind in the Willows*. We went up and down Henley Reach. All along the bank were high-built boathouses, dark cool caves beneath, gingerbread chalets above. The water of the Thames seemed amazingly clean and sparkling, especially when one considers the number of towns and villages that cling to its banks. Old gardens crowded so close that rose petals drifted in the current, but the Thames is kept clean by the watchfulness of the Thames Conservatory which, we were told, is responsible for the health and safety of Her Majesty's swans.

But life had its difficulties. John had packed a decent suit for himself and, although a trifle monotonous, he always looked presentable. The children and I had packed for camping, not for the dining room of a fashionable hotel at the height of the season. Since we had paid for our meals we could not afford to forage elsewhere and had to appear for public scrutiny or starve in our garret.

My main concern was to keep the children as far away from the Red Lion "regulars" as possible, but sometimes my efforts were of no avail. One morning Lucy ran ahead of me into the dining room and discovered an old gentleman reading his *Times* at arm's length. I had explained to her several times that she must not bother him, but before I could stop her she popped up between the old gentleman and his newspaper and asked, "Are you having your peace and quiet?" I really thought he was going to have a heart attack. Perhaps no child had been that close to him for half a century (he was a retired bachelor colonel from the Indian Army). He folded his newspaper and went immediately to his room, and was not seen the rest of the day. After that he gave Lucy a wide berth, although she was as determined as ever to keep up the unseemly flirtation. She may have been making headway. Once, as he stood beside me watching both children at play a safe distance off, he cleared his throat and came out unexpectedly with, "A dear little girl, that!" I was too stunned to reply, and of course after such an outburst of emotion there was nothing for us to do but avoid each other completely.

I often thought of Mrs. S., our friend in Cornwall, during these days and wished that I could talk to her. She had told John that the countryside near Fowey (pronounced Foy) in Cornwall, was the background for Kenneth Grahame's *The Wind in the Willows*. At the time I had thought that there must be some mistake, but now I was beginning to have doubts as to my other information. What had brought us to the banks of the Thames was the supposition that this was the river that dominated Kenneth Grahame's masterpiece, but the longer we stayed in Henley the farther off we seemed from the world of Rat and Mole.

Before leaving the United States, I had read Patrick Chalmers' biography of Kenneth Grahame. Unfortunately I had not brought my notes. All I could remember was that Grahame had been born in Scotland, that his mother had died when he was young, and that he had gone to live with his grandmother somewhere near the Thames. When he grew up he became Secretary of the Bank of England and, presumably, lived in London. None of this was very helpful in tracking down the place where Mole and Ratty had had their picnic, yet the spot had been described so concretely that I was positive that it existed. Then, just before we sailed, an interested friend handed me an old copy of *The Horn Book* magazine in which there was an article by Ernest Shepard, "Illustrating *The Wind in the Willows*." Shepard had visited Grahame in his home just a few months before the author's death. Although Grahame was too weak to accompany him to the riverbank, he gave him explicit instructions as to where he could find Rat's house and Toad Hall, the pools where Otter hid, and the "Wild Wood way up on the hill above the river, a fearsome place but for the sanctuary of Badger's home and of Toad Hall." The artist described how he had spent a happy autumn afternoon rambling about, sketchbook in hand. Later he was able to return and show some of the results of his work. The old man had been pleased and had said, "I'm glad you've made them real!" In his article, Shepard recollected that the two of them, author and artist, had "seemed to share a secret pleasure in knowing that the pictures were of the river spots where the little people lived."

I had counted on being able to reread both book and article when we were actually in England, when I knew the lay of the land. This was not the easy task I had thought it would be, and I began to realize that if we were to justify our week in Henley I must do some detective work on my own. I went to Boots (the chemist-bookstore chain) and bought a beautifully detailed map of the Thames, one and a half inch to the mile. Stretched across our bed and drooping onto the rug, it proved to be almost twelve feet long. I had bought a copy of *The Wind in the Willows,* too, but try as I might I could not orient Ernest Shepard's illustrated end-paper map to the official one. If only I could find one concrete fact to tie the two together! Whom could I ask? There was a library in the Henley town hall, but it was locked every time I went to it. I finally lay in wait for the librarian who, when he made his appearance, said he could remember Kenneth Grahame as living somewhere up on the Berkshire downs, "miles away from the

Thames," even farther from Fowey. He did not have the Chalmers' biography and had never heard of the *Horn Book*. I was more confused than ever.

I went back to the hotel in despair and consulted with John. He, as usual, had a good idea. Why not call the English equivalent of the American Library Association in London? Perhaps someone there could help with the detective work. I got a handful of enormous coins from the office and retired into the booth off the lobby. Telephoning in Britain always seemed inordinately difficult to me. To begin with, there is no classified section in the directory. On the other hand, perhaps because of this deficiency, the telephone operators are terribly efficient and have masses of initiative. I finally got through to the Library Association in London (after a few false starts and forgetting to press the "A" button). A pleasant male voice answered. The owner was interested and courteous. Could I give him a little time to mull the question over and to call back? He did not seem in the least upset that I had asked him to find out where a fictitious water rat had entertained a talking Mole.

When the phone rang again my informant said that he had been looking up what he could find on Kenneth Grahame, but he must confess that his sources were meager if what I wanted was explicit geography. He had in hand *A Critical History of Children's Literature*, by Meigs, *et al.* Did I know it? I said I owned a copy, but it was three thousand miles away. All he could find, he said, was a reference to the small Kenneth's going to live at Cranborne with his grandmother. "That's funny," he continued, almost to himself, "but I always thought he lived in Pangbourne. That's what someone told me once when I was punting up that way. Hmmm. . . .

I'm afraid I'm not much help. But I say! Why don't you go up to Reading? Miss P. is in charge there and she's one of the best children's librarians we have anywhere. A real authority. It's quite close to you."

We awoke next morning to leaden skies and threatened rain and consulted over breakfast as to how we should spend the day. John offered to take charge of the children if I would go to the library in Reading. It was too tempting an offer to pass by. As for the children, John would take them to Windsor to see the Castle. I had never been there, but John had pleasant memories from his own childhood of suits of armor, wide halls and corridors, and a wonderful doll's house that had belonged to Queen Mary. It seemed just the sort of excursion for a rainy afternoon, so after lunch we drove through the streaming landscape to Reading and sought out the library in the center of town. I was to return by bus at my own convenience.

I had telephoned to Miss P. in advance, so she was ready for me with a copy of Chalmers' biography and a stack of old *Horn Books*. She apologized to me for not having a *Reader's Guide* or index handy to facilitate my research (they were upstairs in the adult department) and admitted that the magazines had been shifted about in the storeroom and were out of order. A few had been lost. I gazed at the pile in some dismay: the "Three Jovial Huntsmen," multiplied ad infinitum on identical covers six times a year, year after year, seemed to defy me. I had no idea of the date of the issue in which I had read the article by Shepard. With a sigh I began to arrange pen and notebook, book and magazines on the table before me. The magazines looked as though they were about to topple over so I cut them into two piles. And there, on the top of the newly made second pile, was the very issue I was looking for. Surely this was an omen. I attacked my task with renewed hope.

Miss P., who had excused herself to help some young readers, now came back to my worktable and settled down to a good talk. I tried to explain to her more fully what it was that I was looking for, and now that she could really grasp my aim she was not only interested and sympathetic, but full of the very information I had been seeking. My heart fairly leaped when she said: "Of course you'll want to see Toad Hall. It's generally accepted that that's Mapledurham House near Pangbourne. Kenneth Grahame and his wife were living in a little house in Pangbourne when he died, you know. That's where Mr. Shepard must have visited him."

At last, at last I had hold of a piece of string that led somewhere! I could have shouted for joy. I took out my map and carefully marked a circle around Pangbourne. It was just a few miles along the main road, above Reading. We could drive there very easily. I started to fold up my map again, when Miss P. stopped me, "Now, let's see. Where is Blewbury?"

"Blewbury?"

"Oh, yes," said Miss P. "Bohams, Blewbury. That's Mole's house, you know—though the kitchen undoubtedly belongs to Badger. I've been there several times and even taken a party of school children in to see the kitchen. It's quite a drive —way up on the Berkshire downs. It used to be such a lovely unspoiled little village, but I have heard that it's changing. And the house is in new hands again."

So now I had hold of another piece of string and could tie it to the first. I did not know it then, but in a few more months

Peter Green was to supplant Patrick Chalmers' account of
Grahame's life (written soon after his death) with a new de-
finitive biography studded with facts—and Freud. It is an almost overwhelming job, but now, at last, I can see the meaning of all my little bits of information, now I can see that *all*
my informants were right, if only partially so. But let Mr.
Green explain:

> The core of reality, in this case, is that stretch of the Thames
> which runs, roughly, from Marlow to Pangbourne; and in par-
> ticular the area around Cookham Dene. . . . Grahame never
> drew straight from life, but borrowed piecemeal. . . . For this
> reason it is a task as pointless as it is fascinating to press any top-
> ographical identifications too closely. Toad Hall, for example,
> contains elements from Harleyford Manor, Mapledurham House
> and Cliveden—each supplied part of its *mise en scène*. Elements
> from a dozen river islands, weirs, and backwaters have been
> blended in "The Piper at the Gates"; elsewhere Cookham merges
> into Cornwall, and the Thames . . . flows seaward to Fowey.

We are glad that we went exploring on our own, although
there is no doubt that Mr. Green's book would have made life
much less haphazard for us. We are quite content to think of
Mole's and Ratty's habitat in terms of the illustrations in
which they were introduced to us. If we were led astray, so
was Mr. Shepard and so, later, was Arthur Rackham when
(after Kenneth Grahame's death) Mrs. Grahame did the
honors and showed him about at Pangbourne when he came
to illustrate a new edition of *The Wind in the Willows*. But
Sir Arthur Quiller-Couch, who lived at Fowey, was Kenneth
Grahame's closest personal friend, and Grahame often spent
his summer holidays boating on the river there. Mrs. S. is vindicated. Some of the scenes can be traced to Cornwall.

The trip to Windsor had been a great success and next morning, the skies having rained themselves out, we set forth in high spirits. We rolled through Reading and paid proper homage to Huntley & Palmer's biscuit factory as we went by, feeling that it was an old friend. The road wound through miles of bleak brick, we were led away from the river, and the July sun was hot. We stopped and bought some iced lollies (popsicles) and noticed two soldiers standing guard by a huge arched gate almost across the way. The men looked hot and uncomfortable in their heavy uniforms, and we wondered idly what lay behind the high walls they were guarding. Somehow it did not look like an army post. . . . A prison? We had already started off in the car again when John and I were struck with the same idea at the same moment. Why, of course! Reading Gaol! This was the place where Oscar Wilde was made to pay his debt to society. Ian caught the note of excited self-congratulation in our voices and asked what we were talking about. Who was Oscar Wilde? What did he do? Why was he put in jail? John leaped into the breach. "Why, don't you remember? *That*, my boy, is where poor Toad was thrown into the remotest dungeon of the best-guarded keep in all the length and breadth of Merry England!" He had not really answered Ian's questions, but he had won his attention and respect. He had won my respect, too, but for quite different reasons.

After Reading the road gave way quite suddenly to countryside, and we swung back toward the river, then away again to higher ground. Now we could look down and see the meanderings of the old stream, the low green fields on either hand, and the parklike woods. Surely the Thames is charmingly unique among streams, its landscape almost absurdly appropriate. In Nan Fairbrother's *Men and Gardens* there is a story of an eighteenth-century landscape architect (his standards set by Versailles) who was shown a panoramic view of the Thames. Gazing at this ultimate in "serpentines" he could only exclaim, in simple admiration, "Clever! Clever!" And it was with difficulty that someone finally persuaded him that the entire landscape had not been arranged by Capability Brown, or some other professional "improver." It is not that the landscape looks artificial, it is only that one so rarely sees man and nature in perfect scale and harmony.

We drove under the railroad bridge and into Pangbourne. We took a vote: should we look for Church Cottage (where Kenneth Grahame had lived), or drive up to the Downs, or try for the riverbank? On such a lovely day the vote was unanimous for "messing about with boats." We turned to the right by some little shops, parked our car, and made our way on foot to the end of the street. The street became a lane, and then a dusty footpath, and we came out beside a boathouse. An old man (for all the world like the busy Mole in Shepard's illustration) had upturned a boat on two sawhorses and was carefully varnishing the hull. We waited respectfully for him to finish drawing his gleaming brush a full stroke and while he made a step back, brush in air, to squint at his handiwork. Only then did he notice us.

Would we like to hire a boat? He had several kinds for hire, but it all depended on where we wanted to go, what we wanted to do, and how skillful we were. He cast a doubting glance at Lucy and said that he did not approve of small children in boats. For a few moments it looked as if he would refuse to let us have a boat at all, but we finally settled for a motor launch, despite Ian's loud cries of dissent. He thought it sacrilege to explore Ratty's domain in a petrol-eating putt-putt, but he was somewhat appeased when we explained that we could go so much farther than if we were rowing. The old boatman backed our argument when we asked him the direction to Mapledurham House. He said that it was quite a way downstream and that it would be an effort to get back against the current unless we had a motor to help us. "It's dangerous here," he cautioned us, "and folks as is not used to boats can get into trouble. It's all right to go as far as Mapledurham, but be careful of the weir. It's swift thereabouts and folks has been drowned who got caught in the current." He turned to Ian. "You there! Sit down in a boat!" Then he turned to me. "And you," he admonished sternly. "Keep hold of that little girl. Don't let go of her an instant." We complied meekly while he showed John how to start and stop, to turn left or right and to go into reverse. It was obvious he held a low opinion of our boatmanship.

Directly across from Pangbourne landing a little backwater was almost lost in shadows between the dark bank and an island a few yards offshore. Stunted tree trunks dangled their gnarled roots in the water. We were tempted to explore but No Trespassing signs warned us off. We had turned the boat upstream in order to get a better look at the backwater, so now we continued toward Whitchurch Lock, upstream from the landing. We could see the foaming waters pour over the weir and at the same time watch a boat being taken through the lock beside it. The sight sobered us. The pretty Thames was swift and deep and powerful beneath its surface. What if one should miss the lock and be swept over the weir?

John made a fairly expert U-turn and we headed down-river again, past the boatyard. Just beyond where the old man

was working we saw that a narrow iron bridge spanned the
stream. We had brought along our copy of *The Wind in the
Willows* and the long strip map. Now I could orient book and
map to the actual landscape. "That's the New Iron Bridge," I
said, and tried to show Ian how faithfully Shepard had represented it in his end-paper map for the book. Ian almost
crowded his sister and me off the thwart in his eagerness to
look.

The river broadened out below the bridge and a towpath
wound along the Berkshire bank. Stunted willows and low
bushes grew in profusion, and here and there "Ducks were a-
dabbling, up tails all!" There was no doubt in our minds that
we were very close to Rat's house. We could see small doors
and windows dug into the bank by the river folk, but the sun
was too high and there were too many humans abroad to allow the real residents of the river to show themselves. And
then, under a willow tree that leaned out over the water and
trailed its drooping leaves like a curtain, we caught a glimpse
of something that caused Ian to give a small leap. He caught
himself in time, the boat revealing the smallest tremor of his
excitement. "I think I see Rat's boat," he whispered. John
throttled the motor, then put it in reverse. We were able to
hold our own against the current for a few minutes while we
peered in under the trailing leaves. "There!" said Ian, pointing triumphantly.

A wind had sprung up, ruffling the river, and for a moment
the branches parted. We caught a glimpse of a small boat,
smaller than the other river craft. It was tied to a willow root.
It was not only tiny but delicate, and obviously there was not
room for even one extra person in it unless that someone were
very small. We would not have seen the boat at all if Ian had

not been keeping such a sharp lookout. There was a little dark space in underneath the roots. Perhaps some eyes, set in a brown, furry face, were even now watching us. It was not so much what we could *see* as what we could *feel*. The prickle at the back of our necks confirmed a *presence*. We started downstream again, hardly daring to breathe.

As the current carried us downstream we saw fishermen and campers all along the riverbank. Once we passed a camping punt, the same kind as in *Three Men in a Boat*. The canvas hung in sodden swags and from the comfort of our motor launch I tried to ignore the sight of a harried member of my own sex grimly bailing out yesterday's rain with an enameled saucepan. John was the soul of tact and forbore any remark as we putted past. We came to Hardwick House, a great mansion with grounds running down to the river. We could see the terrace, near the house, where Charles I had used to like to play a game of bowls. Almost opposite, in midstream, was a small island supporting a jungle of twisted, stunted willows. Ian begged to be allowed to explore it, so with some trepidation we came alongside while he leaped off into the mud and hauled himself ashore by hanging onto roots and branches. We circled the island several times, wondering if it were close enough to the weir to qualify as the place where the Rat and Mole had come upon "The Piper at the Gates of Dawn." The current was running more swiftly, it seemed to us, and John decided he did not want to go much farther downstream. Getting Ian aboard proved more difficult than we had bargained for, but we finally managed it, ruining his shoes and socks in the process. He reported no lost baby otters and no goaty footprints in the mud.

Now our boat was going faster than ever downstream, and we all peered anxiously at the Oxford shore in order to obtain a glimpse of Mapledurham House. It was harder to see than Hardwick House had been, set back as it was among the trees, but at last we glimpsed its multifarious chimneys, Tudor gables, and mullioned windows sparkling in the sun. Surely this must be Toad Hall! Grahame describes it as "a handsome, dignified old house of mellowed red brick, with well-kept lawns reaching down to the water's edge. . . ." We easily found the page where Shepard had supplied us with a picture of Rat and Mole gazing at the house from the river, even as we were doing. We decided that although Mapledurham was undoubtedly the model, the artist had borrowed a few details from Hardwick House, too. On their first outing together, Rat told the Mole: "Toad is rather rich, you know, and this is really one of the nicest houses in these parts, though we never admit as much to Toad."

It seems to be generally agreed that Mapledurham is the showplace of this part of the Thames. In the *Forsyte Saga*, John Galsworthy records that Fleur Forsyte once rented a country house at Mapledurham as part of her scheme for climbing higher on the social ladder. (If she ever met Toad, I am sure she wrapped that innocent, expansive animal around her little finger.) Only Alexander Pope, who carried on a curious literary affair with the daughters of the Blount family, has disparaging remarks to make about Mapledurham. According to an account in *The Thames Illustrated*, by John Leyland, Pope quarreled outright with Teresa Blount and was rather miffed when Martha, her sister, withdrew from London society after the coronation of George I and let it be known that she preferred her ancestral Mapledurham House on the banks of the Thames. Leyland quotes the vinegarish lines that Pope wrote as comment on the desertion:

> She went to plain-work and to purling brooks,
> Old fashion'd halls, dull aunts, and croaking rooks;
> She went from opera, park, assembly, play,
> To morning walks, and prayers three hours a day;
> To part her time 'twixt reading and bohea,
> To muse and spill her solitary tea.

I am sad that we did not discover *The Thames Illustrated* until after our return to America. It would have been such a help to us. A huge, portfolio-sized volume, it was published in 1887—two years before the *Three Men in a Boat* made their journey, twenty-one years before *The Wind in the Willows* was published. Despite its size and publication date, I would still recommend it as a guide to the river and the countryside along its banks. What my large-scale twelve-foot map strives to do by cartography, Leyland set out to do with a camera. His equipment must have been primitive by present standards, but he was able to record an almost yard-by-yard portrait of the Thames. The photography is beautiful. At Mapledurham he not only took pictures from the river, but went ashore in order to view his subject from several approaches. His pictures are accompanied by a delightfully meandering but always careful account of the historical and literary backgrounds for his photographs. Besides the anecdote about Alexander Pope and the Misses Blount, he gives other facts about Mapledurham. The house was built in 1581 and fell into Parliamentary hands during the English Civil War. By Leyland's day, the house had become an almost legendary place, known to hold secret rooms and passages, a great staircase, paneled rooms, and walls hung with family portraits. Nowadays, I am told, the house no longer belongs to the Blount family, but has been divided up into sumptuous apartments. At any rate, it is still kept in what appears to be perfect condition. Both the Blounts *and* Toad should be consoled.

We did not want to drift too far downstream because of the weir, and a cloud had been creeping over the sun. In the sudden way of English skies, the blueness disappeared suddenly and at almost the same instant the gray river was spattered by a slanting rain. John swept the boat around, tracing a great arc in our wake, and we headed back toward Pangbourne. Over hot tea at The Swan we reassessed our adventures. We had found Rat's house and Toad Hall, but what we really longed to see was the picnic place. Ian and I were both certain that we had been within yards of it and we got our copy of *The Wind in the Willows* for the hundredth time that day to read aloud the description:

> Leaving the main stream, they now passed into what seemed at first sight a little land-locked lake. Green turf sloped down to either edge, brown snakey tree-roots gleamed below the surface of the quiet water, while ahead of them the silver shoulder and foamy tumble of weir, arm-in-arm with a restless dripping mill-wheel, that held up in its turn a grey-gabled mill-house, filled the air with a soothing murmur of sound, dull and smothery, yet with little clear voices speaking cheerfully out of it at intervals. It was so very beautiful that the Mole could only hold up both forepaws and gasp, "O my! O my! O my!"

The description was so concrete that we were certain that the place really did exist, and that we could find it if only given another chance. Much revived by a good tea, John promised faithfully that we would return another day to continue our search. He was true to his word, but we never did find what we were seeking, although we spent several more halcyon days on the river and came to know the old boatman and be known by him although he never reversed his original low opinion of our boating abilities. I think now that we should have gone on foot along the Oxford shore, or hired a boat at Purley, below Mapledurham, and gone *upstream* through the lock so as not to come upon the weir unexpectedly. I do know, now, that Grahame was describing an actual place, but I did not discover it by punting on the Thames, as I had hoped. Instead, I found it while exploring the pages of Leyland's book. He describes what I am almost certain is the place we were seeking:

> The mill at Mapledurham has been a subject for many artists, and is, perhaps, the most picturesque on the whole river—so picturesque, indeed, with its old brick walls, little windows, timber gables, and tiled roof, and its quaint bridge and surroundings, that some have thought its picturesqueness artificial. However that may be, it is certainly remarkably pretty. There is a small island above the weir—and a very noble weir it is—and then the river opens out wide and beautiful.

One day we drove up on the downs to Blewbury, a delightful little village. When Kenneth Grahame first moved there, he wrote to his American friend, Austin Purvis:

> Blewbury is perhaps the most beautiful of a string of very pretty and very primitive villages stretched along the northern edge of the Berkshire Downs. It is only about 54 miles from London, but 5400 years remote from it in every way. This is the heart

of King Alfred's country, "Alfred the Great" who beat the Danes close by here; about 860, and nothing has really happened since. True, a tiresome innovator called William the Conqueror came along some years later, and established a thing called the Curfew bell, which still rings here during the winter months, to the annoyance of the more conservative inhabitants, who say they used to get on very well before these new-fangled notions; but this is all that divides us from Saxon times.

The present owners of Bohams (the Grahames' house) were busy in the garden. They were pleasant enough but it was clear that they held little regard or sentiment concerning previous owners. Living in an old house where once had lived a Famous Author was an inconvenience to be borne, like bad drains. The Grahames, they said, had left the village after their son Alastair "committed suicide" down at Oxford and Mrs. Grahame had alienated her neighbors by giving his old clothes to the village jumble sale. Peter Green, in his biography, debates at great length whether or not the Grahames' only child fell or jumped in front of a train, but at the time I had only read Chalmers who gives no hint of sinister possibilities. For the first time I felt the chill of deeper currents beneath the surface.

With the owners' permission, we walked around the outside of the house. We wished we could see into the kitchen that Miss P. had hinted at as being Badger's. Could this little dooryard be the entrance to Mole's Dulce Domum? We quickly exhausted the possibilities of Bohams and wandered out into the village streets. *The Wind in the Willows* had been written before the Grahames moved to Blewbury, but the village could very well have been the one where the Animals, trudging through the snow, caught a glimpse of the ca-

nary in its cage and felt the temptations of domesticity. Almost every house was whitewashed, well kept, and surrounded
by flowers. Blewbury was picturesque and prosperous.

I have never seen such beautiful thatch as they had in that
village. Most of it seemed to be new, a fact which struck me
as worthy of investigation. One of the roofs was in the process
of being thatched, although no one was working on it at the
moment. We could see a cut-away section of the roof, almost
like a diagram, which gave us a good idea of how the straws
were tied into bundles, about a foot thick, then laid at an
angle so that rain would run down the outside layer. I stopped
to speak to the owner of the house who, like almost everyone
else in Blewbury, was working in his garden. I saw by his gate-
post that he was a retired Commander, R.N. He seemed
grateful to be able to leave off carting stones for his rock garden and came and stood by me, gazing at his half-finished roof
and mopping his face with a handkerchief. I wondered aloud
about the roofs of Blewbury and asked him if there were any
particular reason for their excellence. I assumed that thatching was a dying craft and suggested that perhaps the village
harbored some old craftsman, perhaps the last of his kind,
who would take the secret with him when he died. No, the ex-
naval officer said, it was a young chap who had taken on the
job. Curious thing, that. He worked in the atomic plant
down near Oxford during the day, but in the evenings and
on holidays he was a thatcher. It was a lucky thing for Blewbury, since his rates were not too dear. The commander went
on to say that it took someone with muscle to do the job
properly. The straw had to be compressed tightly with iron
hooks in order to prevent it from burning—like the pages of a

book, which burn individually, but are difficult to ignite when the book is shut.

I cannot help but muse on the paradox of a young man who works in an atomic plant by day, but who is willing to practice an ancient craft by night. Is he tired of pushing buttons? I like to think that thatching gives him some satisfaction beyond the extra money he earns. Since our trip to Blewbury I have read more about the intricacies and economics of the craft. Lawrence Fellows, in *The New York Times* (September 30, 1962), has written an especially interesting and comprehensive article, "Thatched Roofs Fading from English Scene." Evidently there is no shortage of craftsmen (as I had at first supposed), but of material. With the development of improved agricultural techniques, good wheat straw is disappearing from the English economy. The new strains of wheat have a higher grain yield, but shorter stems. In addition, new fertilizers "burn" the stalks or they are bruised by machines in the harvesting. There is an alternative, but countrymen are slow to adapt to "foreign" ways. Wild reed is the traditional thatching material for the low-lying marsh country of eastern England and the Rural Industries Board is trying to encourage its use in the rest of England. Its advantages are that it is available, it is easier to lay, and it lasts longer. An ordinary straw thatch lasts from ten to fifteen years; a reed thatch can last a century. But there are drawbacks. The color of reed thatch is slightly different (Englishmen are conservative), it takes several years to develop a good ron (or reed bed), and it is a nasty crop to harvest. The reeds must be harvested between November and March. "Not everyone," according to Lawrence Fellows, "takes easily to this kind of seasonal

work . . . standing up to the knees in icy water, with a north-
east wind blowing off the sea, and hacking at butts of reeds
that are almost as unyielding as bamboo."

As we wandered about in Blewbury and up on the downs
behind it, we felt that something of Shepard's illustrations
clung to the scene, although we had no proof that he had
made the same pilgrimage. The houses were all very old and
charming. Under the heavy eyebrows of thatch the windows
seemed to blink in the summer sun, and an air of somnolence
hung over all. Far off we could hear the noise of the mowing
machines, and near a huge barn we saw some men who were
pitching hay from a massive wagon pulled by two patient
Percherons. The men spoke rarely or in muted voices, rather
than spend the effort on anything but hay and sun. It was as
though the village slept under an enchantment. Driving out
of the village we looked upward to where the downs met the
sky. The sky was clear and cool and hot and blue, all at the
same time. It made one dizzy to peer into it. Great white pillars of cloud-temples and towers and Taj Mahals floated
there, as though the ancient hills and great outcroppings of
rock were transmogrified by reflection in a pool. It reminded
me of something, and when we pulled up beside a little inn I
thought I knew what it was. We peered at the darkly painted
surface of the inn sign. Dimly we could discern the coils of a
great serpent, a knight in armor, an upraised sword. Perhaps it
is safe to surmise that this was the sky and countryside depicted by Ernest Shepard in his illustration for Kenneth Grahame's *Reluctant Dragon.*

Another day we explored the village of Pangbourne. We
wanted to see for ourselves the house where the Grahames

had spent their last lonely years. We were standing near the gate, trying to peer into the garden, when a woman and a teen-age girl came around the corner of the house. When we explained why we were interested in the house they seemed pleased and a little proud. They had just bought the house, they explained. Mrs. Grahame had left it in trust with Oxford University, as a memorial to her son, but the University had kept it only ten years as a rental property, then decided to sell it. "I don't think that was quite fair, do you?" asked the new owner.

She opened the gate and invited us to come in. The house was being renovated, but in the meantime she and her daughter were trying to keep the garden, at least, in a civilized state. Near the gate she pointed out a little toolshed and remarked that it had once been the village lockup. There was hardly enough room for one prisoner even if he stood up. Ian, of course, was fascinated.

The garden was larger than one would have thought possible, and exceedingly private—an excellent retreat for the Grahames. A high bank and a thick growth of trees made an almost impenetrable fortress on two sides of it. It had been cut back into a hillside so that the ground was on varied levels. There were unexpected terraces and gardens hidden within gardens. The children ran about in the late evening sun, sniffing and exploring to their hearts' content while we grownups exchanged what we knew about the Kenneth Grahames and their life in Pangbourne. Rather shyly the young girl said, "I found a toad yesterday when I was weeding. He was so big we thought he might be someone's pet." An idea struck her. "Oh, Mummy! Let's call this place Toad Hall!" But her mother was not to be led astray by a girlish whim.

Mapledurham could have that honor. The little house they had bought had been called Church Cottage for over three hundred years and it would be foolish to change it now.

Our hostess asked if we would like to see the inside of the house and of course we were delighted. Church Cottage had once been two houses, placed back to back, but long ago the two houses became wings joined by corridors. This accounted for the difficulty of deciding whether the front door was the one facing the gate and street, or the one that went from the garden directly into a bay-windowed drawing room. The house was decidedly "cottagey" and the fireplace was set back in a curious cozy-nook. It looked rather like Shepard's sketch of the Rat's comfortable hearth. We picked our way through fallen plaster and around dismantled plumbing and came into the comparative haven of another drawing room. Our hostess ran her hand lovingly over the curved marble chimney piece. "We think this might be an Adam," she said hopefully, and I, not knowing a thing about it, concurred willingly.

We went upstairs being careful not to let Lucy fall through the gaping holes where new flooring was to be installed, and discussed the pros and cons of putting a daughter here, and a son (away at school) there, and new closets somewhere else. I must say it was rather nice to talk shop with another housewife. Afterward we went downstairs and out into the garden again. There was a little extension or lean-to which, although attached to the house, could only be entered from the outdoors. This, our guide explained, had been Mr. Grahame's study. It seems to me that we had to go down a few steps to enter it—at any rate it certainly gave one the feeling of having "gone to earth." The room was damp and musty and smothered in spider webs. A tiny fireplace was set diagonally in one corner. The room was empty of desk, chairs, books, but I knew where I had seen it before. It was Mr. Badger's study— the place where he could retire when he was "particular busy," where he could put his feet up before the fire, a red cotton handkerchief over his face, and where he was on no account to be disturbed. Ernest Shepard must have sketched it during his visit.

But Blewbury and Pangbourne were only side excursions. It was to the river that we returned again and again. Once we saw an abandoned boathouse, lonely, cavernous, swept from its foundations by old floods. It was scandalous the way it had been neglected. We decided that it must have belonged to Toad, during his boating craze. Another time we found his caravan, wheel-less, but painted gaily and made livable again by a cheerful young couple, enterprising and much in love. There was always something new, if only a pattern of ripples or a family of moor hens. We never found what we were seeking, but somehow the seeking became more important than the finding. We were content to agree with the Water Rat when he told the Mole that there is "nothing—absolutely nothing—half so much worth doing as simply messing about in boats. . . ."

"In or out of 'em, it doesn't matter. Nothing seems really to matter, that's the charm of it. Whether you get away or whether you don't; whether you arrive at your destination or whether you reach somewhere else, or whether you never get anywhere at all, you're always busy, and you never do anything particular; and when you've done it there's always something else to do, and you can do it if you like, but you'd much better not. . . ."

Even on the last day, having checked out of the Red Lion
bag and baggage, we drove a considerable distance out of our
way to have a final picnic on the riverbank at Pangbourne.
We had bought veal and ham pie (jellied under the crust,
with an egg in the center) and we decided that no food had
ever tasted as good. Even the old boatman shared the spirit of
a farewell party, and for the first time he unbent enough to
talk to us. Yes, he had known Mr. Grahame. No, he had
never read any of his books. He was amazed to discover that
the old gentleman had once been Secretary of the Bank of
England, though he did remember people saying that Queen
Mary had written to Mrs. Grahame when her husband died.
People said that Mrs. Grahame was a little odd. He suddenly
waxed enthusiastic, "But Mr. Grahame was a foine old gentleman, a wonderful looking chap. He used to go for a walk almost every day, rain or shine, walking along the bank in a big
black cape. He loved the river. . . ."

"And messing about with boats," said Ian, speaking around
a mouthful of pie in his eagerness. "Simply messing about
with boats. . . ."

The old man picked himself up abruptly and moved off,
muttering to himself as he disappeared into the boathouse. I
wondered if Ian had offended him, then he came out again
with a paint brush and a pail of varnish. He started toward an
upturned boat on the dock, seemed to change his mind, and
came toward us again.

"It's a funny thing what the lad just said," he told us.
"That's the very way *he* always put it. He'd come walking
down that path and stand watching me when I was painting
or caulking or getting the boats in the water. I was younger
then, but I remember he always said exactly the same thing to

me each time: 'There's nothing, absolutely nothing, like messing about with boats. . . .' I thought it was a joke, like. And now this little lad comes along and. . . . It fair gives me a turn!" He shook his head with the wonder of it, then wandered off again toward the river and the dock. Soon he was hunched beside the upturned hull, completely absorbed in his brushwork. He was still muttering to himself when we left.

7
Johnny Crow's Garden

The day we drove up on the Downs to Blewbury, we decided to go farther on toward another little village with "literary" associations. This was Harwell, the place where L. Leslie Brooke lived during the years when he was illustrating the *Johnny Crow* books and *The Golden Goose Book*. I had written to Henry Brooke, the artist's son, before we left for England and had received a friendly and helpful reply on most impressive stationery. The letter was stamped with the seal of the Minister of Housing and Local Government, complete with lion and unicorn fighting for the crown. Remembering the pictures of those two combatants in *Ring o' Roses* (a collection of nursery rhymes illustrated by Leslie Brooke), it seemed fitting to meet them again in their official capacities. Since then we have followed Sir Henry's career with an air of proprietorship. In 1962 we were happy to see him chosen for the Cabinet with the title of Home Secretary, but we must admit it a bit disconcerting when we see his familiar round face staring at us from the newspapers. This same servant of

134

the crown once served as model for the gardener's child in *Tom Thumb* and for "the little boy that lives in the lane" in "Baa Baa Black Sheep" in *Ring o' Roses*.

Sir Henry informed us that his father had built a house five miles out of Oxford in 1923 and had lived there until 1934. Before that he had lived in London for many years, but from 1899 to 1908 (the years when he was working on the books in which we were most interested) he had lived at Pillar House, Harwell, near Didcot, Berkshire. A farm in Buckinghamshire, where the family stayed during holidays, is also recognizable in some of the drawings.

The road to Harwell wound reassuringly broad over the Downs. Later, I was to recognize the same sweep of road when I saw a copy of *Travels Round Our Village*, an adult book written by Eleanor G. Hayden in 1901, and illustrated by L. Leslie Brooke. In a letter written to Anne Carroll Moore and quoted in the May 1941 issue of *The Horn Book*, he wrote:

> There are chapters in it that I think you might like. As to the drawings which were mostly done at the turn of the century—so long ago that I may speak of them—I think that they have caught something of the hard roughness of the surface of the Berkshire village life that is unconscious of its own underlying humanity. "The Village" was West Hundred, but the book, both in text and illustrations, is an amalgam of three neighboring villages—West and East Hundred and Harwell (where we ourselves lived) and there are few figures in my share that were not drawn directly from, or from memory of, individual inhabitants, if not always from the same person that the author had in mind. Possibly had the illustrations been done with less respect for fact they might have been more amusing!

This last may be true, but the discipline and insight gained before he set to work on the picture books must have been invaluable.

I became aware of L. Leslie Brooke's work and style in what I believe is a most unusual way. At the age of six or thereabouts I brought home from the library a copy of *The Golden Goose Book*. Poring over the pages, I was struck by something familiar in the illustrations. I remembered an old book belonging to my mother and went in search of it. The story of "Prince Toto" was illustrated by "L.L.B.," the initials in a little box in the corner. But I did not need the initials to tell me that this was the same artist. It is as easy to recognize Brooke's humor and style as it is his familiars—toads, geese, cockatoos, mice, grasshoppers, fairies, and so on. These were to populate Brooke's later work, too. But even my innocent eye could note improvement. In the earlier illustrations every square inch of the page was covered, the borders crowded and fussy. The illustrations in *The Golden Goose Book* make wry comment by isolation of objects in an infinity of space. The drain pipe "laid on" to the Third Little Pig's brick house bespeaks volumes about its owner.

My mother's book, a legacy from her childhood, is called *The Parade, 1897: A Gift Book for Boys and Girls,* and is edited by Gleeson White. Besides Brooke, the book includes such artists as Laurence Housman, Max Beerbohm and Aubrey Beardsley. The list of authors includes Richard Le Gallienne, Sir Richard Burton, Mrs. Molesworth and other eminent Victorians. Gleeson White was editor of *The Studio,* the most influential art magazine in London in the 1890s. In the winter issue of 1898, White wrote an article entitled

"Children's Books and Their Illustrators," the first serious criticism of children's book design.

Through the pages of his magazine, White appealed for the importance of being earnest—with children. He made his plea to a most sophisticated audience, an audience whose eye for line and detail had been made sharply aware by such diverse inspiration as a Japanese print, a page in *The Yellow Book*, a gown from Paris, an all white room by Whistler. There was also a new concern for natural form, the viewpoint of *arte nouveau*, both Romantic and scientific.

A young artist living in London in the 1890s would not fail to notice whatever interested the *Studio* crowd, especially if it applied to his own field of illustration. L. Leslie Brooke had a sense of humor and a good eye. He had an almost Romanesque view of leaves and grasses, flowers and small animals, which gave to their shape and textures a jewel-like intensity. Perhaps it was a growing sense of proportion that helped him to unclutter his work. Perhaps it was the influence of the art world and the help of serious criticism. I like to think it was the sweep and reality of the Downs.

We were made to think of Leslie Brooke's *Three Little Pigs* as we drove closer to Harwell. On either hand lay sun-flooded fields studded with the sort of hayricks I remembered from my first trip to England at the age of ten. They seemed to have disappeared in other parts of England. Farmers nowadays evidently find it easier and cheaper to squeeze the hay into tight rectangular bundles by the use of machinery and then to cover the stacks with tarpaulin or corrugated tin. In the fields near Harwell, however, we saw the hay stacked in the old way—circular and thatch-covered—so that here and there we saw what looked like a wattle hut or little cottage, but was really a hayrick. I said something about their looking like doll houses, but John held out for early Saxons. Ian wanted to know if Saxons had settled Jamestown, Virginia, because, if so, he had helped build a little house like that. We had visited Jamestown a week or so before the restored village was officially opened, and a friendly workman had allowed Ian to help pulverize oyster shells for him and add them to his "stew" of mud and chopped straw.

I could see John struggling with his cautious historian's conscience. He cannot bear to oversimplify. "Well . . . yes . . . in a way we could say they were Saxons. But, on the other hand, it was much more complicated than that. . . ."

"I just wanted to know about straw houses," said Ian a bit hastily. He was determined to be polite, but he knew about historians. They do run on. It was Lucy, though, who saved him from a long lecture.

"Piggies live in straw houses," she said with sudden firmness, then was quite put out when we all laughed. After all, what happened to the first little pig was no laughing matter.

Harwell is not as remote from civilization as Blewbury, yet it is still a pleasant little village. A shade more suburban, perhaps, it is not as self-consciously "quaint" and relies far less on whitewashed brick. The architecture is a medley of period and style. The brick is apricot and mellow—the color of Harwell cherries. Most of the houses had gardens enclosed by high brick walls. We could see the tops of trees and decided that almost everyone in the village must have a small orchard in which to grow the famous cherries. Baskets of the translucent fruit were set out for sale along the roadsides and John and

Ian went off to buy some. I took Lucy with me and set off in the opposite direction to look for L. Leslie Brooke's house.

So much of the village was enclosed behind walls that it was disappointing, but at length Lucy and I paused before an ancient cottage that fronted on the main street. It had such a high pitched roof that I wondered if it could have been the model for the one in "There Was a Man":

> There was a man, and he had nought,
> And robbers came to rob him;
> He crept up to the chimney pot
> And then they thought they had him.

A woman was standing in the doorway of the cottage and I asked if we might take a picture. She would give her consent, she said, only if we would wait a few minutes until school let out and we would take her little girl's picture at one and the same time. I tried to explain that I was not a professional photographer, but she appraised my camera and its leather case and I could see that she thought she had struck a bargain.

She was curious about why I should want to take a picture of her house, so I changed my tack and began new explanations, this time stressing the fact that I was a writer—not a photographer—and that I had come to Harwell to seek out the scenes made familiar by a famous artist, an artist who illustrated children's books. She wrinkled her forehead when I mentioned Leslie Brooke and when I asked her if she knew of a place called Pillar House. She had never heard of Leslie Brooke, but Pillar House was just a few doors down the street. She hesitated, perhaps sorry she had admitted as much and afraid I might leave right then. A new thought seemed to strike her. Would we like to come inside?

"Mind the child doesn't trip," she cautioned, as Lucy and I entered the tiny living room. I gazed about enchanted. The house was hardly bigger than the length and breadth of this one room. The beams were so low that if John had been there he would have cracked his head. How clean everything was! I wondered how many hours it took—how many centuries of spring cleaning—for whitewashed walls to achieve the texture of fresh-ironed linen. And the floor! No wonder she had warned us to be careful, for no two flags were of the same height or thickness, yet they were scrubbed to hues of pink and lavender, gray and mauve. Everything was out of plumb —jambs and lintels, sills and mantelpiece. A flight of stone steps wound upward to a loft above. Each step was worn by the feet of centuries.

Now I knew where I had seen all this before. This was the house in which the crooked man had lived, along with his crooked cat, and the cat's crooked mouse. No wonder they had seemed so well content in Leslie Brooke's pictures. For all its craziness, the little house seemed to me the most solid piece of architecture I have known, rooted in time as well as space.

The woman went over to the mantelpiece and moved the jar of flowers there closer to the center. She did it automatically as a woman pushes a strand of hair from her forehead. It must have been a losing battle to keep anything placed squarely on that chimney piece, so shiny and black with age, but this woman was not the sort to give up easily. She interrupted my thoughts by asking, quite suddenly, how old Lucy was. As with most English people, she considered my child enormous.

"My little girl was hardly as old as yours when we moved in

here," she said. "Of course we thought it was only temporary, but you know how hard it is to find housing, especially since the war. We put our name down for one of the Council houses—they're new, you know, with real sinks and electricity laid on. I thought I'd go wild at first. I kept making my husband go check and see where we were on the list, and I used to wheel the baby in her carriage to watch the builders. Not that I always had time for that, though. I like things kept neat and in good order, and it's hard work to keep this house that way."

"Oh, but it's charming!" I burst out. "So small and snug and old." Then I stopped and must have blushed furiously. How patronizing I must sound. What did I know about the heartbreak of keeping house in such a place—I, who with all my gadgets, am yet an abysmal housekeeper? How awful, if one really thought neatness and tidiness so important, to be sentenced to a lifetime of the picturesque!

"Do you have long to wait?" I asked. "You must be fairly close to the top of the list by this time." I tried to make my voice cheerful and sympathetic.

She shook her head and gave an odd little smile. "Oh, we got to the top all right," she said, "but I wouldn't move after all." She must have sensed my astonishment, because she laughed outright. "My husband and all the neighbors thought I had gone clear out of my mind, but, . . ." she paused and let her eyes sweep the tiny room, "I found that living in this house had sort of changed me. I had worked so hard to make it clean and comfortable, and our garden was just coming into its own and I had got the old cherry tree to bloom again. . . . My husband decided to make some repairs before we moved (we didn't want anyone to talk behind our backs after we left) and he cut into the walls. He found the house was much older than we had thought. It must be the oldest house in the village, and what's more, it's built on top of something even older. I went up and took another look at those Council houses and they looked raw and new and ugly, and you can hear the neighbors through the walls. . . . Ugh! I wouldn't have any more to do with the flimsy things. And, of course," she added demurely, "the landlord was only too anxious to renew our lease. He knows he has good tenants, and we made good terms."

When I went outside again, the village street was a maelstrom of dust and school children—thick boots, sturdy knees, rosy cheeks. It was late in the afternoon and traffic was pouring into town from the auto factories and atomic plant down toward Oxford. The village traffic director, in long white "overall," stood in the center of the street, his face the color of Harwell brick. I diagnosed his trouble as high blood pressure, brought about from the constant frustration of trying to direct traffic at the very spot where the ancient Downs-life ends and the Atomic Age begins.

John and Ian rejoined us, and we asked the policeman where we could find Pillar House. He pointed to a house across the street and we all stared at it. The house was whitewashed Georgian brick with a little portico at the entrance. I could not remember having seen it in either *Ring o' Roses* or *The Golden Goose*. To one side of it was a high brick wall which evidently enclosed a garden. The double gate was open and sagging on its hinges. The traffic had suddenly dispersed and the policeman came over to talk to us. He had never heard of Leslie Brooke, he said. The house was now rented by an RAF captain, his wife and two little boys. They were all away for the day and we could not possibly be allowed to enter the gate.

Ian and Lucy were standing in the gateway, the only safe place for them since houses and walls rose abruptly from the street with no sidewalks to stand on. A car was coming, so we all drew back to stand with the children. I stole a good look at the garden. There was something vaguely familiar about it, but I was aware that the Guardian of Britain had his eye on me and I did not dare act too interested. The general impression I received was that the garden was not sacrosanct and that no one would greatly care if we went in. The lawn was mowed—but only just—and what flowers there were were perennials much in need of weeding. Some toy trucks (or lorries) had been left out under a tree and I could see that whoever owned them had been having a glorious time making a network of muddy roads. A battered pail and spade suggested mud pies. Farther back I could see a shed. Something about its roof line tugged at my memory and I knew I must see it.

Ian edged through the gate to get a better look at the trucks and Lucy had her eye on the pail. John was in deep conversation with the policeman when Lucy eluded my grasp and ran through the gate. By the time I had run after her and picked her up it seemed rather foolish to argue whether or not we should enter the Promised Land. I made my way to the back of the garden and stood back to look at the shed. It was obviously being used as a garage. There was a puddle of oil and several old inner tubes and tires about, but at one time the building must have been a stable. No, that wasn't it either. It

looked more the sort of place where a cow and a few chickens
would be kept. A definite picture leaped into my mind and
then I knew I had it:

> Cock-a-doodle-doo!
> My dame has lost her shoe;
> My master's lost his fiddling stick
> And don't know what to do.

I looked up at the roof to see if any magpies were watching
us, as in *Ring O' Roses*. The roof was slate, but the slates
looked fairly new and I wondered if there had once been
thatch. There was something else about the roof that intrigued
me. I walked into the garage and looked up. A large skylight
had been cut into it to flood the interior with light. Of course!
The place had once been used as an artist's studio. This was
probably the place where Leslie Brooke worked, looking out
toward his beloved garden, those early years in Harwell.

Leslie Brooke once wrote to a friend that his three great
passions were children, books and gardens. Johnny Crow's
garden was a much grander and more formal affair than the
plot of ground that lay about Pillar House, but I am sure that
in his years there Leslie Brooke "plied rake and hoe" with all
the enthusiasm of a frustrated Londoner lately removed to
the country. He must have been very proud of his rose trees,
for they appear in several of his illustrations. We see them in
the *Johnny Crow* books and in "The Story of Three Bears."
The best picture in Mrs. Hayden's *Travels Round Our Village* is one of an old fellow in a flat straw hat, leaning on his
hoe and gazing at "The First Bud on the Rose Tree." Only a
true gardener would have sought to capture that moment.

Lucy had run back to be with her father and when I arrived

he had scooped her up in his arms and was holding her over his shoulder. Ian was fairly dancing with impatience. I thought it was because he had been forbidden to play with the trucks but that was not it.

"Look!" he said, excitedly. " 'Simple Simon'! See, here's the pail . . . and the tree (he pointed upward). . . . And there's the way where the door goes out to the garden."

We gazed at where he was pointing and saw that he was quite right. True, there was no circular bench under the tree and the thrifty flower border that flourishes in the pictures had now been beaten into clay, but surely we were standing in the same garden. Leslie Brooke was hard at work on *The Golden Goose Book* while living at Pillar House. Our family likes to think that the garden there reappears in "The Story of the Three Bears." But it is not only flowers that bloom in the climate of that place. Childhood flourishes, too. The antics of the Little, Small, Wee Bear must be very much like those of L. L. Brooke's own small boys and the essential "familyishness" of the Bear family must have been borrowed from a source close at hand. Children are still enchanted by the warmth and coziness and "just-like-us" feeling that permeate the illustrations of the "Three Bears" story. I think that Leslie Brooke would be glad to know that two small boys still inhabit the garden of Pillar House. I do not think he would mind that Ian and Lucy trespassed there.

Although the rest of us were quite content that we had found Johnny Crow's garden, Lucy was not. Where was the "lion with the green and yellow tie on?" And the "giraffe who made everybody laugh?" A few days after our expedition to Harwell we decided to abandon the Henley hotel and go up to London to the zoo. We took train and taxi to the zoo and found, when we arrived, that it is one of the most efficient enterprises in Britain. The British take zoos seriously. I, on the other hand, detest them, but I had happy memories of the London one since I had been taken there at the age of ten by two maiden aunts. *That* trip had somehow involved Hampton Court and a trip by boat, but this was Lucy's day and I knew enough not to combine events with a two-year-old.

Although Lucy had learned to walk miles and had developed a sturdy pair of legs I was delighted to find that someone (Christopher Robin's denizen of "the Superintendent's House?") had thought to provide wheeled strollers for a small fee. There was also a nicely illustrated guide handed to us at the gate which mapped out a short tour, a long tour, and (rather touchingly, I thought) a tour for a rainy day. Unhesitatingly I chose a short tour for a muggy day. I was wilting before we started and it proved to be a wise decision. Lucy and I trudged (or, rather, Lucy lolled and I trudged) over a circumscribed fraction of the zoo territory and seemed to see a great many small animals whose names I did not know (a bidger, a badger, a bodger?) simply because those were the cages where no one else was standing.

I was just as fascinated by the people as by the animals. London is still the center of a great empire, but why do people from Africa and India and such exotic places flock to see their native animals in a London zoo? Is it because they are homesick? Or because they can't see "native" animals in their own countries? Or, as I suspect, is there a sort of identification with the beasts themselves, a kind of symbolized nationalism? I must admit that I felt a real surge of affection for the biffalo-buffalo-bison even though I rarely see one in the suburbs where I live.

I noticed ladies in saris standing transfixed before the tigers' cage and, for all I know, there were Russians gazing at the bears. But the most splendid was an African chieftain staring up at a giraffe. He was over six feet tall and dressed in full regalia. The orange, yellow, and black patterns on the chieftain's full-flowing robes seemed to reflect the markings of the giraffe and to recall the heat and shimmer of Africa. For a long moment man and beast stood staring at each other, haughty and enigmatic, then the man turned and swept an amused glance toward where Lucy and I stood, open-mouthed. Next moment, with long unhurried strides, he set off towards the gate, head and shoulders towering above the rest of the crowd. Now, why had *he* come?

But we were impatient for the chimpanzee's tea party. By some miracle we were able to find John and Ian, buy our tickets, and file into the tiny circus surrounded by benches. All around us were families like ourselves, tired, hot, excited. A keeper led in a pair of chimpanzees and they sat down at a little table in the center of the ring. An assistant brought in the tea—an enormous pot very like the one in *Johnny Crow's New Garden*.

> Till the Chimpanzee
> Said: "Shall I Make the Tea?"

These particular chimpanzees began seriously enough. Tea time in Britain is as fraught with significance as any Zen ceremony, and a reverent hush fell over the audience as the first decorous cup was poured. There followed a second cup, but by this time enthusiasm began to overflow. There followed a third and fourth cup in rapid succession, with more and more tea being slopped over the little table.

An anxious, puzzled look spread over the countenance of the two apes. One of them lifted the lid of the teapot and peered in, as if to see what was causing the leakage. In doing so, he tipped the pot so that more tea spilled out. His friend turned and leered at the audience. Lucy shrieked with laughter. Ian, beside me, was laughing uncontrollably and John suddenly came out with a loud Haw-haw-haw. I looked about us and noticed the other families nearby. Some of the grown-ups were smiling politely, but the children—all those Christopher Robins and prim Alices—looked as tense and grave and anxious as the chimpanzees.

The little girl next to Ian had her hand clutched in a fist, the knuckles up to her teeth. She looked as though she did not know whether to laugh or cry. Suddenly one of the apes reached over and poured a cup of tea on the head of his fellow guest. A gasp—almost a groan—rippled through the crowd, then the second monkey retaliated. A few smiles appeared. After all, this was fair play! The little girl next to Ian took her hand from her mouth and craned to get a better look. The party was growing wilder. With the next peal of laughter from Ian she joined in. All around the ring, in wider and wider circles, the ripple of laughter grew. It was all right to laugh! It was permitted to laugh! It was *proper* to laugh!

> And they danced and they sang, and each visitor's attitude
> Was his very best way of expressing his gratitude
> To Johnny Crow and his garden.

A few days later we set off from the Red Lion at Henley for the last time, John groaning as he carried the suitcases down from the top floor. He kept muttering that someone was putting weights in the bottom. We did not dare tell him that in addition to the slates we had picked up in Merlin's Cave at Tintagel and a score of books we had bought along the way, Ian had started an old iron collection. He had methodically labeled each piece in his collection in his own shaky spelling. My favorite and his (but for different reasons) was "Wench found at bottom of Thames."

We came at length to Aldershot, hot and dusty and anthill busy. The map showed a faint shadow marked "Caesar's Camp" with the modern military center superimposed. Soldiers dressed in heavy brown wool and General Montgomery berets marched on the double about the paths and parade grounds. It all looked frightfully strenuous. Ian was enchanted, but my emotions were nostalgic. Shades of Mrs. Ewing! I could remember my mother reading *The Story of a Short Life* (which was set in Aldershot) and how we all cried both at that and at *Jackanapes*. Mrs. Ewing (nee Juliana Horatia Gatty) was an estimable Victorian writer for children who combined real insight into childhood along with an insider's view of Victorian military life. Perhaps it was because we were military dependents ourselves that my sisters and I took such pleasure in her books. We were neither "country" nor "town" nor "city" but "knocked about the world" much as the barracks master's wife had done in *A Story of a Short Life*.

At last we made our way out of Aldershot and set off on a straight bit of road pointing toward Guildford. Lucy fell asleep on my lap. Ian crawled up on the high deck made by our suitcases piled in the back of the car and fell asleep, too. When he awoke we were driving along a high ridge, the green fields of England spread out on either side.

"Where are we?" he asked. I peered at the *Atlas* and was able to tell him that we were driving along a place called "Hog's Back."

"Hey, really? That's in *Adam of the Road.*" Ian leaned over the back of my seat and looked at where my finger was pointing. "And look—there's Guildford. Isn't that where Adam swam across some river?" His finger traced a wider circle, coming to rest on some wispy lettering on the other side of Guildford. I don't know which of us exclaimed first; "Albury! Albury Heath!"

> A Toad that lived on Albury Heath
> Wanted to see the World.

Of all the books illustrated by L. Leslie Brooke our family's favorite is *A Roundabout Turn,* the story of Jacob Toad. A comfort-loving type with a streak of adventure in him, Jacob is dissatisfied with the confines of Albury Heath and sets out to explore a larger world. He hops as far as the local fairgrounds where a little girl puts him up on the merry-go-round. Poor Jacob! He mistakes the merry-go-round for the world and staggers home a sadder and wiser toad, quite content to live the rest of his life in a less dizzy environment.

Ian and I were both so excited that we woke up Lucy. With a sigh of resignation John pulled to the side of the road. He seemed elaborately unconcerned as he studied the map, then he must have caught something of our excitement.

"That's it all right," he said. "See, there's Shere, right next to Albury. Remember? There's a picture of a hedgehog in the book who carries a market basket with 'A Present from Shere' stamped on it. I always wondered what *that* meant."

He shot the car into gear and started forward again. "We'd better find ourselves a place to stay. It's getting late."

We crept through Guildford and onto the crossroads marked by a half-hidden sign: Guests. We turned off the main road and up the sweep of a long drive. There, set back beyond lawns gone to seed and unkempt shrubbery, was an old Tudor mansion, low and rambling. I went in to ask for reservations while John and the children stayed outside to stretch their legs. A young woman showed me upstairs to a room on the second floor. My heart sank. The room was dark and low-ceilinged and the beds looked neither clean nor comfortable. I did not expect a private bath, but I was made positively downhearted by the news that not only would we have to traverse a long corridor, but go up a flight of stairs as well if we would be clean.

I was just about to back out gracefully when I heard familiar voices from below. I looked out to see Lucy circling round and round in the new-mown grass below us, chanting happily as she ran. Ian's voice seemed much nearer. It took me several minutes to place him. He had climbed up the winding stair of a little summerhouse and had crawled out on its sagging roof, quite near our window. I knew that eventually I would have to forbid him such dangerous pleasure, but for the nonce I decided to pretend I didn't see him. Even from this distance I could tell he was ecstatic. I leaned out from my window to see what he was gazing at. Directly below him was the lawn and the remains of an old terrace. Beyond and to the left was a walled garden snarled by an impenetrable mass of rose briars. Beyond that was another walled garden, and beyond *that* the moss-clotted fruit trees of an old orchard. Down below me I saw John's size thirteen shoes sticking out from the other side of the summerhouse. Since they did not move, I surmised he was taking a brief snooze. I told the girl I would take the room.

Dinner would not be served until eight. Food was imperative for our flagging spirits and, as we were all anxious to explore the fabulous heath, we set off again to look for a place that served a good tea. We putted along the green lanes to the top of a hill, then gave a gasp of delight and recognition. The road unwound like a ribbon before us. On either hand and as far as the eye could see were folded hills. Knots of gorse and heather and bracken intermingled with clumps of trees to make a tapestry of greens, and over all arched the blue sky with a few white clouds floating in it. Surely we were at the very spot where Jacob paused to contemplate his journey:

> But there—it's a long way down the road
> For a fellow that walks as slow as a Toad.

Leslie Brooke's illustration must have been sketched from this very spot.

We came to a crossing: Shere to our left; Albury to our right. We took the right turn, but it proved a mistake. Albury was asleep, its windows shuttered to the sun. There was not one human being in sight, but an antique shop, with an ancient carousel horse out in front, gave us hope that someone, at least, was an admirer of *A Roundabout Turn*. The houses were built so close to the narrow street that it was dangerous to stand there, even with our noses pressed to the shop window, so we set off again—this time toward Shere.

In 1930 Leslie Brooke wrote to Jacqueline Overton:

Report has told you right. I have committed the indiscretion of another book. I hope you may find yourself disposed to introduce Jacob to the same children who know Johnny.

A little later she wrote to him that the children at her library wanted to know, if it were not a secret, what he had meant by "a present from Shere" on the bottom of the hedgehog's market basket. This was his reply, printed in *The Horn Book Magazine*, May 1941:

> You say very kind things about Jacob. I wish you could meet his author, Robert Charles—a most kindly man with a family of growing children. . . . At one time he lived on Albury Heath himself. As to the Present from Shere it is no secret of my own but I suppose I oughtn't to have done it as not being generally comprehensible. The Hedgehog for marketing would go either to Albury Village or to Shere Village, next door, as it were. Shere is sometimes described as the prettiest village in England, which it certainly isn't now . . . but in the 80's and 90's many Americans went down to Surrey to see it. . . . But the real truth is— my wife and her sisters as children spent their summer holidays in the house of an uncle near Shere (they used always to go across Shere Heath to the Fair at Albury Heath one day each summer and always rode the roundabouts) . . . as both author and artist were known in the neighborhood I thought it would be no harm to put that on the basket—just to give local colour. . . .

Having no earlier standards by which to judge, we found Shere Village delightful. It was larger than Albury and certainly more awake. A pleasant stream, adrift with white ducks, ran through the center and the houses were set about a tiny tree-shaded green. Best of all, tea was being served at the most picturesque of the little houses. We made a meal of

homemade scones, fresh-picked raspberries, and thick country
cream. It was amazing how our spirits revived. After tea we let
the children paddle a bit in the stream, then we set off for our
lodgings again. Perhaps it was because we had fuller stomachs
and lighter hearts that we now noticed a large red-lettered
sign at the crossroads: "Albury Heath Annual Fair. Games!
Booths! Prizes!" and a date, three days off.

Some things in life are pre-ordained. Fate had arranged that
we should arrive on Albury Heath in time for the Fair. Even
John could see that. As soon as we had returned to our lodgings at The Gables we made arrangements with the manager
to keep our rooms for a few days longer. For the next day or
two I washed out clothes and hung them in the orchard, the
children played in the garden, and John went up to London
on the train. While he was there he bought a copy of *A
Roundabout Turn* and brought it back to us to refresh our
memories.

In the evenings we went for walks on the heath, confirming
Jacob Toad's estimation of it:

> It's a perfectly charming Heath, of course—
> All this heather, and all this gorse,
> All this bracken to walk beneath,
>   With its feathery fronds to the sky uncurled—
>   It's as jolly a Heath as ever was found.

One afternoon we drove back into Albury to find the antique
shop open. We learned that the carousel horse was just coincidence: the family who owned the shop had never heard of
Jacob! It was a nice family, though, with children about the
same age as ours. They were so interested in both the poem
and illustrations that we left the book with the little boy (it

was his birthday). When we saw the family again they pointed out something we would have otherwise missed: "The Silent Pool," a picture on the wall of Jacob's house. The pool is a local landmark, a regular tourist-trap "lover's leap" sort of place which lies just off the road on the way to Albury. One evening we paid it a dutiful visit and saw for ourselves the curious little hut built out over it, exactly as in the picture.

But at last came the day of the fair. It was a glorious summer day—hot, with a light breeze blowing—and we arrived to find other families pouring through the gates to the fairgrounds. Where they had all come from I cannot guess since the heath was for the most part uninhabited. Most people were walking, although the very youngest rode in disdainful ease, seated in beautifully designed British perambulators, rolling along like royalty.

We cocked our ears for the sound of carousel music, but in this we were disappointed. There was no roundabout at the Albury Heath Fair that year, and had not been since World War II. There were, however,

> . . . tents, and swings, and cokernut shies,
> And a hoop-la stall with many a prize,
> And races, and a band, and cheering.

Ian and John were soon engaged in throwing balls at "cokernuts" while I wandered with Lucy. We were enchanted by a pen-full of pink piglets. The little pigs were to be given away as prizes for climbing a greased pole that towered nearby. We also looked in at the flower show, then went on to the dog show. The dog show, unfortunately, developed into a snarling free-for-all and the judging had to be postponed until all participants—both human and canine—had regained their tempers. The judges then decided to fill the program gap with a children's costume parade, but since some of the children had not yet arrived and others were not ready, this caused a flutter among the anxious parents, many of whom were already upset by the dog fight.

In the midst of all this heat and excitement Lucy sat down to take off her shoes—something she was wont to do in moments of stress. The crowd swerved good naturedly around her, but looking up at the passing parade she must have felt much like Jacob Toad:

> Off he crawled to the thick of things,
>   And the crowds made crawling rather tiring.
> "Dear me," he said, "I wish I'd wings!
> "If this is the World," said he, perspiring,
> "It's inconveniently full of Feet."

It was not very long before a sudden voice said, "Look—how sweet!" and other voices, quite unknowingly, fell into the role with "It's not very safe . . . on the ground. . . ." In another moment Lucy's father swept down upon the scene to put her, not on the merry-go-round, but upon his shoulder. Sleepy and sated, she rode back to the Gables. It was tea time when we arrived and we went into the parlor. Lucy awoke in time to share a pot of tea and to discuss with her family the joys of living on Albury Heath. The rest of us listened to her with new respect. Lucy had pushed literary research to its ultimate. She was the only one among us who had obtained a true Toad's-eye view of the Fair.

8
Looking at History

While we were still living on Albury Heath John and Ian drove down to Portsmouth for the day to see Nelson's flagship, *Victory*. The trip was a great success. Ian, although only eight, was fascinated by the era of Napoleon. He had a good enough grasp of history to understand who Nelson was, and a small boy's bloodthirsty delight in seeing the exact spot where he had lain when he whispered "Kiss me, Hardy," before he died. It was while they were there that John conceived the idea that we should stay a few days in the New Forest. It was not difficult to persuade me. Not only was there the prospect of our seeing wild ponies, but I had happy memories of my mother reading Captain Marryat's *Children of the New Forest* aloud to me years before. Although supposedly bound for Tunbridge Wells, the day after the fair at Albury Heath we packed all our belongings together and set forth in the opposite direction.

We drove into the New Forest from the north and in a little while had come upon a sign pointing toward the spot where William II was killed. We parked our car and walked into a little glen where stood the Rufus Stone, commemorating the event:

> Here stood the Oak Tree, on which an arrow shot by Sir Walter Tyrell at a Stag glanced and struck King William the Second, surnamed Rufus, on the breast, of which he instantly died, on the second day of August, anno 1100. . . .

Although the glen was quiet, peaceful, and sun-dappled, old animosities poisoned the air. How else to explain why our family almost came to blows? I said that the inscription was wrong and that the king's death was no accident. William Rufus had been shot by the wicked Tyrrel on purpose. I knew it as a fact from my English mother. As further proof, I could remember that years ago my sisters, English cousins, and I had acted out the cold-blooded murder as a play. John insisted that no one knew whether murder had been committed. Meanwhile, Ian and Lucy were quarreling because Ian wanted red-headed Lucy to lie down and pretend she was shot, and Lucy would not oblige. Then Ian, overhearing his parents' conversation, said it wasn't a stag that was shot at, but a squirrel. "Ahah!" said John, and quoted from *Kings and Queens*, a book by Eleanor and Herbert Farjeon. Ian joined in:

> William the Second
> He had a red head;
> One day to the forest
> His huntsmen he led;
> A fellow called Tyrrel
> An arrow let loose,
> And William fell dead
> As a Michaelmas goose—
> And nobody knows

> If the fellow called Tyrrel
> Took William's red head
> For the king or a squirrel.

Before we ever planned our trip to England (except in a "someday" sort of way) we had discovered our favorites among children's books on English history. The nice thing about the Farjeons' book is that it helps one straighten out all those crowned heads in English history by giving the facts about each one of them in much the same way that a good grandmother does—only in rhyme, which is easier to remember. We also like the anecdotal approach of *Our Island Story* by H. E. Marshall, a shabby old volume I had had on my own shelves when I was young. *The Story of England* is a newer book by Beatrice Curtis Brown and Helen Arbuthnot. The text is rather dull, but the splendid illustrations by Gustav Tenggren more than make up for that. Another book, called *Looking at History*, by R. J. Unstead, is as full of pictures as a pudding of plums. It has big clear type and a straightforward text that is used, I am told, in British schools. Ian admires it for the neat and careful drawings of armor, costume, and architectural detail. Just for fun, our family likes *1066 and All That*, by W. C. Sellar and R. J. Yeatman. It is a splendid spoof on English history and, I suppose, like a family joke— not much fun unless you know the straight of it.

To a little boy thus steeped in history, the prospect of being able to act out the death of William Rufus on the actual spot was irresistible. Since Lucy was uncooperative, Ian stretched himself full length beneath an immense oak and asked us to take his picture. He was very anxious, please, not to get the Rufus Stone into the photograph. It had not been there on

the day of the famous hunt and Ian, like his father, was a
stickler for authenticity.

Back in the car again, we drove on slowly, stopping often to
let herds of wild ponies go by. Sometimes they merely stood
and stared at us, refusing to budge until they wanted to. It
was obvious that human beings took second place in this old
preserve. At last we came to Brockenhurst where we took
lodgings at The Cloud, a pleasant sunny inn with one of the
prettiest inn signs I have seen anywhere: a green tree, a blue
sky, and one white cloud. Our windows looked straight out on
a stretch of open land with a herd of milling ponies and a
brook that flowed out of the forest.

Ian was so wild to get away from the hotel that I said he
could go for a walk on the moor (or was it a heath? I am
never quite sure). I wanted to walk into the little village to
buy a guidebook and to ask if anyone knew which was the
original of Arnwood, the house in which *Children of the
New Forest* had lived. Later I was cross at myself for wasting
so much time chasing a wild goose when we could have had
a much nicer time exploring the forest paths. After all, the
most interesting part of the book is when Arnwood is burned
by Roundheads and the aristocratic Beverley children have to
live in a keeper's cottage and learn to fend for themselves.
Captain Marryat's book, written in 1847, was one of the earli-
est novels for children and has all the charm of a desert island
story. Captain Marryat seemed to know that the secret of
many successful children's books is that the author gets rid of
the grownups right away, either killing 'em or packing 'em off.

We arrived in Tunbridge Wells late the next afternoon and
took up residence at a large and elegant hotel on the heights

overlooking the town. We reasoned that since the hotel had
sixty acres of park, Ian could roam to his heart's content, and
since it had its own farm, Lucy could be amused by the pigs
and ducks and chickens. The town itself had been a fashionable watering place in the days of Beau Nash and still had the
airs and graces of a well-to-do spa. Our prosaic reason for
choosing it was that it was a rail center and we had shipped
our baggage there. More important to us, it was close to Rudyard Kipling's farm at Burwash and A. A. Milne's house in the
Ashdown Forest. It was also Rosemary Sutcliff country.

Rosemary Sutcliff, who herself writes exceptionally good
historical fiction for children, makes full acknowledgment of
her debt to Kipling's *Puck of Pook's Hill,* and its sequel, *Re-
wards and Fairies.* Ian, too, fell under the spell of these books.
For more than a week, John had been reading *Puck* to him
every night at bedtime. I almost envied his hearing for the
first time how Dan and Una had acted out their version of *A
Midsummer Night's Dream* three times in the meadow, and
how Puck had appeared before them to conjure them back
into the past. Listening with half an ear, I was reminded of
my own childhood enchantment. An older cousin had read
the same stories aloud to a group composed of my sisters,
younger cousins, and me when we were all quarantined with
mumps in a isolated country house in Wales. I remember
how we were made almost drunk on the rare, rich prose and
how time and space seemed to melt away as we were transported back across the centuries.

Not all of Puck's stories quite come off, but surely any child
who is exposed to "Young Men at the Manor" will have a
feeling for the Middle Ages that will last him all the rest of
his life. I wish that teachers who want to explain the concept

of feudalism would read aloud the paragraph in which Sir
Richard tells how and why he followed his overlord to Hastings. Pages of history are condensed to a few vivid sentences.
Any writer would envy Kipling's marvelous skill with details
that are never static, but "magicked" (as Puck would say)
into shifting, shimmering, everchanging life. Simultaneously
with his lucid explanation of the laws of feudalism, he keeps
the story moving by holding before us another picture of Sir
Richard:

> . . . bare-headed to the sunshine, dandling the sword in both
> hands, while the gray horse cropped outside the Ring, and the
> helmet on the saddle-bow clinged softly each time he jerked his
> head. . . .

The wonder of it is that Kipling can fit so much into less than
twenty pages. The framework of his story is like one of those
nests of intricately carved ivory balls that one used to find in
collections of Oriental curios. At first the child is captured by
the outer surface, then by the movement of sphere within
sphere, and finally by the impact of infinity.

The day that we arrived in Tunbridge Wells it began to
rain, and it either rained or threatened to all the time that we
were there.

It was in pouring rain and a state of desperation that we
packed ourselves into the car and headed south to look for
Batemans, Kipling's farm and the site of *Pook's Hill*. The
clouds began to part and break up and there was a sort of di-
luted sunlight that hovered over the landscape. We followed
a road that twisted its way through the soggy countryside with
lushness on either hand. It is hard to realize that England was

once a land covered with great primeval forests that had to be
cleared by resolute pioneers. The section through which we
were traveling is still known as the Weald and lies between
the high chalk lands of the Downs to north and south of it.
Once its clay soil supported a great oak forest that was probably as frightening to the early settlers as the jungles of Africa
were to the nineteenth-century explorers. The Romans called
it the Forest of Anderida and it is described thus in Rosemary
Sutcliff's novels. Conrad gives a good idea of what it may
have been like in his long short story, "Heart of Darkness":

> . . . think of a decent young citizen in a toga—perhaps too
> much dice, you know—coming out here in the train of some
> prefect, or tax-gatherer, or trader even, to mend his fortunes.
> Land in a swamp, march through the woods, and in some inland
> post feel the savagery, the utter savagery, had closed round him
> —all that mysterious life of the wilderness that stirs in the forest,
> in the jungles, in the hearts of wild men. . . .

There are few remains of prehistoric settlements in the
Weald. Even the Saxon settlements (whose names end in
"hurst," for forest and "den," for dell) must have been like
islands, almost submerged by a vast green sea. By medieval
times, however, the oak had yielded to the metal ax and ox-
drawn plow, and the forests were being burned off to make
way for crops. Oak was also burned in the furnaces, for the
smelting of ore had become an important industry.

We took the road toward the village of Burwash, almost
missing a sign designating National Trust property. We
turned down a graveled lane and swung into the wide open
space before a lovely stone house surrounded by gardens and
outbuildings. The house had originally been a Tudor farmhouse but was bought and enlarged by a wealthy ironmaster

in the early seventeenth century. It fell into disrepair when the iron industry, for want of fuel, moved to the Midlands. About 1890 it was bought and restored by an architect who sold it to the Kiplings in 1902. In Kipling's autobiography, *Something of Myself,* he gives an account of his house-hunting in a Locomobile and how he came upon Batemans:

> We had seen an advertisement of her, and we reached her down an enlarged rabbit-hole of a lane. At very first sight the Committee of Ways and Means said: "That's her! The Only She! Make an honest woman of her—quick!" We entered and felt her Spirit—her Feng-shui—to be good. We went through every room and found no shadow of ancient regrets, stifled miseries, nor any menace, though the "new" of her was three hundred years old.

When I say that Kipling's autobiography is disappointing I do not mean that it is not well-written or witty or entertaining, but that in fact he gives very little of himself. So with his house. It is lovely, it is everything that a famous author's house should be, but even so it is difficult to feel that a family actually lived there. The study is exactly as he left it (but so tidy!) and Mrs. Kipling herself embroidered the chair seats in the dining room, the canopy over the bed. There are oriental brasses and silks to remind us of the Indian boyhood and some paintings to remind us that his cousin was Sir Edward Burne-Jones. There are also some plaques by Lockwood Kipling, Rudyard Kipling's father, who illustrated *Kim* and *The Jungle Books.* A mimeographed pamphlet tells one that the dining room is paneled in Cordova leather, the parlor has a Dutch bureau, an English Dole cupboard, and a Flemish tapestry. It is all controlled opulence and carefully considered

taste, and I find it sad to contemplate. It has been said that
Kipling was a vulgar little man who happened to be a genius.
Once he became a successful author and owner of a proper
country house, the genius was throttled. Never again did he
come to grips with intellectual or emotional problems on an
adult level. I like to think that he was much more interesting
than either that house or his American wife would allow him
to be.

We escaped to the garden. The sun had made a grudging
appearance and the grass sparkled with wetness. We followed
a path over to the side of the house, past the reflection pool
and through a hedge. A small new-mown plot, piled with
heaps of unbound hay, contained the graves of family pets.
They were marked with rather touching little headstones.
The children stopped to play in the hay for a few minutes and
then ran forward, coming rather unexpectedly onto a river
bank. This was the River Dudwell. It was much smaller than
I had imagined from the stories in *Puck of Pook's Hill*. I wondered how Kipling's children, the counterparts of Dan and
Una, had managed to do any boating there, until I remembered how they used to pull themselves along by the willow
branches in a birch-bark canoe, and how it scraped in the shal-
lows. It doesn't take very much water, after all, to satisfy a
small boy—or a small girl, either. Lucy had already found a
bridge to sit on and was taking off her shoes. Ian was casting
pebbles into the brown waters. Suddenly he stopped, his hand
half-way back to his shoulder. He was staring at a small
wooden building just across the bridge.

"Is that the mill?" he asked.

We all stared at it. An old mill figures in several of Puck's
stories, especially in "Hal o' the Draft." This one certainly

looked very old, all crouched down beneath its strangely pitched roof, its windows staring out from under beetling brows.

> See you our little mill that clacks,
> So busy by the brook?
> She has ground her corn and paid her tax
> Ever since Domesday Book.

This little mill was not so much clacking as humming. A sleek modern turbine had been installed where once the mill wheel must have been, an obvious source of electricity for the house and farm. Later I was to read that the Kiplings at a dinner party had met Sir William Willcocks "who had designed the Assouan Dam—a trifling affair on the Nile," and that they had mentioned their project for de-clutching the water wheel from an ancient mill at the end of the garden and using its microscopic millpond to run a turbine. He came the next Monday to advise them to tear down the trees and bushes and to slope the banks properly. He also advised them to bury the cable (evidently a revolutionary thought in a country where such things are "laid on") and obtained for them a rejected deep-sea cable which had failed under test at twelve hundred volts—"our voltage being one hundred and ten." It was in connection with this project that a well had to be dug and an old pond cleaned. By the time the well reached twenty-five feet, the owners had been handed a Jacobean tobacco pipe, a worn Cromwellian lateen spoon and, at bottom, the bronze check of a Roman horse bit. In cleaning out the pond the workers dredged up two Elizabethan "sealed quarts" and, in deepest mud, a perfectly polished Neolithic ax head.

The land was soaked in history and when someone suggested to Kipling that he write "a yarn about Roman times here . . . about an old Centurion of the Occupation telling his experiences to his children," he found himself interested, although at first his thoughts did not come smoothly and he discarded several stories:

> I turned my back on the whole thing and walked away. Therefore, the whole thing set and linked itself. I fell first upon Normans and Saxons. Parnesius came later, directly out of a little wood above the Phoenician forge; and the rest of tales in *Puck of Pook's Hill* followed in order.

Almost all the stories in *Puck of Pook's Hill* and its sequel begin and end within the geographical framework of Batemans Farm, although sometimes a tale within a tale takes one as far afield as the Roman Wall or to Africa or to the Americas. Besides the mill, Kipling uses the cone-shaped oast houses, the village church, the fields and woods in the neighborhood as springboards to take the reader back into the past. He describes the hill from which Puck issues as ". . . a bare, fern-covered slope . . . that runs up from the far side of the mill-stream to a dark wood. Beyond that wood the ground rises for five hundred feet, till at last you climb out on the bare top of Beacon Hill, to look over the Pevensey Levels and the Channel and half the naked South Downs." We could see the hill in the distance and set off along the brook to walk to it. We had not gone far, however, before we found ourselves in morass that, in the next few steps, would be over our knees. The mists crept up out of the bog, the sun disappeared again, and it began to rain. We stood up to our ankles in mud, gazing at the unattainable, then wandered disconsolately back toward the house and parking lot.

The next day we drove down to Batemans again, although why we expected any miracles I cannot imagine. The landscape was as soggy as ever. We learned later, by consulting maps and reading R. T. Hopkins' *Kipling Country*, that we could have reached the hill by driving back along the main road and going through another farm (Lynden Farm in the stories; Dudwell Farm on the maps). At least we have the satisfaction of knowing that, according to Hopkins, the hill we saw was the one we sought and that the countryfolk 'round about still call it "Puck" or "Pook's" hill. Very likely the hill was once inhabited by the Flint People (the Dark People, Rosemary Sutcliff calls them), the shepherds and hill people who were living in Britain before the Celts came. Miss Sutcliff writes of them in *Warrior Scarlet*, her story about the Bronze Age. In her introduction she explains that the hero, Drem, lived nine hundred years before Rome was founded—and Celtic Drem thought of the Dark People as being ancient. "The oldest thing in England . . . ," says Puck, when speaking of himself. There is something about that hill that makes the prickles rise on the back of one's neck.

Frustrated in our efforts to reach the hill, we returned to the car and drove about the countryside, peering through the rain. In the village of Burwash, all gray stone and humped roofs, we saw the church and the inn, both mentioned in Kipling's stories. Behind the farm, on a back road, we came across a quarry and wondered if it were where Una saw the gypsy encampment. We tried to find Weland's Ford (now Willingsford) because Weland, "a sort of kin to Scandinavian Thor," is the subject of Puck's first tale. Perhaps we had insulted the Smith of the Gods in some way for our little car wandered about on back country lanes as though it were bewitched.

Finally we decided to head south toward the seacoast, although it hardly seemed the weather for it. Our history buffs wanted to see Hastings, and we thought it would be fun to seek out the castle at Pevensey where several of Puck's most exciting stories took place. Morale was so low that it seemed a good idea to stop first for tea. This was made difficult by the fact that all we had seen for an hour were narrow lanes, green fields, and deep woods. At last we came across a gloomy rustic hut which stood back from the road among dark pines. A faded sign, creaking in the wind, advertised Teas. We might have thought the place deserted but for two enormous trucks drawn up outside, and a spark of light inside.

We were used to being stared at, but this time our arrival seemed to have an electrifying effect. The two truck drivers and the buxom serving wench seemed dumfounded by our arrival. They were all three sitting at one of the wooden tables looking at a map or piece of paper, but now one of the men whisked it out of sight and into his pocket and the wench (she *did* look like someone out of *Tom Jones!*) rushed behind the counter. I asked for tea and cakes. The girl ran her hands down her apron and looked imploringly at the taller of the two truck drivers. He nodded at her, apparently as much in anger as encouragement, and pointed out that there were some packaged cakes on a shelf above the gas ring where she was boiling water for tea.

In a few moments the girl brought each of us a mug and we stared glumly into the steaming brown depths. Ian wrinkled his nose at the bitterness of the stuff and Lucy found hers too hot to drink. I asked for milk, an ordinary request, but the shorter of the two men, who was drinking something out of a mug, gave what might have been a sneeze—or a laugh—and spluttered drops half way across the table top. He was sobered by a glance from his companion and sat wiping his mouth with the back of his hand. The girl went into the kitchen and came back with a can of "condensed"—the kind, said John, that the army used to get in Australia and which is so thick you can cut it off with scissors, like ribbon. Despite this recommendation, the children did not like it. We would have risen to leave then but for a burst of activity. The taller man had summoned the wench to his table.

"I've changed my mind," he said. "I think it'll be better if I take them cans now," and he pointed to four big milk cans that had stood unnoticed in the shadows. "You get 'em over to the door and Al and me will load 'em into my lorry." The girl went over and grasped the handle of one of the cans and pulled hard.

"I can't budge it," she said, then caught Al's eye and dissolved into giggles.

" 'Ere, let me do it," said the tall man, but although he took a firm grasp and really bent his back to it the can barely scraped across the floor. Behind his back, Al carried on a curious pantomime. He would look at the cans, then look at us, then look at the girl—and something in his very manner caused her to burst into helpless, silent laughter. His companion was still struggling with what must have been the heaviest milk cans in the British Isles, when he turned suddenly and caught the revelers in the act.

" 'Ere, 'ere! Get to work now. Give me a hand and look smart. Both of you!" His glance flicked in our direction. We then realized that we had been staring open-mouthed. Finally the cans were hauled out the door and loaded, and the two trucks drove off in a swirl of gravel. The girl came back into the hut and directly into the kitchen. She began putting up shutters and locking doors and windows with such thoroughness that it looked as though she were shutting up shop forever. John asked for the bill and she brought it to us in an absent-minded way, hardly seeming to care whether she was paid. We went off down the road, all agreeing that this had been the most dreadful tea we had had in England.

"I don't like that kind of milk," said our two-year-old, positively.

"I don't either," said Ian. "Why didn't they open one of those big cans and give us some fresh milk? They had it right there."

John grew strangely excited. "Ian's right," he said. "Do you realize that this is the first time since we've been in England that we haven't had fresh milk offered to us?"

"Well, maybe it was too hard for them to get it out of those cans," I ventured. "Those cans were awfully heavy."

"You're right they were heavy," said my husband. "Ian, do you remember 'Hal o' the Draft'? Remember how the Burwash men made cannon for the pirates and hid them in the church, then sent them down to Rye under the wool packs? *That wasn't milk in those cans!*"

"Smugglers!" cried Ian.

"Then I think we should notify the proper authorities," said I, very prim. John and Ian glanced at each other in masculine conspiracy, then began to laugh.

"We can't have half Sussex hanged for a little gun-running," said John, quoting from Puck. And that night, back at the hotel, he read Kipling's "Smuggler's Song" to us:

"If you wake at midnight, and hear a horse's feet,
　Don't go drawing back the blind, or looking in the
　　　street,
Them that asks no questions isn't told a lie.
Watch the wall, my darling, while the Gentlemen
　　go by!
　　　　　Five-and-twenty ponies,
　　　　　Trotting through the dark—
　　　　　Brandy for the Parson
　　　　　'Baccy for the Clerk:
　　　　　Laces for a lady, letters for a spy,
And watch the wall, my darling, while the Gentlemen
　　go by. . . ."

We came out on the main road near the village of Battle and drove through the rolling countryside, trying to imagine what it must have been on that day when the Normans came ashore at Pevensey. They marched inland toward London and were met by Harold's forces on these fields north of Hastings.

　　　　See you our stilly woods of oak,
　　　　　And the dread ditch beside?
　　　　O that was where the Saxons broke
　　　　　On the day that Harold died.

I found myself thinking of *The Golden Warrior*, by Hope Muntz, and wishing that Ian were old enough to appreciate it. It is the story of the Saxon cause at the Battle of Hastings. Even though sympathetic to Harold, it tells why he deserved to lose. I do believe it is my favorite historical novel. The author worked over it for eleven years, making of it a sort of bright Bayeux Tapestry of prose. Surely the children will appropriate it in time. It is too good to leave to mere grownups.

We stopped at Battle Abbey, hoping to glean more information about the surrounding countryside, but it was closed to sightseers, so we drove on toward Hastings. The town was no more romantic than the grimmest "front" on the Jersey shore. Ian was disappointed and pleaded for Pevensey. I had a bad few moments trying to find the town on the map because I looked for it to be along the coast. We finally located it toward Eastbourne, a little inland. Later we discovered that the shallow bay had silted, leaving flat green fields between the village and the sea.

Our luck seemed to change the moment we came into Pevensey. The sun came out in full force just as we rounded a curve in the village street, gilding two battered stone eagles which surmounted a pair of gateposts. We wondered if they had any connection with De Aquila, that wonderful little man whom Kipling describes:

> He was little, like his father, but terrible with a nose like an eagle's nose and yellow eyes like an eagle. He rode tall war-horses —roans, which he bred himself—and he could never abide to be helped into the saddle.

Kipling seems to have fallen in love with his own character, for he allows him hearth space in three of Puck's stories, "Young Men at the Manor," "The Knights of the Joyous Venture," and "Old Men of Pevensey." He is even allowed posthumous influence on a twist of plot in "The Treasure and the Law," which supposedly took place a hundred years after Aquila died. Kipling makes him wonderfully clear to us— always fretting with his gauntlets, poking someone in the ribs with a dagger as he talks, hopping round and round some great horse with one foot in the stirrup. Whether his historic self equaled his literary one we have no way of knowing, but a family named De Aquila did exist and Pevensey was its aerie.

I must say that Pevensey is one of the most satisfying ruins I have ever seen—just tumbled down enough to be romantic, but in good enough repair so that the imagination can build where the eye leaves off. There were curtain walls and round towers, a moat and a drawbridge, all the satisfying details for which Ian's heart yearned. Nowadays Pevensey is a medieval castle surrounded by the brilliant green of the Pevensey Levels, but on that fatal day in 1066, when William of Normandy crossed the sea and came to Pevensey, water lapped almost to the walls of the ruins of a Roman fortress there. One can still pick out the letters in the Bayeux Tapestry: *"Hic Wilhelm Dux in magno navigo mare transivit, et venit ad Pevensal."*

William stumbled as he came ashore, a mishap that might have been interpreted as an ill omen by his followers. With great presence of mind, he reached out to grasp a piece of turf in both hands. Scrambling to his feet and holding it up for all to see, he called out that he was "taking seizin" to all England:

" 'What's taking seizin?' asked Dan, cautiously. And Puck answered:

> "It's an old custom the people had when they bought and sold land. They used to cut out a clod and hand it over to the buyer, and you weren't lawfully seized of your land—it didn't really belong to you—till the other fellow had actually given you a piece of it—like this." He held out the turves.

We filed through a gap in a low outer wall, walked across a meadow and clumped over the drawbridge, our shoes making a hollow sound in the moat. We found ourselves in the grass-grown inner bailey. There was a well in the center of it. As we peered down into its depths we were reminded of the secret well where the treasure was hidden in "Old Men at Pevensey" and found again in "The Treasure and the Law." Kipling described it as being built into the walls and then abandoned because it was tidal. We went in search of a guide to find if such a well existed. He smiled and said that many people asked him that question. He thought there was such a place in the south wall, at least so he had heard, but he could not allow us to look for ourselves because that part of the castle was in poor repair and closed to visitors. Ian asked him if he had ever tried to look for himself. We were shocked to hear him admit that not only was he not curious enough to search for the well, but that he had never bothered to read Mr. Kipling's books! Later, doing a little research of our own, we learned that more than twenty years after publication of *Puck of Pook's Hill* a secret well was discovered in the walls at Pevensey. Kipling was delighted, of course, to have archaeology confirm imagination.

The sun cast a cheerful glow over all of Pevensey. John and I found a bit of wall to sit on while we watched the children climb about the ruins. Ian and Lucy especially liked the dungeony feeling of the North Tower and now that the sun was shining so brightly spent most of the time going up and down the dank steps. John lay back to snooze in the sun and I scanned the guidebook we had bought near the gate. I found that during World War II the interior of the towers were adapted as quarters for the troops who garrisoned the castle. An inner skin of brickwork was built, wooden floors were inserted, the windows were glazed, and roofs put on. All the work was done by the military, but under the direction of the Ministry of Works. The government did not want the Germans to know that the fortress was being used again, so no effort was spared to give it what Edgar Eager, author of *Knights Castle*, would call "a proper yeomanly appearance." I called Ian to me in order to read to him from the guidebook. When at home, Ian's favorite toys were his model soldiers for whom he spent long hours making landscapes or dioramas. He had developed a good eye for the form and texture that goes into making a convincing ruined wall and he was fascinated by the ingenuity displayed to make modern pillboxes look like parts of a ruined castle. He had often put oatmeal boxes and milk cartons to much the same use, and viewed the efforts of the Ministry of Works with the eye of a fellow professional.

"By the grace of God," I read aloud from the otherwise unemotional prose, "These twentieth-century defences were never put to the test, and Pevensey Castle remains untaken by assault." In 1945 the Ancient Monuments section of the Ministry of Works resumed control. It was decided to leave the greater part of the recent military works intact as evidence of an important phase in the long history of the castle. I don't know of any decision that could have done more to strengthen our family's sense of history. We had seen too many self-conscious restorations in our own country coupled with senseless destruction (for example, the tearing down of honest-awful nineteenth-century buildings in order to replace them with ersatz eighteenth-century ones). The men who manned the radar screens at Pevensey were just as brave and just as much part of history as the medieval men-at-arms or the Roman legions who had held Pevensey before them.

The Romans' name for Pevensey was Anderida and it is thus that Rosemary Sutcliff refers to it in her novels of Roman Britain. The Roman fortress covered more acreage than the medieval one which is built into a corner of it. Before crossing the drawbridge, our family had come through a gap in the tumble-down Roman wall and had had to cross a meadow to reach the medieval part of the castle. Now, as we left the castle, we turned toward another gap in the outer wall and went through the Roman East Gate and around in back of the Castle. A sign announcing "Teas" drew us like a magnet toward a cluster of sheds huddled against the wall. We ordered a proper tea this time—scones and raspberries and *real* milk.

To our hostess's surprise we chose to sit as far back as possible from the doorway, in heavy shadow. It was the wall that drew us. At our level it was still of Roman construction, but, peering upward, we could see where the Roman stone and flint left off and the medieval "restoration" began, for in this part of the castle the Normans had full use of the work of their predecessors. We sat and leaned our cheeks against the cool stone and rubbed our hands over its surface, wondering about the men who had built it. This wall had been old when William came. We talked, too, of Dunkirk and what would have happened if the Nazis had made their invasion. "We will fight on the beaches . . . !" quoted John. "That would have meant Pevensey." Perhaps it was not just the cold of the stone that sent shivers down our spines.

Several months later, when I was reading Rosemary Sutcliff's *The Lantern Bearers*, I was reminded of our feelings that day at Pevensey. At the beginning of Miss Sutcliff's story her young hero, an officer in the Roman Cavalry, is faced with the decision whether to remain in Britain and fight the Saxon invaders, or whether to sail away with the Roman legions. Is he British, or is he Roman? He elects to stay, but that night—when the last Roman galley leaves Britain—he climbs up to the platform of the great beacon tower at Rutupiae and, on a sudden impulse, sets fire to the pitch-soaked brush piled there.

> . . . even from the shores of Gaul they would see the blaze, and say, 'Ah, there is Rutupiae's Light.' It was his farewell to so many things; to the whole world that he had been bred to. But it was something more; a defiance against the dark."

Pevensey is not far from Richborough Castle and we could easily have driven there to see the ruins of Rutupiae and the site of that enormous beacon tower which, faced with pure white marble, could be seen for miles out at sea, either day or night. According to Leonard Cottrell's *Seeing Roman Britain*, some authorities believe that the lighthouse at Rutupiae may have been as large and impressive as the Phares of Alexandria. The remains of a second Roman lighthouse are incorporated into the walls of Dover Castle, but we missed that one, too. There is a picture of it in Cottrell's book and he gives clear directions how to find it. He describes it as "a monstrous construction, octagonal outside, and square within; and, entering it by the large archway on the east side, the interior is seen to be hollow, though there are clear enough indications that once there were chambers, one above the other, where those who tended the fire lived like eagles in their aerie high above the world."

Alas! We will always regret that we did not know about those lighthouses when at the time we were so close. It would have been a simple matter to drive over to see them. But something of their meaning shone through to us that day at Pevensey, shines through still in the Book of Common Prayer! "As it was in the beginning, is now, and ever shall be, world without end. Amen."

9
Little Countries of the Mind

Besides Puck and Pook's Hill, we had Pooh and the "Enchanted Place at the Top of the Forest" in mind all the time we were in Tunbridge Wells. Soon after A. A. Milne died in 1956, *Life* magazine published photographs of his house and garden in Sussex. This had emboldened us to write to the publishers of the Pooh books—both British and American—to ask for help in the search for clues. We wanted to find out for ourselves if at least some of the storied places on the maps in the end papers of the Milne books actually existed and, if so, to search them out. We had given the post office at Tunbridge Wells as our forwarding address and were most excited, therefore, when John brought back to the hotel an invitation to visit Mrs. Milne at her home at eleven o'clock Sunday morning. "I am always happy to meet friends of dear 'Pooh,' " she wrote, and signed herself, "Daphne Milne."

Mrs. Milne had given as her address a little village at the edge of the Ashdown Forest. We had some difficulty in finding the house. We drove up and down an earth lane several times before it occurred to us to plunge into a leafy tunnel

180

that led off down a bank. In an instant we emerged in another world—a wide sweep of gravel drive looking out toward garden and meadow, with copse and spinney beyond. Farther off, half-hidden by low rain clouds, we could see the hills of the Ashdown Forest. Close to us, huddled under the bank, was a wonderful old steep-roofed farmhouse. There is a sketch of it in *Now We Are Six*, seen from a distance as part of the background for "Buttercup Days." Now, seen thus closely, it seemed smaller, cozier, more secret somehow than either Shepard's sketch or the photographs in *Life* had led us to expect. This was the house where Christopher Robin had lived, this was "The House in Another Part of the Forest."

Mrs. Milne came out to the terrace while we were disentangling ourselves from the car. She was tall and white-haired and elegant and dressed in several shades of green. She suggested that since we were still in our outdoor clothes we might as well tour the garden. As we walked about I found myself getting it mixed up in my mind with a place in a book by Kenneth Grahame, not A. A. Milne. It was like the Mole's garden in *The Wind in the Willows*, but instead of Mole's gallery of plaster statuary ("Garibaldi, and the infant Samuel, and Queen Victoria, and other heroes of modern Italy") the garden abounded in stone images of Christopher Robin and Pooh and Piglet.

Then we found ourselves all talking. The children were telling Mrs. Milne about their own Pooh and Piglet (stuffed) and John went back across the wet grass to the car to fetch them and Mrs. Milne asked would Ian please not talk so fast, because she could not understand American accents, and where did he get that dreadful hat? Ian's ears were turning rather pink when John came back with the animals and Mrs.

Milne looked them over carefully, noting that Pooh's nose was torn and that one eye was missing. We explained that Lucy had chewed off the nose several months before, the eye's disappearance was a mystery. According to Milne's autobiography, "The animals in the stories came for the most part from the nursery. My collaborator had already given them individual voices, their owner by constant affection had given them the twist in their features which denoted character, and Shepard drew them, as one might say, from the living model. They were what they are for anyone to see; I described rather than invented them. . . ."

Mrs. Milne now turned her attention to Piglet. "But he's too big!" she said, genuinely surprised. "He's much too big. Piglet is supposed to be small, you know—small enough to fit into your hand or put into your pocket. Oh, no, this is not Piglet!" She was quite right, of course. Piglet was of a size so that he could be slipped into Christopher Robin's pocket when Christopher went off to school. He had to be so small that he could fool Kanga (although only for an instant) into thinking that he was Roo. Even Eeyore makes a virtue of his size, although ambiguously: " 'About as big as Piglet,' he said to himself sadly. 'My favorite size. Well, well.' "

A soft rain had begun to fall so we ran for shelter. The garden was conventionally lovely, but we were quite unprepared for what lay inside the house. Mrs. Milne opened her door to all the colors of spring. In some of the pictures in the *Pooh* books Christopher is shown as living inside the trunk of a tree. Perhaps a house in a tree trunk would look something like this. A subtle translucent effect was achieved by the use of all the spring-leaf shades—from pale yellow walls to palest greens, deeper greens, rich golds and the red of two Chineselacquer chests set in opposite corners of the room. An arrangement of fresh-picked branches of leaves brought in from the woods served to heighten the effect.

"I am house proud," Mrs. Milne announced happily, seeing my response, and I could believe it and be glad. The room was of a peculiar shape with little nooks and crannies. Perhaps it had been made from several rooms. The mantel ran the breadth of the huge chimney over the hearth, then unexpectedly turned a corner to run at right angles along the side of the chimney. The fireplace itself was a tiny, tiny little mousehole of an opening at the hearth, set with bits of kindling and miniature pine cones. Above it, in ever-widening radii, half circles of brick were set to repeat the half-moon shape at the base. Ian had walked around the bend of the chimney piece and was staring at a small oil portrait of Christopher Robin. The picture was propped against the chimney, and Christopher was propped among many pillows. "Done when he was sick in bed," said Mrs. Milne. "Sneezles and wheezles?" asked Ian, and she seemed pleased.

Next Mrs. Milne showed us some pillows she had made for her gold-colored couch. They were patchwork, but the patches were cut from velvets, silks, satins, and brocades, the shades ranging from rich amber to old malmsey. I wanted to ask if one of them was a remnant from James James Morrison Morrison's mother's golden gown, when Mrs. Milne interrupted my thought to say that Mr. Shepard had come to visit a few months before to make supplementary drawings for a new edition of *Pooh*. He had been so enchanted with her needlework that he had included the pillows in one of his new color sketches. She went into the next room and brought back a large fat volume, *The World of Pooh*. She showed us a picture of Pooh doing his Stoutness Exercises, the pillows on a chair beside him. She had a pen with her, and on the flyleaf of the book she wrote: "To Ian Bodger from Christopher Robin's mother, Daphne Milne."

The sun was making a watery reappearance outdoors and it was time to go. We stood out on the drive, discussing the best places for a picnic. The Enchanted Place at the Top of the Forest would have the best view, but Pooh-stick Bridge was nearer. "Besides," said Mrs. Milne, "small boys like water." We drove down the lane as she instructed and parked the car near the gates to a large poultry farm. We set off on foot across the fields, following a path through the wet grass. A pair of turkeys and a goose started toward us. Lucy clutched my hand a little tighter and I tried not to think of those formidable geese that had frightened us in Cornwall. Ian was braver. He waved his battered Pooh in the air and shouted, "Shoo!" Surely these must be the "silly old dragons" described in "Us Two" in *Now We Are Six*.

> "Let's look for dragons," I said to Pooh.
> "Yes, let's," said Pooh to Me.
> We crossed the river and found a few—
> "Yes, those are dragons all right," said Pooh.
> "As soon as I saw their beaks I knew.
> That's what they are," said Pooh, said he.
> That's what they are," said Pooh.
>
> "Let's frighten the dragons," I said to Pooh.
> "That's right," said Pooh to Me.
> "I'm not afraid," I said to Pooh,
> And I held his paw and I shouted "Shoo!
> Silly old dragons!"—and off they flew.

"I wasn't afraid," said Pooh, said he,
"I'm *never* afraid with you."

The big birds ran off and a moment later our feet struck
the boards of the fabled bridge. It was quite an ordinary
bridge, really, but it gave us more of a thrill than any of the
famous bridges that straddle the rivers of England. "Now
we're really living in a book," said Ian, and even Lucy knew
that we had "arrived." Pooh and Piglet were propped up
against the bridge rail and watched in what we interpreted as
contented silence while the children threw twigs and branches
into the muddy stream below. The sedgy waters were disappointing in that they did not afford a really rousing game of
Pooh sticks, but there is always satisfaction in knowing that
one is doing the right thing at the right place at the right
time. John and I unwrapped ham sandwiches we had had
packed at the hotel and handed them around, then settled
our backs against the bridge posts, the better to watch the
scene before us. The sun had come out and steam was rising
from the woods, the fields, and even the bridge. "This is the
life," said John, and lay down full length on the bridge. Soon
he was gently snoring.

But what goes up must come down. In no time at all the
steam turned into mist, the mist into rain. John woke with a
start and a snort and we all scrambled back into the car.
Down the lane we went again, back onto the main road. Mrs.
Milne had said that the Enchanted Place described in *The
House at Pooh Corner* would be about two miles away and
that we could recognize it by the pine trees. But we found ourselves in a *forest* of pine trees, obviously some sort of new
plantation set out by the government to confuse us.

As the road began to climb, however, the soil seemed to

heave itself up in sandy enbankments and the trees thinned
out so that now and then we could glimpse the way ahead.
And then, on the very top of the forest, we saw a hill which
stood out all by itself. It was crowned with a circle of pine
trees, quite different from the shaggy little fir trees we had
seen below. These were old trees, bare and wind-swept and
full of character, and it was strange how the very moment we
saw them silhouetted against the sky line we knew that they
were the ones in Shepard's illustrations.

The road seemed to lead straight to the foot of the hill,
then turned off at such an alarming angle that we were afraid
we would lose our bearings. We pulled to the side of the road
and tried to decide what to do. Lucy was asleep, so John
stayed behind in the car with her, and Ian and I proceeded
straight ahead on foot. Straight ahead meant straight up. The
air was stifling, the way steep. Ian and I clambered up the hillside, clinging to gorse and bracken as we went, then slid down
into a little gully on the other side. We soon discovered that
there was not one hillside, but a series of dunes. It was all
right for Christopher to expound the glories of "upping and
upping," but I soon found myself short of breath.

Even Ian was slowing down. I made a last desperate rush to
catch up with him so that together we could crawl over the lip
that jutted out from the top of the hillside. I lay there gasping
for a moment, then found myself gazing into the pale blue
eyes of a startled picnicker. He was sitting in the lap of civilized luxury. A primus stove hissed beneath a kettle, his family
lay or lolled about in attitudes of ease and comfort, a radio
blared from the dashboard of the Morris Minor parked on
the roadside beside him. The road was wrapped around the

brow of the hill. Above us was the tuft of pine trees to remind us where we were. The trees were guarded by a strand of barbed wire.

I stole a glance at Ian and saw incredulity mixed with disappointment. Still panting, we tried to pretend we had clambered up the sandy precipice merely to look at the view. On another hill nearby were some steel signal towers. Far below us stretched green fields and hedgerows, the land tilting toward the distant sea. At our feet a geodetic marker had been sunk into the ground to give the compass points and the number of counties one could see from there. Months later I came across a paragraph in Christopher Trent's *The Changing Face of England*:

> On the heights of Ashdown Forest I could find the faint marks of prehistoric entrenchments, one at least pin-pointed by a circle of pine trees planted by romantic antiquaries of the last century. Nearby the skyline has been transformed by the tall masts of a wartime radar station.

Perhaps it would have helped to know that early Saxons, fighting their way clear of the Weald, had found this spot to make their camp. We had come to seek the ghost of a little boy and his stuffed bear, but there were older ghosts abroad on that hillside.

I felt a tug at my sleeve. "Aren't we going to go in?" asked Ian. He pointed to where the barbed wire trailed toward the ground. I held down the wire with my foot while Ian clambered over, then he did the same for me. Together we walked toward the center of the little grove of trees. It was very quiet, like a church. All of a sudden we realized that we could no longer hear the blaring radio. "It *is* enchanted!" said Ian, and we sat down to rest. It was curiously comfortable, and I thought of the description in *The House at Pooh Corner*:

> Being enchanted, its floor was not like the floor of the Forest, gorse and bracken and heather, but close-set grass, quiet and smooth and green. It was the only place in the Forest where you could sit down carelessly without getting up again almost at once and looking for somewhere else. . . ."

The breeze stirred through the branches and fanned our hot cheeks. Ian turned over on his stomach and kicked his heels in the air. After a while he began to gather together a store of little pine cones which littered the soft sward beneath the trees. He filled the pockets of his mackintosh with them, then filled his trouser pockets. We rested a while longer then, by mutual consent, rose and walked back toward the dip in the barbed wire, blinking in the strong light as we came out near the picnickers. We plunged off the side of the road and, slipping and sliding, made our way over the shoulders and slopes of the dunes, back to our car. We stopped then and looked back toward the hill, thinking about those last few paragraphs in the Pooh books when Christopher Robin bids farewell to childhood and the right to go Anywhere, do Nothing:

> So they went off together. But wherever they go, and whatever happens to them on the way, in that enchanted place on the top of the Forest, a little boy and his Bear will always be playing.

Lucy was still asleep, but John yawned and stretched as we opened the car doors. Ian reached into his pocket and held out a pine cone towards him.

"What? What's that?" asked John.

"It's a pine cone," said Ian. And then, rather shyly, "It's a sort of seizin." But whether it was to England or the Enchanted Place he did not say.

From Tunbridge Wells we telephoned ahead and made reservations at the Northampton Hotel, partly because we had to be assured of rooms during the August Bank Holiday weekend, and partly because it seemed as good a place as any to use as headquarters while we explored the Midlands. But mostly we chose it because of what T. H. White had written of his heroine, in *Mistress Masham's Repose:*

> She lived in an enormous house in the wilds of Northamptonshire, which was about four times longer than Buckingham Palace, but was falling down. It had been built by one of her ducal ancestors who had been a friend of the poet Pope's, and it was surrounded by Vistas, Obelisks, Pyramids, Columns, Temples, Rotundas, and Palladian Bridges, which had been built in honor of General Wolfe, Admiral Byng, the Princess Amelia, and others of the same kidney.

Northampton did not seem at all wild. Indeed, it was disappointingly civilized, and the hotel was the dullest and most modern in which we stayed during our entire trip. It occurred to us that the libraries would be closed over the holiday, and that if we intended to find out about Malplaquet (the name of the place in *Mistress Masham's Repose*) we had better move fast. John set out almost at once to the library. He came back most disappointed. He had not been able to find anything in Northamptonshire that remotely resembled T. H. White's description. Being a good reference librarian, he had checked in *Who's Who* to find if White had ever lived anywhere in Northamptonshire, but found no clue. "The closest he ever came was when he taught school in Buckinghamshire, the next county over," he said.

It began to look as though we had come on a wild-goose chase and, what was worse, we were stuck. Until the Bank Holiday was over there was no place to move since every hotel and inn in England would be filled to overflowing. Resignedly we decided to dig in and make the best of it. The next afternoon, since Lucy was sleeping, Ian and I decided to explore the city and to find the library in order to follow up any clues about the location of Malplaquet. John suggested that I try talking to the children's librarian and to the young man in the reference department. The day before he had seemed interested if not particularly helpful.

The Northampton children's library had an extensive collection, high standards, several professional librarians and, most important, a copy of *Mistress Masham's Repose*. When, however, I asked the librarian if she knew where I could find the place described in the book, she assumed a kind and patient air. The book, she explained, was pure fiction and read aloud to me several of T. H. White's extravagances to prove her point. I began to feel a little foolish. Soon she would be explaining to me that there *are* no Lilliputians! I do not think she would have been in the least impressed if I had countered with *The Geography and Chronology of Gulliver's Travels* by Arthur E. Case (Princeton University Press, 1927). Professor Case writes of an "old gentleman" who, soon after the *First Book of Gulliver's Travels* had been published, reported that he had held conversation with a seafaring man who had told him exactly where lay the neighboring countries of Lilliput and Blefuscu. The old gentleman planned to go home at once to consult his maps! Professor Case places the two little countries between New Holland and New Zealand—conveniently expunging Australia in order to do so. I should not have been abashed by that librarian!

She was very kind, however, in allowing me to take a copy of *Mistress Masham* upstairs to the reference room. Leaving Ian behind in the children's room, I went in search of the young man whom John had consulted the day before. I found him without difficulty and he immediately recalled John as an American searching for interesting ruins in Northampton-shire. This time I had something more tangible to offer him. The moment I opened my copy of *Mistress Masham* and read out the paragraphs describing Malplaquet, a great light seemed to dawn. He *did* know such a place, but it was not in Northamptonshire at all. It was Stowe House, the family seat of the Buckinghams—over in Buckinghamshire, of course. "It's simply enormous. Drove the chaps broke, you know. Had to sell it off for a school. . . ." It was then I remembered what John had found in *Who's Who:* T. H. White had taught at Stowe School, Bucks.

The young man fairly glowed with excitement and enthusiasm. Stowe, he explained, is one of the newest of the great public schools, having been founded in 1921. In order to reach its present state of eminence in such a short time, it makes a point of being unusually severe not only with the boys who go there as students, but with the public and parents as well. No one is ever allowed to visit, except (and here the young man fairly burst with excitement) on such occasions as when the school is empty of students: Easter, Christmas, and the August Bank Holiday. "And then only with special permission," he hastened to add.

"Do you think we could get it—the permission, I mean?"

"Well, you *do* sound most frightfully American," he said. "It's worth a try. You could say you were doing research. Americans always are. Didn't your husband say something about Pope or Swift? I know for a fact that Pope used to stay there. He wrote a couplet about it. I'm not so sure about Swift. . . . Anyway, you could telephone, there's no time for a letter, and *try* to get permission."

He went off to fetch me a telephone book, but that was not all he brought back with him. In his arms was a huge, bound volume, more than a foot high. It was the list and description of articles for sale on occasion of the auction of the Duke of Buckingham's estate. He opened the vast tome on a slanted lectern for me and left me to take notes. Fascinated, I turned the pages. Everything had been put up for sale, from the dining table (described by White as being "long as a cricket pitch"), to crested chamber pots. T. H. White must have consulted the list when he described the wonders of Malplaquet at the beginning of the book, and when he chronicled the bewildered Professor's search for the lost Maria. The Professor had wandered through endless rooms filled with unused and useless objects. T. H. White all but quotes the bill of sale, using the same capitals and florid prose that the auctioneer adapted to describe the neoclassical magnificence. Here is the official description of the First Day's Sale (there were twenty-one days in all):

> The Gardens and Grounds at Stowe included in this lot are of world renown, being 272 acres in extent, enclosed by a sunk fence nearly three miles in circumference. Hill, valley, streams and lakes with superb views, vistas and groves laid out by Great Architects and Landscape Gardeners of bygone days are in full maturity.

Within the gardens, the water spreads out into a broad lake known as the OCTAGON LAKE which, dividing itself into branches, flows through the valley East and West, one end being concealed amidst a maze of woods where it falls over some artificial ruins and forms a second or lower lake known as THE LAKE. Upon the upper lake are three small islands on one of which, embosomed amidst evergreens, stands Congreve's Monument.

OTHER MAGNIFICENT BUILDINGS, TEMPLES AND MONUMENTS of Historical interest are beautifully situated in the grounds commanding wonderful views from one to another, or over surrounding parklands.

They include the Boycott Pavillion at the SW corner of the gardens, the Temple of Venus, the Statue of Queen Caroline, the Bell Gate Pavillion, the Temple of Friendship, the Palladian Bridge, The Rotunda, The Temple of Bacchus, The Museum, The Temple of Ancient Virtue, Captain Grenville's Monument, the Gothic Temple, The Doric Arch, The Temple of British Worthies, the Gothic Cross, the Cobham Monument, the Queen's Building, the Temple of Concord and Victory, and the Vale of Pastoral Poetry, and others. . . .

In addition to the above, in the grounds are The Shepherd's Cave, the Pebble Alcove, and Dido's Cave. The Latter has been the Scene of Royal Hospitality on More than One Occasion; George the Second passed many Festive Hours at the Place. . . .

Ian and I returned to the hotel to tell John of our success. John decided it would be best to call Stowe School to gain permission to enter the grounds. Accordingly, he went down to the lobby to telephone to Stowe and was soon back with the report that we had permission "to do research" there. The caretaker would be told that we were coming. We would be allowed to explore the grounds to our hearts' content, but on no account would we be allowed in any of the buildings.

We set out under cloudy skies, driving south again. We turned off the main roads and by means of our trusty Bartholowmew eventually came to a forlorn finger post marked Stowe. A mile or two brought us to a castellated gatehouse guarding the way to the Oriental Bridge. We remembered from *Mistress Masham* that it was at "this collossal Structure" that Captain Bidell, captor and exhibitor of the Lilliputians, "fell Victim to Intoxication," dismounted from his horse, and fell asleep. According to the book:

> "It was a moonlight Eve. The Torrent could be plainly seen issueing from the Other Sea, and all about the Land appear'd deserted. The Resolution to escape was taken on the Spot. . . .
>
> Cables were rapidly made fast, the Strait Ropes of the Exhibition proving suitable. The Sheep and Cattle, slung from these, were quickly lower'd to the Ground. . . . It was the plan of Flimnap to transport his little world by Sea, until some Refuge on the further Shores could be discovered.

The Bridge took us high over a reed-choked waterway, then down onto a bleak drive on the other side. We drove almost a mile and then, suddenly, we were in the courtyard of an enormous building. Surely it was as big as New York City's Metropolitan Museum of Art—perhaps bigger! We sat in the car for a few minutes, dazed by the magnitude. We saw no sign of a human being so we got out of our car (now tinier than ever, it seemed) and walked over to an archway in a wall which extended from the house. On either side of the arch was a niche holding a small pillar which at one time must each have held a bust or statue. Ian immediately installed himself in an empty alcove and posed as a piece of statuary. We all jumped when the gravel crunched behind us. An old man, obviously the caretaker, asked what we thought we were doing? A silly grin froze on Ian's face. I don't know why we felt so foolishly guilty, but with Ian leaning on a denuded pillar it seemed rather difficult to explain that we were engaged in literary research.

Something in our accents (or perhaps our behavior) led him to ask if we were "the Americans." Having accepted our identification and warned us that he had been instructed to let us look through the grounds, but not the house, he asked us what in particular we wanted to see? We looked at each other in consternation. How could we tell him that we had come to look for Lilliputians—or, at least, the place where they lived. This man probably did not know that somewhere nearby, on an island in a lake, there was a summer house or neoclassical "repose" inhabited by descendants of Lilliputians who had colonized it in the eighteenth century.

"We'd like to see the lake," said John.

The old man scratched his head and looked up at the dripping skies. "Well, you might as well go through the building. It'll save you half a mile or so around the east wing."

We turned and gaped up at the multipillared palace looming ahead. We felt like pygmies—or Gulliver in Brobdingnag. The caretaker led us up broad shallow steps. We crossed a terrace and ascended more steps, this time guarded by lions. Our guide led us into a vast rotunda. Ladders and paint-spattered dropcloths leaned or drooped forlornly among the peach-colored marble pillars. The librarian in Northampton had told me that even in its days of glory, part of the building was always being painted or repaired and had never been in repair all at once. We were not allowed to linger. We followed our guide through another pair of doors and found ourselves standing in a great neoclassical porch. All that had gone before was a mere back entrance. Now a landscape, a prospect, a whole world stretched before us, perspective marked by obelisk and monument. A green lawn sloped down to two lakes, "Quincunx" and the "Other Sea," and far, far beyond loomed a replica of the Arc de Triomphe, final punctuation point at the world's end.

"It's a mile down to the lakes," said the old man from behind us.

Our little party pulled itself together and toiled down the steps. It seemed foolish to stay in the open rain, so we made for the Wilderness of the east and sought shelter beneath the thick-branched yews. The land was marshy but we pushed on through briars and nettles until we came to a ruined temple. Plaster, fallen from the ceiling, lay about on the floor, and here and there the laths showed through. "That's its skeleton," said Ian, in morbid glee. I remembered that the librarian in Northampton had told me that when one of the Dukes of Bedford had found Roman ruins on his estate, the neighboring Duke of Buckingham had ordered that bigger and better Roman ruins be built at Stowe.

We pushed our way through the Wilderness and came out on a sedgy shore which we followed along until we came to a boathouse. A leaky punt (Maria's?) was moored there, badly in need of a bailing scoop. We walked further, our wet shoes squelching at every step, and came upon a low isthmus that divided the two seas. The water ran under the narrow earth lane there and tumbled through the artificial ruins of a "Gothick arch," falling in a "Cascade" from the Upper to the Other Sea. Now, with the geography of Malplaquet spread before us, we tried to reconstruct the saga of those desperate Lilliputians. Having escaped from Captain Biddel at the Oriental Bridge, they had made an "Ark" from the receptacle in which they were usually carried and had towed it upstream. The quiet waters of the Other Sea had enabled them to embark their cattle, and they had made their "Way by Navigation" to the east bank where they hid themselves beneath the overhanging branches of a "prodigious Tree."

> Next Evening, shelter'd by the Darkness, our Ark, as we may call it, having been hoisted with incredible pains along the Cascade to the Upper Sea, a Scout, who had been sent ahead in Order to survey the Country, return'd with Informations about the secret Island where we have ever since continued. . . ."

We made our way through the low, wet bushes that edged the Upper Sea and came upon another ruined temple. It was desolate, damp, and flaking. Nearby was a plank bridge, a mere two or three yards long, which we crossed to reach a little island. Was this the site of *Mistress Masham's Repose?* For a moment we were disappointed. It seemed so accessible. Besides, there was no little pavilion, not even the ruins of one. All we could find were the remains of a campfire, and a great stone urn surmounted by gargoyles that peered out at us from the nettles.

The clouds lifted a little from the lake and we were able to gaze out across a sort of sargasso sea choked with duckweed. We thought that we could discern another island, a much larger one, but so overgrown with briars and nettles that until now it had been lost against the background of the Wilderness on the far shore. We retraced our steps across the plank bridge, along the shore, and across the isthmus. We squelched past the boathouse and the floundered punt. There was a peculiar light that shone upon the lake and made it difficult to see properly, but we satisfied ourselves that there really was an island at which we were looking. Larch and cypress trees had thrust their way up and up on the island and we could see that nettles and brambles were almost woven across it, making a sort of curtain. A cold wind shivered across the lake. Was that the shape of a domed roof beneath the vines? Perhaps in sunlight we could have caught a glimpse, a gleam, from the hidden Repose, but now the clouds lowered once again and we would have to run for it if we did not want to be caught sopping. I thought Ian would be bitterly disappointed, but it was he who consoled us.

"But don't you understand?" he asked. "Don't you get it? If we can't see anything it sort of proves it's there!" His thinking may not have been strictly logical, but no doubt what he meant was that if the Repose is difficult to see, difficult to reach, there is some hope that somewhere on the island there still exists a colony of Lilliputians.

Despairing of making our way back to the car through the Wilderness and around the east wing, we had cut slantingly across the lawn (now pocked with golf bunkers) and walked along the Chestnut Avenue. We had tried to find a northwest passage through the labyrinth, had succumbed to a few moments panic when we kept coming back to the same door marked New Chemistry Laboratory, and had finally made our way back to the roadway that passed between the palace and some new brick buildings hidden among the trees to the west. I suppose it wasn't really so far across the courtyard to our car, but something about the immensity of those curving pillared galleries seemed to make our progress a journey across the Steppes. Time and space were so out of kilter that I felt we had been gone for weeks, not hours.

We came at last into Buckingham. The hands on the town clock had just passed three and we found that we were ravenously hungry and made our way directly to The Olde Gaol House Tea Room which stood in the middle of the town square. We entered somewhat timidly. To the right, just inside the door, a cellar yawned with twisting, corkscrew steps leading down to ominous darkness. Ian paused and peered hopefully downward, but no groans were heard. We continued into a snug little parlor where we sat and ate incongruous pink-frosted cakes and gazed out on a slit of courtyard which made a triangular atrium in the middle of the building. Prisoners must once have used it to take the air, their faces turned upward toward the tiny wedge of sky. Weeds and mosses grew among the flagstones and a gangling tree made pathetic supplications toward the light.

It was not until we had paid our bill and were out in the car again that we bethought ourselves of John Bunyan. We should have had tea in the Duke of Bedford's gaol, said John, in order to see where *Pilgrim's Progress* was written. It could not be more than twenty miles away; perhaps we could take it in on the way to Leighton Buzzard. As it turned out, we could not have done so, for the old County Gaol of Bedford was demolished in 1801. According to *State of the Prisons in England and Wales*, a report written by John Howard in 1785, the Bedford gaol was very similar to the one in Buckingham, where we had tea. Bunyan spent twelve years in the little prison in Bedford, a martyr to the cause of freedom of speech and conscience. His wife and children must have suffered as

much as he, although he tried to make a living for them by
making and selling lace. Sometimes he was allowed a few
hours to attend church or to see his poverty-stricken family,
but mostly he spent the dreary hours scribbling away at his
great allegory. Self-taught and untraveled, he transmogrified
his familiar Bedfordshire, studding the landscape with place
names that still grip the language.

Ian first came upon the tale when he was five years old and
we lived in a university town whose large cooperative grocery
store sold books along with bread and cheese. Books, in that
community, were regarded as everyday essentials. You can
imagine the temptation whenever I found myself there with
the change from the weekly shopping still in hand! It was at
such a moment that I came upon Ian sitting on the floor near
the children's bookshelf, immersed in a beautifully printed
picture book, illustrated by Robert Lawson. Knights and
castles, giants and dragons, and a host of grotesque characters
more inventive and intriguing than any comic book held him
riveted to the spot. I finally decided it was worth the ransom
to get him home and counted out the money. I frankly admit
I had been bored to tears by Bunyan when assigned to read
his work in my teens, but rereading Mary Godolphin's version
of the text "retold and shortened for modern readers," I
learned to appreciate it as straight adventure fare for five-year-
olds. For weeks afterwards every mud puddle was a Slough of
Despond, every San Francisco street a Hill of Difficulty.

If we had known what to look for, we could have seen
Houghton House, the original of Bunyan's "House Beautiful"
at Houghton Conquest, near Ampthill, or we could have

searched out Bunyan's cottage at Elstow. But we were ignorant and, besides, in too much of a hurry to reach Leighton
Buzzard. We wanted to see if we could find Fairbank Hall
and to find out if we could reconstruct the saga of *The Borrowers*. Borrowers, according to Mary Norton, are a race of
tiny people who live under floor boards or behind wainscots
and who live by "borrowing" from the human beings who inhabit the same house. Erasers, safety pins, nail scissors, name
tapes, fountain-pen tops, postage stamps—all the paraphernal-
ia of life that so mysteriously eludes us—is somehow put to
use in a Borrower's life. Borrowers live off human carelessness
and folly, Usually, like the members of the Clock family in
Mary Norton's story, they led lonely lives of quiet desperation, characterized by ingenuity and courage. Since they do
not like to be surprised, they prefer quiet households with set
schedules.

The Borrowers in Mary Norton's precisely realized tale live
under a clock in an old house whose owner has been bed-
ridden twenty years. When a small boy arrives and upsets the
household, the Borrowers are forced to flee as refugees. Their
adventures are further chronicled in *The Borrowers Afield,
Afloat*, and *Aloft*. In a letter to her publisher Mrs. Norton had
written that she and her brothers were brought up in a square
old Georgian house, very like Firbank Hall. From clues
gleaned from her books we were quite certain that it was near
Leighton Buzzard, Bedfordshire. We felt like young Kate
who, in *The Borrowers Afield*, pleads with Mrs. May to take
her to Firbank:

> Even if we couldn't go inside, you could show me the grating
> and Arrietty's bank; and even if they opened the front door only

ever so little, you could show me where the clock was. You could
kind of point with your finger quickly. . . .

Mary Norton, as a child, showed talent as an artist, but
when she was in her teens she was suddenly fired with the de-
sire to become an actress, an ambition she eventually realized.
She has an excellent eye for detail coupled with a fine sense of
theater. Her protagonists are tiny but their emotions are on a
human scale. Surely Arrietty is one of the most charming
heroines in or out of literature. I often wish that the very real
Anne Frank, hiding from the Nazis, could have known about
her. How she would have warmed to the description of Arrietty scribbling away in her diary beneath the floor boards,
listening to borrowed conversations on the other side of the
wall. Anne and Arrietty share the same zest for life, the same
faith in the ultimate goodness of mankind.

Mrs. Norton's sense of theater includes not only drama and
characterization, but props and setting. The incongruity of her
tiny characters and their use of human-sized jetsam is never
lost sight of. She makes us look at the most mundane object
with fresh and speculative eye. It is her capacity for "making
do" and improvisation that captures the charm of childhood,
when play is serious business. Clifton Fadiman, in an article
in *Holiday* magazine, claims the spirit of play as explanation
for the British preoccupation with the small, the snug, the
understated. English folklore and literature abound with little
people: fairies, pixies, goblins, elves, dwarfs, sprites, spriggins,
Lilliputians, Hobbits, Borrowers. There must be something
about an island nation that engenders a genius for the miniature: the Japanese can make a landscape in a dish; the British
excel in literary microtomy. It is almost as though everyone on
"this little isle" has a private world into which he can with-

draw and explore—himself, perhaps? Surely his relationship to others.

When Maria of Malplaquet (in *Mistress Masham's Repose*) found her first Lilliputian and brought her, wrapped in a handkerchief, to the old Professor, he advised:

> . . . people must not tyrannize, nor try to be great because they are little. My dear, you are a great person yourself, in any case, and you do not need to lord it over others, in order to prove your greatness. . . .

T. H. White was all his life concerned with the clash of Might and Right, the relationship of Big and Little. One might say that this is the central theme of English children's literature; indeed, of English history. It is well to remember that Anne Frank was held, and finally crushed, by men who had never known—or had lost—all sense of proportion. If such a sense—a common sense—is created through play, then we must learn to respect play's importance and give it free reign.

We did not find Firbank Hall that day, nor Perkin's Beck, nor Mrs. May's cottage. The town library was closed because of the holiday, and so were the shops. There was no one to ask, and even if there had been I doubt that we would have found much more specific information about Borrowers. Speculation we could supply ourselves and, looking at the map, we found ourselves doing so. Buckingham (and Stowe House) is quite close to Leighton Buzzard, connected by a network of waterways. Suppose that Spiller (huntsman, voyageur, Borrower-extraordinaire) should discover the colony of Lilliputians at Stowe? What if he should link the economy of the Lilliputians with that of the Hendreary family at Little

Fordham? Little Fordham is rich in manufactured goods (borrowed, not made); the Lilliputians are agricultural, raising cattle and sheep to their own scale. Spiller with Pod's help, could carry on trade between them. Later, when Arrietty and Spiller have married and have stalwart sons of their own, they could engender a race something like the Vikings or the Phoenicians. They could explore strange streams, perhaps find colonies of other little people!

I went, one day, to the British Information Services on Third Avenue in New York City. I told the librarian there that I would like to see the ordinance maps (one inch to the mile) of Buckinghamshire and Bedfordshire. What sort of information was I looking for, she inquired politely? I stared back at her, stone-cold-sober: "I wish to explore the trade possibilities between a colony of Lilliputians at Stowe House, Buckinghamshire and a clan of Borrowers near Leighton Buzzard." Not a flicker, not a ripple, of amusement crossed her face.

"Quite so," she said politely. But I caught her gaze upon me as I bent over the maps.

10

Forests, Moors, and Gardens

The day after visiting Stowe and Leighton Buzzard, I was caught up again in the business of packing while John studied maps and plotted our course as though we were to embark on a polar expedition. Time and money were running short; it was only two weeks until we had to be back aboard our ship at the Cunard docks in Liverpool.

The drive to Nottingham was a long one. Lucy dozed and we kept Ian's spirits buoyed by visions of sun-lit glades in Sherwood Forest, the ghosts of men in Lincoln green flitting through the greenwood. At home we owned a first edition of Howard Pyle's *Robin Hood*. Even before he could properly comprehend Pyle's version of the old stories, Ian had pored over the marvelously detailed black and white prints and incorporated some of the details into his own drawings and block-building.

Everything in Pyle's illustrations is meticulously observed. He had a great feeling for clothes and armor and must have collected a great wardrobe in which to dress the knights and peasants and pirates he liked to draw. Some of the same clothes may be seen in the illustrations of his disciple and pupil, N. C. Wyeth, and to this day the rag-tag ends of that wardrobe sometimes reappear and may be recognized in Andrew Wyeth's paintings. There is no doubt that the clothes were well made in the first place. No one ever detailed a thonged sandal more lovingly than Howard Pyle. Hose and jerkin, kirtle and petticoat are all limned with the respect that one good craftsman pays another. The miracle is that he was able to suffuse his work with light and movement and the grace of humor.

There is something so solid in Howard Pyle's work. He obviously loved cobblestones and tiles and dressed stone and thatched roofs, although he never left his native shore to see Europe until the last year of his life. Much has been made of his "authenticity," but if you look at his drawings carefully you can catch him out—in his American love for shingles, for example. Such curious anomalies could have been corrected if he had gone to "see for himself." His castles and his landscapes have the qualities of a particularly vivid dream. Like Stanford White's architectural creations, they are an American dream.

Ian had fallen in love with Robin Hood. As soon as he was old enough (or perhaps a little before) to understand the gist of the tales, he went about the house with a mouthful of "Methinks" and "Forsooths" to chew on. Then someone gave him a set of records for his birthday—a jolly, swashbuckling version put out by Young People's Records. Some of the songs were in the pleasantly spoofing spirit of Gilbert and Sullivan. It was one of these songs that we tried to remember now, driving along the road to Nottingham. John was especially good in one of the choruses: "Venison and hot bread and nut brown ale. . . ." He put his heart and soul into it.

We came to Nottingham in the late afternoon and took an instant dislike to the place. It was grimy and gray and clogged with traffic and seemed to have all the disadvantages of modern industrialism without the compensations of law and order. I have never seen such miserable driving. What the town needs is a good sheriff! High above the town, on a bluff, stands the Castle of Nottingham. Remembering how Robin Hood had been clapped into the dungeons there and, later, how he had been rescued by his Merry Men, we stopped to explore. The site, overlooking the Valley of the Trent, gave us a sweeping view and some idea of the power held by the renowned Sheriff of Nottingham. The castle itself is more Georgian than medieval. Later we found that it is but one of a series of fortifications built on the hill. The hill itself is honeycombed with caves in which the remains of Stone Age men have been found. Even more exciting (we thought), the caves give access to medieval dungeons. It seems incredible that a handful of men could have stormed the castle, but if there was a secret way into the deepest and darkest dungeons, all sorts of possibilities are opened up, and the story gains validity. If not Robin Hood himself, then at least someone at some time may have been rescued from that formidable rock. It is a matter of historical record that in the fourteenth century a band of murderers hired, it is believed, by the young Edward III, entered the castle through a secret passage in order to slay Roger Mortimer, the Queen Mother's favorite. The Castle of Nottingham is not a hospitable place. The rightful dukes have chosen not to live there since the previous structure was burned by the Luddites in the eighteenth century.

Down below the castle, in a little park on Castle Road, we

found a memorial to Robin Hood which was placed there in 1952 by a private philanthropist. Around the walls of the little park were four bronze plaques in low relief depicting incidents from the Robin Hood legend: Robin Hood and Little John fighting on a bridge; Robin Hood, Maid Marian and Friar Tuck fighting Guy of Gisborne's men; Richard Lionheart joining the hands of Robin Hood and Maid Marian; and Robin Hood shooting his last arrow. There were also two statuary groups, about half life-size. In one of them was Alan-a-Dale "playing the harp to Will Scarlet while watching Robin Hood shooting," the other showed Little John, Friar Tuck, and Will Stukeley during "an idle moment in Sherwood Forest." In the center was a larger-than-life-size figure of Robin Hood, his bow bent but curiously empty. We discovered later that the town fathers of Nottingham had been much upset by the theft of Robin Hood's arrow some months before. No amount of detective work or public pleading had been able to restore it. How embarrassing! The bronzes had been given to commemorate the visit to Nottingham of the Queen (then Princess Elizabeth) during the city's quincentenary celebrations. No less than the Duchess of Portland had presided at the unveiling. But to our family, at least, the sight of that foolishly empty bow was proof that the mischievous spirit of Sherwood Forest is not yet dead.

We left Nottingham behind us and drove into open countryside again. Our way wound now through a copse of young fir trees, now through a waste of sand and shale interspersed with mine machinery. So this was Sherwood? I had expected something comparable to the parklike New Forest or, at least, the lush greens of Kent. I had read that once Sherwood and Barnsdale Forests stretched all the way from the Midlands to the sea—more than fifty miles—and that a squirrel could cover the entire distance without touching the ground. Except that we passed a sign declaring "Thieves Wood School for Boys" there was nothing to reassure us that we were indeed in Robin Hood's old haunts. I had not expected to find virgin woodland, but neither had I expected this mottled scenery. What had happened?

According to the little guidebook I purchased next day, there have always been stretches of sand and gravel in the forest—"forest" originally denoting land uncultivated or uncultivatable. In the thirteenth century the king's writ dispossessed lesser lords in order to extend the royal hunting reserve and even more land reverted to the wilderness. At the same time, coinciding with the rise of the home weaving trade, there occurred an agricultural revolution. Much land was deliberately reduced to sheep pasture so serfs and villeins were driven from their homes. The dispossessed, both lords and peasants, preferred to take their chances in the free life of the forest to the alternates of starvation or ignoble town life. According to legend, one of these, the Earl of Huntington, became a forest outlaw, known to us as Robin Hood.

The pasturing of sheep seems to have had a two-fold effect on the forest. On the one hand, the sharp hoofs and close-grazing habits of the sheep caused erosion of the soil so that nothing would grow, hence the sandy wastes. On the other hand, when the thickly wooded parts of the forest were cropped close and the land fertilized by sheep droppings, even more of the land was cleared for cultivation. However, the Black Death further depopulated the region and the forest was little broken into until the enclosures of the last two hundred years. The wooden walls of generations of ships origi-

nated in Sherwood. Not only were there the famous oaks, but
the soil was particularly suited to the ash, and there were
groves of birch. Eventually, however, the splendid trees died.
In the nineteenth century the growth of cities and towns
drained off the water table, and oaks which had stood for
hundreds of years withered at the roots. Vast tracts of virgin
land were put to the plow and then, with the advent of the
collieries came final violation. The greenwood of Robin Hood
and his Merry Men became the dreary countryside of the
D. H. Lawrence novels. Lady Chatterley replaced Maid
Marian.

We spent the night at Forest House, Ollerton, the sort of
small family hotel I had been longing for. The beds were
comfortable, the atmosphere blessedly warm and homelike.
While I busied myself with giving Lucy her bath, I listened
with half an ear while John and Ian talked of Robin Hood. It
is always a delicate business to explain why Robin Hood—
lawbreaker and a robber—is a good man. But John was undaunted. Carefully he explained to Ian the peasant's complete
lack of rights before the law. A villein had even fewer rights
against his lord. If he were so foolish as to lodge a complaint
there was no place to plead his cause except in the manorial
court, where cases were decided by the lord himself—or his
bailiff.

"Why didn't he go someplace else?" asked Ian.

"Because the law wouldn't let him. And if he tried to get
another source of income—say he knew a little carpentry or
blacksmithing—the Statute of Labourers forbade employers
to pay him very much, so he was condemned to be poor all his
life. It was even worse if he lived in a royal forest. He lost
even his ordinary rights under common law, and he had to pay

protection money to the keepers of the forest. He could be imprisoned for crimes against vert (timber) and against venison. In fact he could be thrown into a dungeon just for *looking* a little greedy."

"Why didn't he run away and hide?" Ian asked. "That's what *I'd* do!"

"Some of them did do that. They went deep into the forest and they found other men there who had been outlawed. Some of them were really bad men, but most of them were probably just poor peasants who did not think of themselves as being bad. They were still loyal to the king and thought of themselves as being good men on the side of justice. Like Robin Hood and his men."

The next morning, after breakfast, we repacked our suitcases and put them in the car, bought a guidebook from the tobacco shop across the way, and set out to explore. We decided to walk to the Major Oak. We came to a sort of park at the end of the village street. Other families were strolling ahead of us on the well-trodden path so that there was no fear of losing our way. As we walked we gazed curiously at the view on either side of us. There was a great deal of underbrush and second growth, with here and there the silhouette of some old forest giant looming through the mist. For the most part the oaks seemed but battered ghosts of their former selves, some of them not able to put forth one green leaf. "Mouldering towers noble and picturesque in their decay," is how Washington Irving described them. That was more than one hundred years ago. They've mouldered considerably since.

At last we came to the Major Oak (sometimes called the "Queen"), the oldest and largest in the forest. An enormous old man sat in front of it, collecting sixpences a look, although this was ridiculous. Even *his* bulk could not hide what we had come to see. The tree was tremendous—and very much alive! The broad trunk was split near the roots, but the great sinewy branches stretching parallel to the ground supported other branches and their tributaries and twigs and leaves in a miraculous green canopy. The tree was so old that the acorn from which it grew might have been shaken from the parent tree on a day when Robin Hood himself climbed its branches, yet so new that the buds for next year's growth were forming beneath the leaves.

Being native Californians, we had seen the giant redwoods, but they are architectural in effect, more like pillars of some great cathedral than living, growing trees. The oak tree flourishes outward rather than up and seems almost to welcome the companionship of humankind. The branches are broad and stairlike. A man could live in one of those old oaks; with small precaution he could sleep there. What a wonderful place for a lookout or an ambush! It was easy to imagine with what trepidation a convoy of merchants or monk-landlords would ride through those woods on the way to Nottingham or Southwell Minister. They would be too frightened, no doubt, to appreciate the beauty of the endless sun-dappled glades. Each giant oak must have loomed like a monster, waiting to pounce.

It is generally agreed that whoever the historical Robin Hood might have been (and there is probably no end to argument on this point), the name affixed to him was not his own. Robin Hood (or Wood, or 'ood, or Goodfellow—have it your own way) was the self or spirit or half-remembered god of the greenwood. Robin Hood's day came on May Day or

Whitsuntide. Often the church was decorated with green branches and the floor strewn with fresh rushes. In many parishes the king and queen of the May became Robin Hood and Maid Marian and there was an actual enactment of some of the ballads from the *Lytel Geste*. Christina Hole, in *English Folk Heroes*, suggests that the wide geographical diversity of place names related to Robin Hood is probably related to these rites. Similarly, the several graves attributed to Little John might be confused with various local giants who played the role in the May Day revels.

Robin Hood may have been any one of several outlaws who fled to the greenwood, and who took unto himself (or was given) the name of its spirit. Perhaps he was a veteran of Agincourt where he learned to use the bow with a skill that became proverbial. He is far more likely to have been a yeoman than a knight. The early ballads make no mention of his being of noble blood. Maurice Kean, in *History Today*, has written an excellent article on "Robin Hood and His Merry Men" in which he shows the limits of the peasant's outlook. The peasant was not truly a revolutionary. His faith in his sovereign was unshakeable. Robin Hood's role was not to destroy, but to right the wrongs of, the old system. This is probably why so many of the stories end with Robin's going to the king to make his peace. It is also why later tradition invested him with nobility. A peasant could never lead peasants.

Robin Hood was not the only outlaw hero who fled to the forest to live on the king's venison. As old as any of the ballads of Robin Hood is the ballad of the three outlaws of "merry Carlisle": Adam Bell, Clum of the Clough and William of Cloudslee. A good version of their escapades may be found in Barbara Picard's *Tales of the British People*. But even older is *Coke's Tale of Gamelyn,* a manuscript of which was owned by Chaucer. The ancient ballad describes Gamelyn's life and adventures as an outlaw leader in the forest. Later Gamelyn appears as one of Robin Hood's men in Sherwood Forest. Christina Hole writes that Much, the Miller's son, was probably an earlier hero too, whose legends (rather than himself) attached themselves "for rations and quarters" to Robin Hood's band. She also advances the theory that the original of Maid Marian is probably Maud Fitzwalter, who on refusing the proposals of King John, was poisoned by him and forthwith became a sort of Anglo-Saxon resistance heroine. King John was *not* a good man—he "had his little ways!"

Christina Hole puts the place names of Nottingham and Yorkshire in a special category as being connected with the historical Robin Hood, rather than the ritualized Robin Goodfellow. Both she and the little guidebook we had bought at the tobacconist's mention "Robin Hood's Larder," an old tree not far from the Major Oak. We dutifully went in search of it, but I cannot swear which of the leafless trunks that we saw that day was the one where Robin hid his venison. It might have been wise to drive over to Cresswell Crags to see the caves where Robin and his men are said to have hidden (caves and small boys being such a successful combination), or perhaps we could have sought out Kirklee Priory farm in order to see Robin's grave. Instead, we went to look for Friar Tuck's Well.

The children having had a good run through forest glades, were quite cheerful about wedging themselves back into the car. Ian, especially, was eager to see the place where Friar Tuck had spilled Robin into the river. According to our guidebook, the Friar's well was at Fountain Dale, not far from

Mansfield. We set off, chatting all the while of Friar Tuck and how the location of his cell was described in Howard Pyle's version of *Robin Hood*:

> "Now, good uncle," quoth Will Scarlet at last, when they had walked for a time beside this sweet bright river, "just beyond yon bend ahead of us is a shallow ford which in no place is deeper than thy mid-thigh, and upon the other side of the stream is a certain little hermitage hidden amidst the bosky tankle of the thickets wherein dwelleth the Friar of Fountain Dale!"

Robin Hood goes ahead to look for the Friar, but as he creeps through the undergrowth to the ford he discovers "a stout, Brawny fellow" seated with his back against a willow tree eating a meat pasty, drinking Malmsey from a pottle, and carrying on an intermittent dialogue with himself. When this lusty fellow at length bursts into song, Robin joins him in the chorus and is forthwith challenged to a duel as penalty for eavesdropping. There follows a battle of wits in which Robin thinks to persuade the man to carry him across the river, but ends with a ducking instead. It is only when the man discovers the true identity of Robin that he reveals himself as Friar of Fountain Dale, and asks to join Robin's band.

A man walking his collie along the road gave us directions to the gate. We entered and drove along a drive that ran through a rough meadow toward the house. Several metal caravans were standing in the deep grass under the trees. A woman hanging clothes on a line strung from one of the caravans to a tree gave us directions. She took it quite for granted that we wanted to see the well.

Following directions, we set off through a veritable forest of rhododendron. The path led along the margin of a dark, still pond that lay depressingly motionless beneath the shadows of overhanging willows. The name Fountain Dale would suggest a valley of gushing springs, but the water seemed just to seep up from the ground in rather a messy way. Christina Hole writes that Friar Tuck's cells stand at Copmanhurst in the woods of Fountain Dale, on the banks of the little River Rain in "a remote spot" in the Nottinghamshire woods. The spot was remote enough, an appropriate place for a hermit monk, but for the life of us we could not reconcile it with Howard Pyle's "sweet bright river." We came at last to the well, choked with brush and stones. Farther on we came to some stone steps which led up to a little iron gate and the ruins of a little chapel. We were rather disillusioned by the time we got back to the car. It had all been rather anticlimactic.

But as we drove along we became more cheerful. We decided that although Friar Tuck may have lived at Copmanhurst, he probably met Robin Hood farther downriver. That would explain why Robin did not connect him with the hermitage or recognize him at first. Quite satisfied with this solution, we turned our attention back to Robin Hood. Did he actually exist? Maurice Kean writes: "It matters not so much who or what he was as what people thought him to have been." But driving through Nottinghamshire that day, we decided that there really was a Robin Hood and that he lived in Sherwood Forest. Having spent almost a whole summer chasing other will-o'-the-wisps, we had found them to be satisfyingly concrete when they were actually nailed down. I have great faith that folk memory has perpetuated a historical figure —a man of flesh and blood—who was not so very different from our image of the outlaw. Perhaps, in those grim times, he was not quite as jolly and generous as the nursery tales would have him, but he did represent a force against oppression. "He is the people's Arthur," writes Maurice Kean. I am one of those incurable souls who persists in believing in both.

It was a long drive to Harrogate. We had chosen it for our destination because, on the map, it appeared to be at the very edge of the Yorkshire moors. It was to see a moor that we had come to England! Ever since reading Frances Hodgson Burnett's *The Secret Garden* when I was ten I had wanted to see Yorkshire; reading the Brontë novels when I was older had intensified that longing. Then, the past winter, when it seemed that spring would never come, I had read *The Secret Garden* aloud to Ian so that now he was as eager as I to see "how the heather looks."

We had expected Harrogate to be a manufacturing town with dark satanic mills; instead we found an elegant watering place whose shops and restaurants and big hotels catered to fashionable ladies and tweedy gentlemen. Harrogate, besides being a spa, is a racing center, too. On several respectable door fronts we saw signs advertising bookie establishments. Our favorite read: "Thomas Todhunter. Family Bookie. We Served Your Grandfather."

We found rooms in a pleasant little hotel on Coldbath Road, and the next day we called the reference librarian at Leeds to ask if he could furnish any clues as to the whereabouts of the huge old house that Mrs. Burnett described so concretely in *The Secret Garden*. He told us that as far as he could discover there was no information extant on Misselthwaite Manor, but that the "secret" garden itself was reported to be one in the Cheetham Hill district of Manchester, many miles away and not in Yorkshire at all. He gave Margharita Laski as reference and later we were to read her book, *Mrs. Ewing, Mrs. Molesworth and Mrs. Hodgson Burnett.*

Frances Eliza Hodgson, according to Mrs. Laski, was one of a family of five children who, after the death of their father, was forced to move from the fashionable Cheetham Hill district of Manchester to the shabby gentility of a house in Islington Square. It was while leaning out of the windows of her new home that Frances first saw the garden of the deserted house next door and began to weave stories about it. Mrs. Laski's little biography is an astringent one. Not so the life of Frances Hodgson Burnett described in *The Romantick Lady*, a hymn of adoration written by her son, Vivian Burnett, the original model for Cedric Errol, Little Lord Fauntleroy. But despite his lamentable prose, Vivian Burnett does furnish another clue to the whereabouts of the garden. For a short time his mother owned the estate of Maytham Hall at Rolvenden, Kent, where there was an old walled garden, answering to the description of the one in *The Secret Garden.* She planted it with roses and used it as a private retreat where she did much of her writing. The garden is also described in a short story, "My Robin" and in an adult novel, *The Shuttle.* I have been able to find no evidence that Mrs. Burnett ever visited Yorkshire, but such was her delight in contrasts that she showed no hesitation in picking up a lush, almost tropical, garden in Kent and setting it squarely in the Brontë country.

Mrs. Burnett had evidently read the Brontë novels and profited by her reading. Miss Laski points out that she may have borrowed from Charlotte Brontë's fragmentary *Emma* to give herself a starting point for Sara Crewe (also known as *The Little Princess*). In both the Brontë novel and Mrs. Burnett's the plot begins with a spoiled and petted child being left at a young ladies' seminary where she lives as a star pupil. The death or disappearance of the father who left her there is followed by the dwindling away of funds to pay for board and tuition, and by the heroine being plunged into virtual slavery. Charlotte Brontë died before she could finish her novel, but Mrs. Burnett was able to utilize the idea and to spin the tale out to a satisfying conclusion, employing her favorite plot tricks of the "different" child, impoverished gentility, a sleight-of-hand transformation, and the triumph of goodness and intellect over shoddiness and evil.

Having been so successful with one plot idea borrowed from Charlotte Brontë, it was only natural that Mrs. Burnett would turn to the same source again. I do not mean, in any way, that she took over the plot entirely; I only wish to indicate that certain elements in *The Secret Garden* derive from *Jane Eyre*. They are used in an utterly fresh and unique context congenial to childhood. The arrival of Mary Lennox at Misselthwaite Manor is too reminiscent of Jane Eyre's arrival at Thornfield to be pure coincidence. Mary was only ten, Jane almost twenty, but both were markedly plain young females who had made reputations for being "sour" and "contrary." Both were orphans, and both came into a new life in a mysterious manor house on the Yorkshire moors—a house where the master was "abroad" most of the time, and the place run by servants. There is also the parallel of the tray-carrying nurse who issues from a door concealed behind a curtain or tapestry, and the mysterious "cry in the corridor" that makes one's blood chill in the night.

I suppose that an American's approach to English literature must always be oblique. We share a language but not a landscape. In order to understand the English classics as adults, we must build up a sort of visual vocabulary from the books we read as children. Children's literature is, in some ways more important to us than it is to the English child. I contend that a child brought up on the nursery rhymes and Jacobs' *English Fairy Tales* can better understand Shakespeare; that a child who has pored over Beatrix Potter can better respond to Wordsworth. Of course it is *best* if one can find for himself a bank where the wild thyme grows, or discover daffodils growing wild. Failing that, the American child must feed the "inward eye" with the images in the books he reads when young so that he can enter a larger realm when he is older. I am sure I enjoyed the Brontë novels more for having read *The Secret Garden* first. As I stood on those moors, looking out over that wind-swept landscape I realized that it was Mrs. Burnett who taught me what "wuthering" meant long before I ever got around to reading *Wuthering Heights*. Epiphany comes at the moment of recognition.

A week after leaving Northampton, when we were staying at Harrogate, in Yorkshire, John and I decided to drive over to Haworth, the village where Charlotte and Emily Brontë had lived and written their famous novels. We wanted to see the parsonage where they spent most of their lives and perhaps walk across the moors to the farmhouse which is said to be the counterpart of the one in *Wuthering Heights*. We did not expect Ian to be much interested since he was too young to know or appreciate the Brontë novels.

As we made our way up the steep, cobbled streets of Haworth we wondered why anyone would ever set a village in such an inhospitable spot. Although it was on a height, the village did not seem to want to look out at the world. Rather, it turned inward to the fold in the hillside, one shop window peering into another. The church and the parsonage are at the top of the hill, barely separated from the rest of the village. The front of the house looks onto the fore-shortened vista of a sunken garden and a churchyard to the side of it. It was a pleasant surprise, therefore, to step into the hallway and find it flooded with light from the moors that roll away from the rear of the house. According to Elizabeth Gaskell, Charlotte's biographer, the Reverend Patrick Brontë was afraid of fire and would allow no curtains in the house. Sunlight was a welcome visitor.

We went through the house, which has been made into a museum. It holds a motley collection of memorabilia, some of it far-fetched in any connection to the Brontës. To the left of the entrance hall was a living room with a fireplace, and to the right was the Reverend Patrick Brontë's study. Farther down the hall, behind the study, was the flagged kitchen where Tabby, the Brontë's old housekeeper, held sway; and across from it, a storeroom. Although there were no curtains at the windows, faded turkey rugs partly covered the polished floors. The furniture was mahogany, upholstered in black horsehair. Victorian gloom was dissipated by the quantity of light allowed to enter and the delicate shades of gray and white which had been chosen for walls and woodwork. The whole house had an air of cheerful austerity.

Upstairs were two large bedrooms, each with an adjacent smaller room. Part of the upstairs hall was partitioned off into a cupboard-like space that looked out over the front door to the garden and churchyard. This was known as the children's study. It was here that the four children—Charlotte, Emily,

Branwell, and Anne—spent long hours, their heads bent over minuscule scraps of paper, their grubby fingers busy with pens and crayons.

"What are you doing, children?" asked the Reverend Patrick Brontë.

"Just playing, papa. Just playing. . . ."

Ian had become bored with the tour of the house and asked permission to go downstairs. We thought he would probably go out into the garden, but when we looked for him we found him bent over a museum case, peering through the glass.

"Hey, come here!" he called, when he saw us. "I've found something interesting. I think there was a boy living here, and he was *just like me!*"

We, too, bent over the glass case. We saw a tiny scrap of paper, a little more than two inches square, on which a child had drawn some soldiers engaged in a battle. The drawing *did* look like one of Ian's, but a neat little card attributed the work to Branwell Brontë. Across the top of the drawing the artist had written: "Battell of Wehglen." Even the spelling was similar to Ian's! There were other things in the case—tiny volumes, surely written under a microscope. They had strange titles: *The Revenge: a Tragedy in Three Acts* by Young Soult (In two Volumes); *History of the Rebellion in My Army; Blackwood's Young Men's Magazine; List and Description of the Provinces of Angria.*

What did it all mean? At the time all I could guess was that these were some writings and drawings the Brontës had done as children and which the museum, patently unselective, had put on display. It did not occur to me until later that these works had any connection with the Brontës' adult publications, except as foreshadowing of the genius to come. I assumed that they were the usual juvenilia, of interest mostly to Ian because he was a little boy interested in Napoleonic soldiers. On that afternoon in Haworth I was as ignorant about their importance as the Reverend Patrick Brontë had been, but due to Ian's insistence I determined to pursue the matter as soon as I could find a good library. Months later, when we were home again, our whole family was to become fascinated by the childhood of the Brontës.

What did the Brontë children do upstairs in the little room over the front door? A year after their sisters, Maria and Elizabeth, died, when Branwell was not quite nine years old, his father brought home a box of soldiers from Leeds and put them by his son's bed. He brought presents for the little girls, too: a box of ninepins, a toy village, a dancing doll—but it was the "Twelve Heroes" that caused the most excitement. Early next morning, Mrs. Gaskell tells us, Charlotte pounced on the tallest and handsomest of the lot and proclaimed: "This is the Duke of Wellington! This shall be the Duke." Emily chose "an oddly serious little fellow" whom she decided to call "Gravey," and Anne chose a soldier whom she named "Waiting Boy." Branwell may have been taken aback, but once having established that the soldiers were really his he could be generous. Each sister could keep her favorite as long as she remembered who was master, or Chief Genius. Bending over the remaining nine wooden figures, he picked out one for himself: "Bonaparte." The other soldiers were given such names as Goody, Naughty, Cracky, Cheeky, Monkey, all according to real or fancied characteristics. Toys were not turned out by an assembly line in those days, as witness Andersen's story of the lead soldier with only one leg. Some spark from the craftsman-creator must have lingered in the lineaments and stance of each tiny figure, giving it integrity and individuality and a sort of life of its own.

For a year the Brontë children played with the soldiers, staging battles and re-enacting the great campaigns of Napoleon and Wellington. After all, Waterloo was only a dozen years past and children all over England must have been playing much the same games. Branwell, because the soldiers were his and because of his masculine interest in military science, was the acknowledged leader and director. By the next summer, however, constant warfare had palled and a new game was invented, a game called "Our Fellows." The soldiers were divided and renamed. Each of the genii took unto himself an imaginary island and peopled it with inhabitants six miles high. Exaggerated stories were invented to fit the fabulous characters.

By November, Branwell was grumbling that he had nothing to do, so now Charlotte took charge. Each child took for himself a new island, one actually to be found in Father's atlas. Branwell chose the Isle of Man; Charlotte, the Isle of Wight; Emily, the Isle of Arran; Anne, the Isle of Guernsey. According to the rules of the game, each child was allowed to populate his island with any heroes he wished. Now the names of authors, statesmen, editors, scientists, explorers— most of the great names to be found in the newspapers of the day—emanated from the little room upstairs. Sometimes the soldiers took on the characteristics of these public figures, but just as often the great names were bent and twisted to fit the characters of the Twelve Young Heroes.

The heroes went on a voyage to Africa. Maps were drawn and redrawn, the four islands were given made-up names, the whole world was divided among the four genii. Magazines, newspapers, histories were issued for the benefit of the Twelve. The geography and history of Glasstown became more real than the geography and history of Yorkshire; the inhabitants of Angria were better known (and known better) than the villagers of Haworth. Long after the last soldier had become lost or broken the "play" continued. Fantastic as it may seem, the novels and chronicles of Angria exceed in length and volume all the published works of the Brontës. F. E. Ratchfed, of the University of Texas, has published a bibliography of the Brontë juvenilia, entitled *Web of Childhood* in which he discusses this curious microscopic literature with scholarly thoroughness. Many scenes and characters, he points out, have been lifted whole from the unpublished body of work to be born anew in the adult novels.

Since our return from England there has been published a children's book about Branwell's soldiers. In *The Return of the Twelves*, a modern-day fantasy by Pauline Clarke, eight-year-old Max Morley finds twelve wooden soldiers under the attic floor in a Yorkshire farmhouse not far from Haworth, the village where the Brontës lived. Warmed by his small-boy affection, the little figures come to life. They talk to Max of the time, long past, when four genii—Branwell, Charlotte, Emily, and Anne—loved them and ordered their destinies by imagining marvelous adventures for them. Max soon learns that he may not interfere with the sturdy independence of the Twelves, else the soldiers will "freeze" and become lifeless wood again.

The book becomes most exciting when Max decides to help the Twelves return to their old home in the parsonage at Haworth. Pauline Clarke describes the Twelves' trek across country and the stir it causes as rumors of their march seep through the countryside. One of the soldiers is observed and captured by a farmer who claims he saw the little figure filling a tiny sack with grain from the henyard. Two little girls, "rapt in some secret game," hear a rustle in the "silvery green-gold world of the oats" and see a column of little men winding their way through the forest, singing "The Grand Old Duke of York" in thin, cautious voices. The two children run home to tell the grownups, but of course they are not believed. However:

> Their fathers made excuses to take strolls along that field, and even lay down (when they hoped no one was looking) and gazed, feeling foolish, into the oats. Once down, they thought how possible it all sounded; the world of the nodding grain was so secret and reminded them of their boyhood. . . .

Something there is, in every Englishman. . . .

The day after driving over the moors to Haworth parsonage, we left our hotel at Harrogate and took the road to Darlington to see a favorite uncle of mine. Uncle Roger was a bachelor, but he knew what a little boy would like—and a little girl, too. First of all he walked us down to the train station, solemnly paid a penny each for our entrance fee, and proudly showed us George Stephenson's tiny, shiny locomotive which stood in the middle of the platform. We were enchanted. It so happened that we owned a copy of *Early British Railways*, a King Penguin book by Christian Barman, so that we could appreciate the fact that this was the first British railway engine and that the track section it was set on had been part of the original Stockton-Darlington line.

The track was of such narrow gauge that it looked like a toy, but by peering over the side of the platform, where modern trains came hissing into the station, we could see that it was the same width as used today. George Stephenson had been ordered to make his track "as wide as a country cart." With characteristic thoroughness he rounded up one hundred local carts, measured their axle breadths, divided by one hundred, and came up with the average: 4 feet, 8½ inches. From that day to this the measurement has stood as the standard gauge for British railways. Quite early in the history of railroading Stephenson had a chance to change his track width to 5 feet 6 inches, a gauge used by Spain, Portugal, India, and Argentina. But old George was obstinate and I, for one, am glad of it. English railways are tailored to fit their landscape. Like everything else in that landscape they have grown out of the past and are in harmony with its scale. In more romantic moments I like to think that the measurements of those old carts had been, in their turn, set by the width of the Roman roads.

After our visit to the railroad platform, Uncle Roger took us to a restaurant and treated us to a glorious tea. I suspect that the scones and cream cakes were as much a treat for him as for the children, at least he acted as though they were. But then, he attacked everything in life with such zest that we found ourselves caught up in the same spirit. I do not know when we have laughed so hard. I am convinced that every child should have an English bachelor uncle. Married uncles (American or British) are usually someone else's father and tend to have a reasonable, responsible, well-adjusted way of looking at life. But a bachelor uncle is like Mr. Wiggs in the *Mary Poppins* book (remember the laughing scene?), and

Captain Flint in *Swallows and Amazons,* and Great Uncle Matthew in *Ballet Shoes.* There is a touch of Bertie Wooster and Edward Lear and Professor Dodgson about him. Such uncles are not to be confused with contemporary playmates, but neither are they like parents. They are a breed apart. By very definition, bachelor uncles should be dying out, but let us hope that even unto our children's children there will be a hard core of ebullient eccentrics who answer to the name.

We spent the next night at Morepeth. We had chosen a respectable hotel, but there was a circus in town and the Saturday night crowd was unusually large and noisy. We were kept awake by a row in the bar downstairs. The next day, being Sunday, John went to church, Lucy took an extra nap, I babysat, and Ian disappeared. When John returned from church we packed the car and then set out to look for Ian. We found him down by the river playing with some of the children from the circus. His trousers were rolled up to the knees, his new shoes were ruined by the river, but he was having a wonderful time. It was the first time he had found anyone his own age who would play with him since we left the New Forest. The circus children had told him that they did not like to play with "townies" but since he was an American they had received him as a fellow outsider. I am sorry that I was cross with Ian for making us get a late start. If I had talked less and listened more I might have heard some interesting echoes of Noel Streatfeild's *Circus Shoes.* It is not often that one is accepted by circus people. Ian had been honored.

We decided not to take the shorter route inland to Edinburgh, but to follow the curve of the coast. We came to Alnwick and saw a castle tower surmounted by great armored warriors silhouetted against the sky. I suppose they had been put there to frighten would-be invaders into believing that the castle was manned by giants. We did not stop to find out, but pressed on in search of a place where we could stop to lunch. We were old travelers now who knew that it was all but impossible to buy an evening meal in Britain on a Sunday. We stopped at a little place near Beal and had a hearty luncheon. Hardly had we rearranged ourselves in the car when we saw a fingerpost pointing to the Holy Island of Lindisfarne. How could we resist? To anyone with a passion for books and the making of books, the name of Lindisfarne has a special magic.

Lindisfarne is a mist-shrouded island off the coast of Northumbria, famous for its abbey. When Rome fell and barbarians swept over Europe, scholars and craftsmen from as far away as Byzantium fled to the Holy Island and found refuge there. In that remote and hallowed place the monks labored to keep alive the story of Christianity and the memory of Greco-Roman civilization. They copied out the Christian gospels in their scriptorium and illuminated the vellum pages with unique motifs, blending the traditions of La Tène Celtic ornament with those from the Mediterranean. The result was the famous Lindisfarne Gospel, considered by many bibliophiles as the most beautiful of all illuminated manuscripts, second to not even the Book of Kells.

The glory of Lindisfarne was short-lived, however. Viking pirates swept over the Holy Island in 793 A.D. and in 875 A.D., forcing those monks who were not killed outright to flee elsewhere.

To be so close to the Holy Island yet not to see it was unthinkable! John turned the car along a narrow road toward the sea, explaining as he did so that I must not expect to see the famous manuscript in such a remote and unprotected spot. He was quite certain that it was safely deposited in the British Museum in London. As we neared the coast and saw the green island ahead of us we realized that it was separated from the mainland by a tidal spit or causeway. The tide was out; we would have to get over and back within the next few hours or we would be stuck until next low water. Even my enthusiasm was fast running out. There were no tracks to follow, no way to know where we might get bogged down in soft sands or caught in a cove. The island loomed above us, with seemingly no place to seek safety if the tide should change. Then a small panel truck marked Coast Guard came careening past us. We followed it around a headland and came to a low spot on the end of the island where we could see a road, and a village with a little church and the ruins of the monastery.

We parked our car and made our way over to the ruins. They had been declared an ancient monument and were under the guardianship of The Ministry of Works. We bought a guidebook at the gate and wandered about, reading the guidebook, trying to find the scriptorium, and watching to see that the children did not break their necks on the tumble-down stones. Even now it was oddly impressive to find these immense ruins in such a remote place. What must the original abbey have seemed to the local crofters and fishermen of the seventh century? Now sea gulls perched on the lacelike arches and the blue sky was the only roof overhead. The sound of waves reminded us that our time was limited by the tide. We called the children and made our way back to the gate. We came into the little village just as the church bell began to toll and the church doors opened.

The next moment we felt that we had been transported

back into the Middle Ages. A brown-cowled monk, quite young and at least six feet tall, came out of the church carrying a cross. A rope girdle encircled his waist, his big feet were incongruously shod in ordinary seaside sandals. He walked solemnly toward us, then turned toward the churchyard. Behind him came six pall bearers, staggering under the weight of a coffin. They were all dressed in black trousers and black fishing jerseys and everyone of them had a beautiful, strong, medieval face that looked as though it had been carved from stone or wood. Sorrow was engraved on every face, but it was a private sorrow, each man seemingly wrapped in his special thoughts. The other tourists and ourselves did not exist. Priest and people had stepped backward into time: What we saw could have been happening a thousand years ago. As long as I live I will never forget the faces of the men of Lindisfarne.

But we were bound for Scotland. We scuttled back across the Causeway and drove north along the great highway. Hardly had we crossed the Tweed when we spied an enormous sign painted in jagged letters on the side of a stone barn: "English go home!" The paint looked as though it were barely dry. It was enough to give one pause. I think that Ian was rather disappointed that there was no one at the border to back up that challenge—he would have liked to see just a *little* blood shed—but he was comforted by the knowledge that all about us great battles had been fought. We drove on through the Lammermuir Hills, knowing vaguely that it was "Scott country," and in the late afternoon came to Dunbar. Although we could have easily made the distance into Edinburgh before nightfall, we found ourselves hesitating. A sign on a large and imposing house informed us that there were rooms to let. John pointed out that we were probably on the very site of the Battle of Dunbar, where Cromwell's men beat the Scots. That was enough for Ian! He is a true battlefield buff. We could not have budged him another step.

The next morning (again!) we could not find Ian when we were ready to set out. When we asked our landlady to tell us where we could find the nearest children, she suggested a row of Council houses several fields away. The sound of boyish voices upraised in argument soon led us to our son. He was having a wonderful time, but was perfectly happy to climb into the car with us to continue into Edinburgh. He explained his morning's activities as we drove along. He had gone out after breakfast to explore the battlefield. He had hoped to find an old pike or a Roundhead helmet—some little trinket overlooked these several centuries. Eventually he had wandered across the fields and found himself in the back gardens of the Council houses. "It was real neat," he said. There were slides and swings for the little kids, and the older boys had a tent. They were playing cowboys and Indians and had been hospitable enough to include Ian in the game. Eventually he asked whether they ever played "Battle of Dunbar." They said they played it every day—*after* cowboys and Indians. If Ian wanted to play it now he could be Cromwell, the rest of them would be Scots. No one else would join Ian because no one wanted to be on the losing side. In vain Ian explained that Cromwell had *won* the Battle of Dunbar. When we came upon them, the boys had been arguing the truth of Cromwell's victory. "Do you know what they said?" Ian asked. "They said that maybe tomorrow they'd play it my way." Even Ian could see the humor of it. It had been fun "hacking around" he said. "They sure are good kids. . . ."

We drove into Edinburgh, turned off Prince's Street, and drove along South Bridge. I had a copy of *The Lady*, an incredibly genteel women's magazine, in hand. I had saved it because it carried so many "personals" and classified advertisements announcing rooms to let by "impoverished gentlewomen" all over Britain. There were half a dozen Edinburgh addresses, one of them on a pleasant terrace leading off South Bridge. Besides the one advertised, we found several houses with Rooms or Bed and Breakfast signs discreetly placed in parlor windows. One of them—oh joy!—had a walled garden where I could see clotheslines in abundance. This was the place.

Our main objective in Edinburgh was to go in search of Robert Louis Stevenson—or, rather, Robert Louis Stevenson's garden. There has always been a special affinity between Ian and the author of *A Child's Garden of Verses*. When he was less than a year old I used to read "Windy Nights" to him at bedtime. Of course the most that he got from the poem was the rhythm, but he loved it and would rock his crib at a gallop. When he was six or so, and fascinated by pirates, his father had read him *Treasure Island* and, later, *Kidnapped*. He responded so enthusiastically that John brought home several biographies so that we could learn more about Robert Louis Stevenson.

Ian took especial pleasure in the fact that Louis liked old maps, pirates, knights, toy soldiers, elaborate games of history and make-believe just as he himself did. Of course, Ian may like all these things *because* we read Stevenson to him at such an early age. It is hard to tell. Another bond was that Louis, even as Ian, had difficulty in learning to read. Both little boys had been incessant listeners, almost from their births. Both

could soak up reams of poetry and folklore, they were both interested in "adult" history and—on some occasions—would
listen to newspaper articles or editorials. Both could dictate
long, involved and quite coherent stories of their own. But
when it came to actually reading or writing they were the despair of school teachers and far behind their fellows. Ian was
just issuing from the dread labyrinth that represented his first
few years at school, and it was a comfort to him to know that
his hero (his friend, really) had suffered even as he.

We decided to go first to 8 Howard Place, across the city
from us, which our guidebook listed as a memorial museum.
Although this was the house where R.L.S. was born, his family left it when he was barely three. We found the place clut-
tered with memorabilia. There were locks of hair and pictures
of ancestors, scenes from motion pictures based on the novels,
photographs of Stevenson's yacht and his house in Tahiti.
There were also photographs of the house in Monterey, California, where he had lived for a short time and which we had
visited just the year before. When we, in innocent pride,
mentioned this to the museum caretaker, he countered: "Aye!
Often we have people who say they have visited Stevenson's
house here or there in America. Seems like you Americans
think you own him even more than we do." Well, not more,
perhaps—but as much. I remember how much satisfaction it
used to be to me to sit in Portsmouth Square in San Francisco
and to reflect that Stevenson had once sat there too.

The next morning we decided to sally forth and to spend
the morning in search of "a child's garden of verses" and the
house where Stevenson had lived when he peered out the
window at "Leerie going by." A little research had revealed
that after leaving the house at 8 Howard Place, the Stevenson

family had moved to 1 Inverleith Terrace, a house long since torn down. Just as well, evidently, because its exposed position and poor drains had caused the learned doctors to suggest that if little Louis's health was ever to improve his parents must find better housing. The only pleasant memory of the place was that it was there that "Cummy," faithful nurse and future dedicatee, first came to live with the Stevenson family.

Robert Louis Stevenson was six years old when his family moved to Number 17, Heriot Row, within easy walking distance of the shops on Prince's Street. He was a strange little boy, frail and thin with long narrow face, cold hands, cold feet, and an old fashioned quaintness of manner. He was born cold, and all his life he would seek warmth and sunshine. Number 17 faced upon a southern exposure in almost the very center of a row of houses looking out on Queen Street Garden. The houses were modern (that is, they had been built during the Napoleonic Wars), but they were heated solely by fireplaces. In a latitude the same as Labrador's a small body wracked by coughs and colds must have struggled mightily to exist. If it had not been for the loving skill of Alison Cunningham the only memory of Louis might have been "upon the whole a family happier for his presence." There might have been nothing else to mark the fact that he had ever lived.

The house was easy enough to find. Just a few squares back from Prince's Street the silver-gray houses were steeped in privacy and classical serenity. A plaque affixed to the right of the door of Number 17 informed us that this was, indeed, the former home of Robert Louis Stevenson, but that it was also a private residence and not open to the public. We wandered across the street and peered through the palings into the Queen Street Gardens, trying in vain to picture young Louis at play there. Somehow he did not fit.

Where was the "dark brown river" wherein to float leaves and chips of wood? There was not even a fountain, much less a brook. Where was a place for a child to "go up in a swing?" No tree in that garden looked as though it had ever been hospitable to a child. And who would dare to dig a hole in the grass, to hide his toy grenadier? No, this was not the garden we sought. I began to wonder if Louis, out of desperate longing, had "made it up." He was such an imaginative child that perhaps the poems reflected what he would have liked to have had. No! I told myself firmly. The whole genius of A *Child's Garden of Verses* lies in its common-sensical reality, the concreteness of its detail. Children would not respond to it as they do if the imagination were not tethered so firmly to the five senses.

We turned and looked back at the house across the street. There was no doubt that this was the place of the "indoor" poems—the winter nights, the firelit hearth, the counterpane strewn with toys, the wistful face peering from the window, watching for Leerie to come along "with ladder and with light" to spark the gas lamps all down Heriot Row. Almost, we could see the long, pale little face at the window now, half hidden by the curtains.

And then, almost as though we had willed that it should happen, the sturdy figure of a man came "posting down the street." He was carrying a ladder. He stopped in front of Number 17, propped his ladder against the lamp post, and began to climb up. We must have looked as though we had seen a ghost. Leerie! We raced across the street and stared up at him, open-mouthed. I suddenly realized that we were being very rude.

"We . . . we thought you were Leerie," Ian said.

The man's face crumpled into a smile. "On account of *him?*" he asked, jerking his thumb at Number 17. "No, laddie. My name's MacIntyre—Andrew MacIntyre." He opened a little door in the lamp.

"Isn't it too early to light the lamp?" asked Ian.

"Aye, laddie. I'm just cleaning it and trimming the wick a wee bit."

"Do you like your job?"

Andrew MacIntyre stopped his work and peered down at Ian in astonishment. Like it? He had to think about that. He pushed back his cap and scratched his head for a moment. "Aye, laddie," he said at last. "It's a wee cushy job except in bad weather." Then he descended his ladder, hoisted it over his shoulder, and rounded a corner at the end of Heriot Row. We would still be convinced that we had seen a ghost except for the fact that I took a photograph of Andrew MacIntyre while Ian was talking to him. Ian was disappointed when the picture was returned to us, showing a prosaic Scot of flesh and blood. He had hoped that the film would be blank. A snapshot of a ghost would be even more exciting than that of an Edinburgh lamplighter.

The following day we drove out to Colinton Manse, the house where Stevenson's maternal grandparents had lived and where he had played with his "dozens of cousins" in the most normal and natural relationship of his childhood. In the winter months little Louis lived an isolated sickroom life at

Number 17 Heriot Row, his only companions his lighthouse
engineer father, an invalid mother, and the Calvinistic
common-sensical Scottish nurse, Cummy. Cummy was not
one for fraternizing with her fellow nursemaids and rarely took
her charge across the street to play in the fenced formality of
Queen Street Gardens. One suspects that Louis would not
have enjoyed the atmosphere there, either, or the decorous
play on graveled paths, but much preferred Cummy's astringent company and conversations. She took him for long brisk
walks, well bundled against the cold. Down Heriot Row and
Moray Place they often went, to browse among the headstones
of a little graveyard and to walk along the public footpath
that borders the Water of Leith. This was the same river that
flows past his grandparents' house out at Colinton; the very
stream where, in summer, he launched green leaves as boats
to float "away down the river, a hundred miles or more."
Summertime and Colinton must have seemed very far away.

To Louis, Colinton was another life—as different as Jekyll
is to Hyde. In his poems it seems such a different clime that
we expected it to be miles from Edinburgh, but to our surprise we found that it was in the nearby Pentland Hills, actually within the city limits. Even in Louis's time it was comparatively easy to reach. Colinton is a tiny little mill village in
a steep vale. Louis's maternal grandfather was minister there.
We had to ask directions to the manse and were directed up
the hill to the kirk. We felt rather foolish—of course the
manse would be next to the church.

We walked down the steep street and around the curve of
the churchyard wall to where a gate opened to a sweep of
lawn ("a well of sunshine" sun-starved Louis had called it).

We clicked the gate and walked up the drive, past a huge, old yew tree to the house. A pleasant white-haired woman came to the door to greet us. The house itself, she explained, had been remodeled since Louis's day, so there was not much reason for going inside, but we were welcome to explore the grounds as much as we pleased. She thought she had some pamphlets relating the R.L.S. writing to their sites—now dear me, where had she put them? She bustled away while we turned to carry out her suggestion.

The children had already found a swing under the yew tree, but it was steeped in dark shadows, hanging in a veritable cave, and did not seem to answer to the description in the poems:

> Up in the air and over the wall,
>   Till I can see so wide,
> Rivers and trees and cattle and all
>   Over the countryside—

We saw some other trees behind the house and walked around to a little orchard. This must have been where the cherry tree grew, we agreed, which Louis had climbed "to look abroad on foreign lands." Ian was all for doing the same thing, but his father warned him off: hospitality can be pressed too far.

We went back to the front of the house and wandered about the lawn. A little wind was blowing. "Like ladies' skirts upon the grass," I quoted involuntarily. Perhaps a few ghosts lingered. I thought of that pleasant life when grandparents, aunts, and uncles came out of the house to sit about the lawn and to watch Louis and his sturdy Balfour cousins roll and

tumble like kittens in the sunshine. Louis's mother was the
youngest of thirteen children. Oddly enough, so was his father. Louis did not lack for cousins.

The lawn was ringed by shrubbery and already my children
were finding it an exciting unadult world to explore. Our
hostess came out from the house bearing a small pamphlet
and a warning. "Mind the water gate," she said. "I wouldn't
like the baby to tumble in." I glanced at the pamphlet and
read:

> Over the borders, a sin without pardon,
> Breaking the branches and crawling below,
> Out through the breach in the wall of the garden,
> Down by the banks of the river, we go.

The lawn dipped sharply at its far end, and we followed our
guide through the shrubbery to where another gate led to
some steep steps. We peered down in astonishment. The
Water of Leith foamed and swirled in the narrow vale between two hillsides. We opened the gate and went down the
steps. The most amazing thing about the water was its color:

> Dark brown is the river,
> Golden is the sand.

I had never understood those lines before. The water was not
muddy. It looked like good, fresh coffee—brown and sparkling. We learned later that the color of the water is caused
by an infusion of peat.

A tiny golden beach was caught in the crook of the river's
bend. It was a perfect place to play.

> The river, on from mill to mill
> Flows past our childhood's garden still;

But ah! we children never more
Shall watch it from the water-door!
Below the yew—it still is there—
Our phantom voices haunt the air
As we were still at play,
And I can hear them call and say:
"How far is it to Babylon?"

Ian was already down on his hands and knees, launching forth
a fleet of ships—chips of wood and green leaves set forth to
swirl around the bend, over the weir, and out to sea at Port of
Leith on the other side of Edinburgh. He and Lucy chattered
happily, their voices almost lost in the babble of the water.
The Opies, in their scholarly *Oxford Dictionary of Nursery
Rhymes*, point out that in English folklore "Babylon" often
refers to Baby Land—"childhood's garden." Did Robert
Louis Stevenson know that? Or did he choose the word because it contains within itself the sound of waters? Almost, I
could hear those "phantom voices" and I was reminded of
another time when Ian had seemed to play with Louis's ghost.

He was three years old at the time and we were living in the
cowboy and cotton country of the San Joaquin Valley in California. I had forbidden him to play with anyone because he
had a cold, but he so stubbornly insisted that he was going to
play with "that boy who likes blocks" that I restricted him to
his room. I expected loud rebellion, but there followed a
whole morning of silence. It was so complete that I was guilty
of the thought that Ian might have disobeyed me and gone out
to play. At length, so little was my faith, that I opened the
door to his room. There was Ian, with all his blocks spread out
on the floor. Roads, harbors, castles, and cities had been constructed so that they all led up to a sort of platform on which

stood an open copy of *A Child's Garden of Verses*. It was the Golden Press edition, illustrated by the Provensens. There, on the open page, dressed in Victorian sailor suit, was another little boy, perhaps a bit older than Ian. He, too, was playing with blocks. His pictured edifice somehow had been conjoined and incorporated within the pattern made by the three-dimensional blocks strewn about Ian's bedroom floor.

It was with a faint prickle at the back of my neck that I was reminded of Stevenson's poem to the reader:

> As from the house your mother sees
> You playing round the garden trees,
> So you may see, if you will look,
> Through the windows of this book,
> Another child, far, far away
> And in another garden, play.
> But do not think you can at all
> By knocking on the window, call
> That child to hear you. He intent
> Is all on his play-business bent.
> He does not hear; he will not look
> Nor yet be lured out of this book.
> For long ago, the truth to say,
> He has grown up and gone away,
> And it is but a child of air
> That lingers in the garden there.

Be that as it may, I am convinced that Ian had somehow summoned "that child" and had been playing with him all the long morning.

11
Beyond the Door

As we drove south and westward into the Lake District the mountains fell away on either hand, as though moved by an enchantment. There was a feeling of breaking and entering. Rosemary Sutcliff, in her novel of Viking resistance, *The Shield Ring*, explains that even the Domesday Book stopped short of the Cumberland Fells. For thirty years, for a whole generation, the Norman conquerors could not penetrate into this remote mountain fastness. To this day the map is sprinkled with Viking names and terms—Eskdale and Buttermere (after Jarl Buthar) and Aiken's Row.

We stopped for lunch somewhere near Thirlmere. Far above us a white plumed stream dropped silently to a hidden ledge, then leaped again into the valley below. I said that it reminded me of the falls at Yosemite, but Ian had a far better feeling for the literary. Perhaps, he said, it was Swallowdale, that wonderful camping place described in Arthur Ransome's book of the same name. The Ransome books had held him in thrall all the previous winter and I, reading them aloud to him, had found them just as exciting as in my own childhood.

I had had secret adult doubts, however, as to whether any limited stretch of countryside could have so many perfect lakes and waterfalls and hidden caves and lost mines. Now, gazing about me at lakes and mountains, I was willing to capitulate.

Just above Grasmere we came to a crossroads. To our left lay Wordsworth's cottage, a place I had absolutely promised myself to see. To the right, around the other side of the lake, curved a secondary road posted with a "notice to motorists":

THIS ROAD CLOSED IN WINTER. THROUGH PASSAGE IS POSSIBLE BUT HIGHLY IMPROBABLE IN WET OR INCLEMENT WEATHER.

How could we resist such a challenge—and such nicety of language? Bumping along over the ruts we were reminded of a story of the Irish hero, Oisin, and how he had come to a crossroad where three roads converged. The road to the right, rocky and steep, led up to Heaven. The broad road straight ahead led straight to Hell. But a third road, almost hidden by trees and flowers, was the "tangled, twisty path to fairyland." This was the road that Oisin chose—and we did too.

We came out on the main road near Clappersgate, crossed a bridge, and went on to Hawkshead. Hawkshead was a close-huddled little town, its shops connected by archways. It seemed hardly a bustling metropolis but it had served to impress the country cousin in Beatrix Potter's *Tale of Johnny Townmouse*. I wonder if Johnny Townmouse pointed out the house where William Wordsworth went to school. It would seem in character for him to be a namedropper.

We were looking for the village of Near Sawrey. We skirted around Esthwaite Water and almost drove through the vil-

lage before we knew we had arrived. John actually had to stop
the car and to put it in reverse so that we would not by-pass
the village. It was while we were creeping backward that we
saw a National Trust marker, half hidden in the hedge, that
told us that the entire village was under the guardianship of
the Trust and that Beatrix Potter's cottage at Hill Top Farm
was open to visitors.

We parked our car and went through a familiar-looking
gate in the hedge. The path to the farmhouse was surely the
very one from whence Mrs. Tabitha Twitchit fetched her kittens indoors to wash and dress them. The same view, with a
policeman walking toward the house, can be seen in *The Tale
of Pigling Bland.* We came to the large front door and peered
into the dark, cool interior. A short, pleasing little person clad
in brown tweed came to greet us. For a moment I thought of
Mrs. Heelis (Miss Potter's married name) but it was no
ghost. Mrs. Susan Ludbrooke, the caretaker at Hill Top,
proved to be a unique and interesting person in her own right.
Unlike some caretakers I have known, she proved much better versed than the visitor about the subject of her trust. Not
that she was gushing or sentimental. She had copies of the
Tales spread out on a table in the center of the old kitchen in
order to help us refresh our memories, but she expected her
guests to be intelligent, not sloppy, in their interest. Beatrix
Potter would have approved.

We had told Lucy that we were going to Tom Kitten's
house, but we were unprepared for her total acceptance of the
fact. Just as in Caldecott country, at the beginning of our trip,
Lucy took it for granted that one could step into the pages of
a book. She had never doubted the veracity of Miss Potter's
world, so lovingly depicted in all its detail. Why should she?

She knew that it would be this way. She had been here before.

The door, half ajar, was the one through which Cousin Ribby came with basket and umbrella. The oak dresser, directly opposite, was the very one past which Anna Maria scurried when she was on the way to the kitchen to steal some dough to make a roly poly pudding. Only the grate and chimney piece seemed unfamiliar. Mrs. Ludbrooke was swift to step in and explain that Miss Potter had considered the range too modern and had replaced it with an older and much simpler grate. After all, she had left the house to the National Trust not as a memorial to herself, but to show future visitors the interior of a typical Lakeland farmhouse. Ian and Lucy peered up into the chimney, even as Tom Kitten had, and discussed whether or not one could actually climb it to the roof or wriggle from it into a secret passage.

Instead, Mrs. Ludbrooke offered to accompany us upstairs. We paused a moment on the first landing, enjoying the prickly sensation that we had been there before. Surely our hands had rubbed over that very post and banister? The work was simple and unpretentious—no knobs, no scrolls, no ornate carvings—but the craftsmanship had dignity. No wonder Beatrix Potter loved the Lakeland cottages. There is a feeling for material and, always, a sense of proportion. The same could be said for the artist who immortalized them.

The upstairs bedrooms proved rather disappointing. They were crowded and "museumy" and set about with glass cases. We had had enough of museums. Ian agitated to press on farther, up to the attic, so that we might find the piece of skirting-board with an * painted on it. In *The Tale of the Roly Poly Pudding* Beatrix Potter had used such a mark to indicate where Samuel Whiskers had kept poor Tom Kitten a prisoner while Anna Maria set about to roll him into a roly poly pudding. However, Mrs. Ludbrooke was quite firm about not allowing visitors beyond the second floor.

When Miss Potter was forty-seven years old she married her solicitor, Mr. William Heelis, against her parents' wishes. After that she kept the little cottage behind Tower Arms only for her own enjoyment and amusement and, as Mrs. Heelis, moved to Castle Cottage in the fields across the road. At the time, she claimed that it was because the new house was larger and more comfortable for her husband. All of this was quite true, but one suspects that also she could not bear to disturb the complete and perfect little world into which she had escaped during the unhappy years when she gave allegiance to her cold and unsympathetic parents. She seems to have had a premonition that others would want to seek out that world, too. Margaret Lane, her biographer, writes that even on her deathbed she left minute and sometimes impractical instructions that nothing was to be changed. I would not be at all surprised to learn that Ian is quite right—that one day she took paint and brush and carefully painted an asterisk on the skirting-board in the attic. Perhaps it is there now, only waiting for some child to come and find it.

We lingered for a few moments longer to look at the wax dolls (so ghastly pale in their glass cases) and at a doll's house complete with the immortal plaster doll's food that Hunca Munca and Tom Thumb stole in *The Tale of Two Bad Mice.* The doll's house is not the original one, however. Miss Potter had given that one away to Winifred Warne many years before in that "other" life when she was engaged to Norman Warne, the publisher. If Norman Warne had not died quite suddenly during the engagement she would have become

Winifred's aunt and—who knows?—the mother of Winifred's cousins. There was a photograph of Winifred and another one of Little Lucie of Newlands, the little girl to whom *The Tale of Mrs. Tiggy-Winkle* is dedicated.

This interested us especially since there has always been an identification of red-haired Lucie of Newlands with our own Lucy. The day before Lucy was born I bought a copy of *The Tale of Mrs. Tiggy-Winkle* to give to Ian as a present. By mistake (I was somewhat excited) I packed the book in my suitcase and took it off to the hospital with me. I had never read the book before, but desperate for reading material during the long hours of waiting I turned to the works of Miss Potter. I decided forthwith that the book was meant for a little girl and a few hours later I was able to present it to my daughter as my first gift to her. That day at Near Sawrey we learned that the original Lucie had been Lucie Carr and that she was one of the small daughters of the Vicar of Newlands.

Mrs. Ludbrooke thought we had been rash not to make reservations in the Lake District during August, but she suggested we try our luck at the little inn at Far Sawrey. The proprietress there listened to our plight and kindly allowed us to use a room vacated for one night by some regular guests, but only on condition that we set about at once looking for lodgings elsewhere. Tired as we were, we drove back toward Ambleside and spent the evening in search. We finally found a beautiful old house near the northern end of Lake Windermere. We were shown an enormous room that had once been the nursery. The only catch was that the room was on the top floor of the house, a long climb to up under the carved eaves. When we walked over to the bow window, however, the whole of Windermere stretched before us. Lights winked from the shore and far down the lake the dusk closed in over cardboard silhouettes of mountains. Directly at our feet, it seemed, were terraced gardens, an old boathouse, and the mouths of two little rivers emptying into the lake. What a perfect place to play! I fumbled for my purse to make a deposit. We'd take it!

The next morning we moved all our belongings to the new hotel, then we decided to drive back to Sawrey. Margaret Lane, in *The Tale of Beatrix Potter*, has written:

> If Beatrix Potter had been a poet, the eight years following the purchase of Hill Top, when she came and went and experienced her solitary happiness in Sawrey, would have been her lyric years. As it was, being an artist of a different sort, she produced no fewer than thirteen books for children—each of them having in its way the shapeliness and quality of a poem . . . no fewer than six are intimately concerned with Hill Top Farm and Sawrey. . . . *Jemima Puddleduck* is her poem about the farm itself. . . .

Hill Top garden is, of course, Jemima Puddleduck's. When I said something to Lucy about its being the scene of Peter Rabbit's adventures, too, Mrs. Ludbrooke corrected me in shocked tones. To see Mr. MacGregor's garden one must journey to Tenby, in Wales, where Beatrix's uncle used to live. The house is called "Gwynanog" and has been turned into a girls' school. Mrs. Ludbrooke had heard that the garden, the potting shed, and the gold-fish pool are still in existence.

We went out the gate of Hill Top and found ourselves admiring a flamboyant garden next to the Tower Arms, the very same in which Duchess was standing when she received the invitation in *The Pie and the Patty Pan*. Diagonally across the main road was a cottage with an arched doorway with stone seats built in under the arch. We decided it must be the porch to Ribby's house, the entryway where the Duchess stood so expectantly, armed with a bouquet of flowers. Across the village street we recognized the *Ginger and Pickles* shop. A faded sign, barely discernible, leaned against one wall: It said something about ". . . Taylor . . . Joiner." There is a John Joiner in *The Tale of the Roly Poly Pudding* and the dedicatee of *The Tale of Ginger and Pickles* is "Old Mr. John Taylor who 'thinks he might pass as a dormouse' (Three years in bed and never a grumble)."

We walked around behind the shop to the walled lane that runs past the village over the fields to Castle Cottage. It must have been busier when Sawrey still had its own post office, but the view still looks much the same as when Tom Kitten climbed to the roof of Hill Top to "get out on the slates, and try to catch sparrows." The lane, hardly more than a path, runs past a series of gay, old-fashioned gardens crowded with pinks and snapdragons and magnificent tiger lilies. All along the way, the doorways were a delight. Beatrix Potter loved to dwell on just this sort of detail. *The Pie and the Patty Pan,* especially, is full of studies of doorways and dooryards, as though the artist had a sketchbook full and was just waiting for the right story to come along in order to put them to use.

Miss Potter liked gates, too, as you will see if you look through her books. There are all kinds of gates throughout the village, but the iron ones look as though the same hand had wrought the vines and tendrils. Instead of giving one the feeling of sameness, however, it is like a thread of music running through the village. Here, on Post Office Lane, we found yet another iron gate, and Lucy insisted on climbing it to see the tiger lilies on the other side. ("They're growing simply fierce," her father told her). A large orange cat came picking along the wall to see what she was doing. The August sun beat down, the hills were golden with uncut hay. For one moment the scene fused forever in my memory: flame-haired Lucy, the orange cat, a garden full of tiger lilies. Then Ian called out: "Hey! It must be Ginger from *Ginger and Pickles!*" And the spell was broken.

Ian was tired, hot, and disgruntled. He was bored with looking at doorways and old furniture and obviously pined for something more robust. "How about finding Mr. Tod's house?" he asked, and that seemed a splendid idea. I have found *The Tale of Mr. Tod* to be a great success with small boys. Its plot and action contain an abduction, a daring rescue, and a really smash-up fight that, like those free-for-alls in old movies, stirs the audience to helpless laughter:

> The vases fell off the mantelpiece, the cannisters fell off the shelf; the kettle fell off the hob. Tommy Brock put his feet in a jar of raspberry jam.

That last line always gets 'em!

There is undoubtedly more plot to *Mr. Tod* than to most of the other *Tales* (although anyone who has ever read *Peter Rabbit* knows that Beatrix Potter could handle plot superbly). The characters have substance too. Mr. Tod we have already met as the "elegantly dressed gentleman" with "sandy whiskers" who seduced Jemima Puddleduck. (Shades of *Adam Bede* and *Tess of the D'Urbervilles!*) Mr. Tod is also a sort of British version of Joel Chandler Harris's Br'er Fox. It is interesting to note that in 1895, five years before her first little book was published, Beatrix Potter had tried her hand at illustrating *Tales of Uncle Remus,* a collection she greatly admired.

Tommy Brock is an equally strong and earthy character—in every sense of the word. Less elegant than Mr. Tod, he has all the guile of the incorrigible poacher. Both characters have about them more of the smack of *Jorrocks* and *Pickwick* than they do of *Uncle Remus.* They are thoroughly English. It is interesting to note that "tod" means fox in Old English and "brock" is the old word for badger. Beatrix Potter took a delight in words. It is characteristic that she be interested in the older, simpler forms of language, just as she admired country furniture and country architecture.

We left Post Office Lane and went back to the main street of the village, this time pursuing it to where it ran into the hillside at the far end. Looking back over our shoulders we discovered ourselves to be in the same position as was Samuel Whiskers on page 67 in *The Roly Poly Pudding* as he gazes back for a last glimpse of the hastily abandoned Hill Top. We left the street and took a path that led up toward the fields. The farmhouse at the end of the village had been built partly into the hillside. As we passed it, I glanced down and realized that the kitchen windows were actually at my feet. The window ledge, cheerful with geraniums, struck me as familiar. Surely it was the model for the kitchen window in Mr. Tod's house. I wondered if a rabbit had ever peeked in there, and decided it was quite possible.

The path was steep, the day hot and muggy. We were fast losing enthusiasm when we came to a little springhouse built into the hill. We sat on the roof to look out over Esthwaite Water and to listen to the cool trickle of water running somewhere far below us. We pushed on up the hill, not sure what we were looking for, and came to the edge of a wood. It was cooler here under the trees, and a faint breeze stirred along the hilltop. There were stone outcroppings covered with moss, and at one place someone had cut through the turf into the rock. It may have been the cellar of a long-extinct house or, perhaps, a small quarry.

Ian and Lucy were positive that they had found the foundations of Mr. Tod's house, and I must say that the place looked rather like the illustrations on page 26 in *The Tale of Mr. Tod*. Slabs of corrugated tin were lying about on the grass and the children set about to roof over one corner of the house. They worked mightily, heat and tiredness forgotten. John and I lay about on the moss watching their frenetic activity in stunned amazement. We were too hot to move or care. Gradually, however, we found ourselves drawn into the enterprise. John helped to lift one of the heavier pieces of corrugated roofing while Lucy and I, frightfully domestic, worked together to clear out one corner of leaves and tumbled stones.

The stones and the natural wall behind them were black with soot: someone had once built a fire there. And then, under a pile of wet and soggy leaves, we found what we had been looking for—solemn archaeological proof of tenancy. Lucy held up a tiny china teacup, orange and white and gold, Oriental in design and of such small size that no ordinary adult could be interested in it. It might have belonged to a child, but it seemed much more sensible to suppose that it was the cup to be seen on page 79:

> Tommy Brock was sitting at Mr. Tod's kitchen table, pouring out tea from Mr. Tod's teapot into Mr. Tod's tea-cup. He was

quite dry himself and grinning; and he threw the cup of scalding tea all over Mr. Tod.

We told ourselves that we had found the only piece of crockery to survive that dreadful battle. Schliemann at Troy could not have been more proud.

Teacups naturally turned our thoughts toward tea. We remembered the sign in the window of Ribby's cottage, in the village below, and started down the hill again. Near the springhouse we found an old pail, battered and pitted, that we had not noticed on the way up. "Wait a minute," said Ian, and dashed up the hill again. He returned a few minutes later, breathless but triumphant. "It's for the chimney," he explained. I hope that when Mr. Tod next came up Bull Banks he was pleasantly surprised.

We had promised Ian that as much as possible we would devote the next day to Arthur Ransome's books. Accordingly, we went into a bookshop in Ambleside to purchase a copy of *Swallows and Amazons*. We had written to Arthur Ransome before we left the United States, but had received a polite return from his publishers explaining that Mr. Ransome did not answer letters or grant interviews. They were inclined to believe that he lived in the Broads (in eastern England) nowadays, but had no evidence. . . .

It was while we were standing about in the bookshop, studying and discussing the familiar map in the end papers of Ransome's books, that we fell into conversation with the bookseller. Arthur Ransome? He'd come into the shop last Tuesday. . . . Marvelous old chap. . . . Where was he staying? Oh, somewhere in the Lake District. . . .

John said he'd stay and do errands in Ambleside while the

rest of us went back to the hotel. Back in our room Ian and I set ourselves to try to orient the map on the end papers of *Swallows and Amazons* with the big one-inch-to-the-mile map of the Lake District and the view from our window. Surely the lake described was Windermere, turned on its side. If so, we were at the North Pole (or near it) and the Amazon must be over to our right. Why, there it was! The little River Rothay came wandering down through a delta of high reeds, almost at the foot of the garden. Beckfoot, the home of the Amazons, must be near at hand.

Without more ado we set out for a walk, leaving a note for John. Ian had made friends with a boy slightly older than himself who had read all the Arthur Ransome books and who was more than willing to go with us. We set off along the road toward Hawkshead, crossed a bridge, scrambled under some barbed wire, and squelched along in the mud. We had come to explore the mouths of the River Amazon, but we found it impossible to get near without sinking over our knees in the mud. The only sensible thing to do was to make for higher ground. We climbed up on a little hillock crowned by sheltering trees. I asked our new friend, Tommy, which of the Ransome books was his favorite. "The one I read last, of course, *Picts and Martyrs!*" It was only later, peering at the map, that we could make out some tiny, shadowy letters in the approximate place of our little hillock: Pict house. Had this been Ransome's inspiration?

At the time, however, it seemed as though we had not spent a very fruitful morning. Nothing was proved, nothing was unproved. The Rothay certainly seemed as though it must be the Amazon, but we had not found a house to answer to the description of Beckfoot. How literal should we be? I was washing clothes when John came back from Ambleside. He looked thoroughly smug. Had he remembered toothpaste? He beamed. That's not all he had. He pulled a piece of paper out of his pocket. He had found someone who knew someone who thought he knew someone who might be able to give directions to Arthur Ransome's house. The directions were complicated, they seemed vague and at the same time they were concrete. A prophet is as unappreciated by his own wife as by his own country.

"Are you sure?" I asked. "How did you manage. . . ?"

"Because," said John, "I am the best researcher extant!"

That afternoon we drove over to Bowness to hire a boat in order to explore from the water. The boatyard looked strangely familiar, then I recognized Bowness as the Port o' Rio and the steep-roofed boatyard as the very one where Captain John had to leave the *Swallow* for repairs after she struck a rock off Wild Cat.

We turned our boat toward the north end of the lake, then squinted first at the shore, then at the big map, then at the maps and pictures in our Ransome books. There was our hotel, right under Loughrigg Fell. The River Rothay came down the east side of the Fell. Then, instead of going straight into the lake, cut across in front of the hotel, almost at right angles to its former course. Instead of entering the lake directly, it ran as a tributary into the River Brathay, a stream entering from the west. Together they formed a reed-fringed lagoon, then wound through a green delta before discharging into the lake. How much better it would be to explore by boat! Looking at page 305 in the English edition of *Swallowdale* we were happily confirmed in our hypothesis that this was, indeed, the Amazon.

But where was Beckfoot? Anxiously we scanned the shores of the lake. According to Ransome's map the Blacketts' house should have been in the fields where we had gone that morning. The only house nearby was much too grand—perhaps it was the Brathay Hall indicated on the one-inch map. Then, farther south than it should have been, we saw a whitewashed house with tents pitched on the lawn near the lake. Surely this was Beckfoot! It was a classical Lake District dwelling with a peaked roof over the door. Not far off, anchored in a cove, we found a houseboat. Surely *this* belonged to Captain Flint! We were content in every respect except that we had not been able to find Wild Cat Island. Every island we found in Lake Windermere was either too small or too civilized. Belle Isle, the largest one of all, had houses built on it. We tried to persuade ourselves that they were new, but actually they were solid Victorian structures that must have been there in the time of the childhood of the Blacketts' Great Aunt.

It was all very well a few nights later for John to make the handsome offer to drive me to see Arthur Ransome. He promised to take the children off my hands while I conducted the interview, but *I* was the one who would have to beard the lion in his den. Arthur Ransome sounded as though he might well be the counterpart of Captain Flint, uncle to Amazons, and Captain Flint had a peppery tongue. Also, he did not like to have his privacy invaded. But John was not to be balked. He had gone to a great deal of trouble to get the information and directions for me, and he had made up his mind absolutely that I was going to interview Arthur Ransome. Reluctantly I consented. We drove through the long twilight toward the southern end of the lake. The map was spread out on my lap and I looked with misgivings at the vast region of howe and fell and scree and moor and mountain and dale and holme and thwaite and common and waste and knott and forest. How did he expect me to find one lone man in all of this?

We had to drive the whole length of the lake, then turn north again (there was probably a quicker way, but we decided to follow the directions to the letter). We left the main road and began to watch for landmarks. We passed some men working in a little wood. A fire glowed before a tentlike structure of logs. A patient pony stood nearby, with sled attached, as the men worked to fill a last load before darkness closed in. "Charcoal burners," said Ian, bouncing up and down with excitement. "Gee, I wish we weren't going tomorrow! Maybe they'd let me stay in their hut. You know, like Roger did when he hurt his ankle. . . ."

We came to a place where a farmhouse overlooked a little crossroads and John stopped the car. "Get out here," he said. "I'll let the kids play in the brook and you ask at the farmhouse. The man I talked to said that after we got to this point you'd just have to ask. . . ."

I got out of the car and glanced back wistfully at the rest of the family. I was still dressed in high heels and a ridiculous frock with a low neck—proper garb for dining in state the last night of our journey. I felt a little strange as I walked up to the farmhouse. The house and barnyard looked familiar. Could this be Swainson's farm? Some men who were finishing up chores paused politely to answer my questions. Mr. Ransome? Aye, they knew him. He lived farther up the road, half a mile perhaps. I could ask as I went along. . . .

I came to a house perched high on the bank, smaller and more modest than most farms in the district. I almost passed it by, then decided to ask directions of a woman digging in the garden. Did she know where Mr. Ransome lived? She left off her digging and came over to speak to me. I noticed that she was not English, Russian, perhaps. I learned later that this was Arthur Ransome's Russian-born wife, Eugenia. Haltingly I tried to explain my appearance. I was an American, I was writing a book about children's authors, I had tried to reach Mr. Ransome through his publishers. . . .

She said Mr. Ransome was out at present—fishing. He did not grant interviews and he did not especially care for Americans. If I wanted to wait for him I could sit on the wall. She went back to her digging and I sat on the wall, kicking my heels. I would give Mr. Ransome five minutes to appear, possibly ten, and then rush down the hill to join John and the children. I could always feel that I had made an honorable attempt at an interview without actually having to go through with it.

There was the sound of a car, a very ancient car, coming up the road. "There he is," said my hostess, and I slipped down off the wall prepared to do battle or run, I was not positive which. A tall old man came through the gate. He was wearing brown tweed knickers, a brown tweed Sherlock Holmes hat stuck about with trout flies, and a Norfolk jacket. A great white mustache swept down from his nose. A Victorian Viking!

"What's this?" he asked. "What's this?"

"Arthur, this is a young woman from America. A journalist. She wants to interview you."

The blue eyes looked me over sternly. "Interview?" he said. "Interview? I don't give interviews." Suddenly he reminded me of my father—blue eyes, mustache, forty years at sea.

"I think you are quite right," I heard a voice saying (could it be mine?). "I wanted to hear it from *you*—not just from your publishers—and I'm awfully glad you told me at the outset." I tried to edge around him, to get out the gate.

But now he was giving me another look. "Well, young woman, what are we waiting for? You'll catch your death, sitting around on walls. I'm just going to put my rod up, then I'll get some chairs." He was back in a moment and the chairs were arranged so that we could look out over the purpling hills. "We could go inside, but it's getting dark and we have no lights, of course. Besides, I like to sit here every evening at this time and watch the sunset. Now?"

I hardly knew how to begin. I hated to ask him questions that were too personal. I was not certain how he felt about telling the whereabouts of the places in the stories. I decided to advance cautiously. Was Windermere the lake where most of the adventures took place?

He sighed. People often asked that. Yes, it was, but things were scrambled somewhat, of course. He hated to be too literal. People had always taken him too literally. The stories were written for fun and to please the grandchildren of some old friends. But at least one woman took his stories so seriously that she had actually written him a long letter to ask about the Walker family. She thought it perfectly dreadful that children should be left to the tender mercies of a father

who sent such a telegram as BETTER DROWNED THAN DUFFERS
IF NOT DUFFERS WON'T DROWN. "I think she thought I might
be the father. I think she would have had some society after
me. Silly woman!"

Determined not to fall into the same category, I abandoned
the literal tack altogether. How about his boyhood? Had he
spent most of it in the Lake Country?

He brightened visibly, then almost dashed my hopes with
an emphatic, "I only wish I could have." His father was a professor at Leeds University. The family had come to the Lakes
only for the long vacation. "My poor mother," he said. "We
never brought any toys with us—we weren't like modern children. We didn't need a lot of extra playthings when we had the
Lake. But at the last minute, hurrying through the railroad
station at Leeds, my mother would remember the rainy days
and a houseful of children. She used always to stop at a little
stand and buy us transfers, packages and packages of them."
He paused and peered at me from under shaggy white eyebrows. "Do you know what transfers are?"

Almost involuntarily I cupped the palm of one hand and
brought it down with a smack on the back of the other. He
laughed. I seemed to have pleased him. "Perhaps modern
children are not so different after all," he said, giving me the
compliment.

"The Lake Country was a different place then," he went
on. "Not crowded with all these trippers who come just because it is a place to come to and who never care at all about
it, really, but just dash through on those dreadful motorcycle
things. There were not automobiles, of course, and we were
quite isolated, except for our own families—and the Lake.
The Lake was everything. I remember we used to arrive at

night and we could hardly wait until next morning to rush down to the water's edge to dip in our hands. Dip them in up to the wrist, you know. I suppose it was a kind of ritual, to show we could come back." He paused again, looking out over the miles and miles of mountain turning crimson and mauve and purple before our eyes.

"When I was a boy? I went to school at Windermere, that was before I went to Rugby. I ran away from school one day. I was trudging along the road when the coach came along. There were still coaches then. The man on the box was the friend of an aunt of mine, so he stopped the coach and hauled me up beside him and took me home. I remember my aunt used to be very fond of archery. She had friends who lived on Belle Isle, and in the afternoon the ladies would stand about in their long skirts and bend those great bows. . . . Well, the old people are dead now, and all we young ones have scattered hither and thither and grown old ourselves. But we always come back to the Lake. . . ."

He paused and pointed out toward the mountains. The Old Man of Coniston, the highest peak in the Lake District, stood out against the sky. That must be the Katchenjunga of the stories, I thought. "Do you see that skyline? When I used to be correspondent for the *Manchester Guardian* I sometimes thought I might never see England again. But I could always close my eyes and see that skyline—every peak of it—silhouetted against a sort of screen in my mind. I am never tired of looking at it. Even in Manchuria I could close my eyes and summon it at will."

He was silent for so long that I thought the interview was over and I pushed back my chair intending to leave. He must have heard my chair scrape, for he put out his hand and said,

"I notice you brought one of my books. Wait a minute while I fetch a pen and an electirc torch." He was back in a moment and with quick, deft strokes sketched in a little pen and ink drawing of *Swallow* and wrote his name underneath. I was terribly pleased and told him that Ian would be the envy of his friends.

He seemed surprised. He said he didn't know that American children still read books. He had been told that they couldn't read at all, that they only watched television. "I've watched it myself," he said, but it had seemed like journeying through strange country on a very fast train. "It's like seeing everything through a little slot. You can never climb down or go back once you are aboard. . . ."

I laughed and said I thought that a wonderful description, but that American children still read books. Be that as it may, he said, his books were almost out of print in America, although they had been popular enough when they were first published there.

I asked him if the books were still popular in England, and told him about Ian's friend, Tommy, who claimed that his favorite was always the last one he'd read. He seemed pleased, then went on to say that as well as in England, he had an enthusiastic following in Czechoslovakia. "I keep getting letters from the children there," he said. "They pass the old copies around among themselves and manage to hold on to them somehow. Of course Hitler banned them. He didn't like his youth groups to know what English children were really like. We were supposed to be effete."

I decided to make one last try about the maps. Was Ambleside the North Pole? "Yes, well near it. . . ." Was Bowness really Rio? "Yes." Was this house Holly Howe?

"No." Where was Swallowdale? At once he became vague. The stories rather scrambled things about. . . . I mustn't be too literal. . . . The same for Wild Cat Island. . . . I realized that he was not going to give out any information except to confirm what we had discovered for ourselves. He walked to the gate with me and he hung over it a minute or two, watching me walk down the road.

"Come again," he said, "or write to me. . . ." I had gone a few yards farther when he suddenly called out, "Wait a moment. I've decided I like you. Wild Cat Island is not in Windermere at all—it's borrowed from another lake." And he gave me its name.

Lucy was already asleep in the car, but John and Ian were waiting impatiently for me. What had kept me so long? I was bubbling over the interview and could hardly wait to tell them about it and to show Ian the sketch in his book. Had I been able to find out about Wild Cat Island? I told Ian what Mr. Ransome had called out to me from over the gate. To really *know* was a sobering thought.

"I don't think it would be fair to tell," said Ian.

The last day at Windermere we drove over to Newlands to see the countryside described in *The Tale of Mrs. Tiggy-Winkle*. It was a long way we had mapped out for ourselves —all the way past Derwentwater (where Squirrel Nutkin had his adventures), then to Swinside and beyond. Once again we marveled at the scenery and several times let the children out for a run. Water, in any form, is irresistible and in this country there were so many gills, becks, brooks, streams, tarns, rivers, meres, and lakes that even Ian could be satisfied.

The countryside became extravagantly romantic. Even our big one-inch map seemed uncertain as to which roads were paved, which were not, and what was a mere footpath. We took a wrong turn just after Swinside and ended up in a sheep pasture. We just sat there, in the car, while some strange looking little sheep came over to investigate us. They were smaller than most sheep and their fleece had a different cast to it—almost bluish. I still remember their faces—not stupid at all, but sweet and intelligent. John walked off to a farmhouse to find out where we were. "Skelghyl," he said, when he came back, and then we remembered what it said in the book:

> "What are these dear soft fluffy things?" said Lucie.
> "Oh, those are woolly coats belonging to the little lambs at Skelghyl. . . . And here's one marked for Gatesgarth, and three that come from Littletown. They're always marked at washing!" said Mrs. Tiggy-Winkle.

These were Herdwick sheep, the little breed that has tripped over the fells since prehistoric times. Their fleece is of such quality that until the invention of linoleum it was highly prized for the toughest carpets. Beatrix Potter, as Mrs. Heelis, became an enthusiastic supporter of the breed. As demand for the fleece declined she fought valiantly not to have the little sheep driven into extinction. She even had her clothes woven from Herdwick fleece (it's almost waterproof) and could be seen tramping about the roads and footpaths in disreputable hat and long woolen skirts, often with a pointed stick in hand to pick up the litter left by careless trippers. Margaret Lane writes that Miss Potter was a familiar sight at cattle shows and sheep fairs. She raised Herdwick sheep herself and judged them herself (the first woman to do so). She was known and respected throughout the district not as Miss Potter, heiress, nor as Beatrix Potter, author-artist, but as Mrs. Heelis, the most knowledgeable sheep farmer in the Lake Country.

John turned the car around by making a wide arc in the pasture, then headed back toward Swinside, where we took the other fork in the road. We drove through Little-town without knowing it, and came to a halt before a little church. This must have been Newlands, the very parish where Lucie Carr's father was the vicar. If we had kept on we would have come to Buttermere and Crummock Water. It is just as well that we had not read Rosemary Sutcliffe's *Shield Ring* at that time because Ian would have given us no peace until we saw for ourselves where the Vikings built the "Road to Nowhere" up Rannardale Beck from Crummock Water in order to fool the Normans, and where they fought their last, lost battle. Since then, studying the map carefully, we have been able to see how Butersdale (Buttermere) is hidden, and have been most intrigued by some shadowy letters that spell out "Crag houses." What does *that* mean?

At Newlands, John turned the car around once again and we drove back along the road. We came upon two houses built so close together that they almost connected. A barn and a farmyard were across the road from the living quarters. An old couple was sitting in the garden of one of the houses so we asked them if they knew where we could find Little-town. They shook their heads. They were from London and hardly knew where they were themselves. Their son had sent them here for a holiday. They sounded so pathetic that I realized that Napoleon on St. Helena could not have been more lonely. Brighton or Blackpool was more their cup of tea.

Lucy and I crossed the road to where a young woman was throwing out grain to a yardful of clustering hens. I asked her if she could tell us how to get to Little-town and she, rather surprised, told us that we had arrived. "Little-town" was the name of the farm. Several children, about Lucy's age, were playing in the yard, but they were far too shy to accept her overture of friendship. I asked the woman if she minded if we looked about.

"You know," I said brightly, "Mrs. Tiggy-Winkle and all that. . . ."

She looked at me as though she thought me daft. "Mrs. Tiggy-Winkle?" she said.

I tried again. "Beatrix Potter wrote a book about this farm and this barnyard and a hedgehog who took in washing at Cat Bells. . . ." (At least I had seen Cat Bells on the map. I must make a *little* sense!) Still she shook her head. We were not speaking the same language. Fortunately her husband came into the barnyard at that moment.

"I've just brought in the ram. Going to saw off its horns. . . ." He broke off suddenly when he saw me. By this time I felt a little shy. His wife tried to explain why I was there, speaking carefully so not to let me know that she knew I was mentally deranged.

"This lady," she said, "Says that there is a book written about Little-town."

"Aye, lass," he said to his wife, "it's true. A friend of Mother's, she did it. Mrs. Heelis, it was. I'll show you the book when you remind me. It's in mother's box."

"And show it to your children, too," I could not help adding. "It's really for them. Children all over the world know this farm. We've come all the way from America just to see this barnyard. . . ." But I could see that the young farm woman was still not convinced. She called her children to her and I saw her giving a long look at Lucy. Lucy was dressed in corduroy overalls (*her* little girls wore nylon dresses), and Lucy had bare feet. I had noticed that farm children all over England nowadays wear nylon. It must be so easy for a busy farmer's wife to wash and dry. I do not begrudge any housewife her leisure, but I did feel a pang for something more aesthetic:

"'There's one of my pocket-handkins!" cried Lucie—"and there's my pinny!"

Mrs. Tiggy-Winkle ironed it, and goffered it, and shook out the frills.

"Oh that *is* lovely!" said Lucie.

I suppose that Lucy's garb was just as out of place in that scene as were the nylon dresses. Both the farmer's wife and I were held by common bond: each of us was in desperate need of a Mrs. Tiggy-Winkle, that "most excellent clear starcher."

Lucy had taken Sally Henny Penny's advice too literally and was, in truth going "barefoot, barefoot, barefoot." A henyard was no place for her, so I took her across the road again. Ian and John were watching through the slats of a pen as the young farmer (he must have been terribly strong) wrestled with a huge old ram. He finally got him down far enough to grab a saw and to begin sawing off the pointed horns. The noise was dreadful. The ram bellowed and baaed, and the sound of the sawing rasped through the still damp air, bouncing off the hillside. Partly to get away from it we decided to try to find the famous path that Lucie took when she ran along the mountainside to Mrs. Tiggy-Winkle's.

A turnstile was set between the two houses. Ian was through it and up the hill like a shot, losing himself in the mists that shrouded the hillside. The scene most certainly answered to the description in the book: "A hill that goes up—up—into the clouds as though it had no top!" We seemed to be walking through a cloud at that very moment. I looked at Lucy. Her face was aglow, transfigured. She had walked into another world, a place compounded of mists and watery sunshine, of reality and make-believe. To John and me, watching, it was uncanny to be in that place, with Little-town's chimney just below us, and a red-haired Lucy running ahead of us along the path. I felt like pinching myself to make sure that we were not still at home, that we had not, for a moment, slipped off into a doze while starting to read page 17 in *Mrs. Tiggy-Winkle:*

> Lucie scrambled up the hill as fast as her short legs would carry her; she ran along a steep path-way—up and up—until Little-town was right away down below—she could have dropped a penny down the chimney!

But it was growing late. We had to get back to the hotel to pack. Tomorrow we would drive to the Cunard docks at Liverpool and next day we would be sailing for America. Lucy still trotted along the path, expecting any moment, we realized later, to come to "that door into the back of the hill called Cat Bells." The sun was growing stronger now, the mist withdrawing as though an unseen hand were gathering back the folds of a curtain. We heard someone shouting at us and looked up to see Ian standing knee-deep in heather. The whole mountainside, as far as the eye could see, was steeped in bronze and purple. "Hey!" he shouted, *"Now* I know how the heather looks!"

But Lucy, on the long drive back to the hotel, was still not satisfied. "Where did Mrs. Tiggy-Winkle go?" she asked.

"Next time you can look for her," I said.

"Next time all by myself," said Lucy. "Next time I'll *find* the door. . . ."

Index